The Philadelphia Inquirer

Playing A Round

―――

The guide to Philadelphia-area golf courses

With Joe Logan

Books by The Philadelphia Inquirer

Lost at Sea:
The Atlantic Claims 10 Men
By Douglas A. Campbell

Crisis on the Coast:
The Risky Development of America's Shore
By Gilbert M. Gaul and Anthony R. Wood

Beyond the Flames:
One Toxic Dump, Two Decades of Sorrow
By Susan Q. Stranahan and Larry King

Philly's Final Four
UConn Rocks the Cradle of Women's Basketball
By the staff of The Inquirer

FAQ:
Sound Answers to Real Computing Questions
By John J. Fried

A Christmas Quartet
By Chris Satullo. Illustrations by Tony Auth

ISBN 1-58822-007-9

Cover photograph of Pine Hill Golf Course by Michael Plunkett.

Table of Contents

Pennsylvania
Berks County

1. Arrowhead Golf Course 11
2. Flying Hills Golf Course 14

Bucks County

3. Bensalem Country Club 18
4. Fox Hollow Golf Club 22
5. Middletown Country Club 25
6. Northampton Valley Country Club 28
7. Five Ponds Golf Club 31

Chester County

8. Downingtown Country Club 36
9. Hartefeld National County Club 40
10. Honeybrook Golf Club 44
11. Kimberton Golf Club 48
12. Pickering Valley Golf Club 52
13. Tattersall Golf Club 55
14. Wyncote Golf Club 59

Delaware County

15. Golf Course at Glen Mills 64
16. Paxon Hollow Country Club 68
17. Springfield Country Club 71

Dauphin County

18. County Club of Hershey 76

Lancaster County

19. Hawk Valley Golf Club 82
20. Pilgrim's Oak Golf Course 86

Lebanon County

21. Iron Valley Golf Club 90
22. Royal Oaks Golf Club 94

Lehigh County

23. Bethlehem Golf Club 98
24. Center Valley Club 102
25. Locust Valley Golf Club 106
26. Olde Homestead Golf Club 109

Montgomery County

27. Cedarbrook Hills: Short Course 114
28. Center Square Golf Club 117
29. Hickory Valley Golf Club 120
30. Horsham Valley Golf Club 124
31. Jeffersonville Golf Club 127
32. Limekiln Golf Club 130
33. Macoby Run Golf Course 133
34. Mainland Golf Course 136
35. PineCrest Golf Club 140
36. Skippack Golf Course 143
37. Turtle Creek Golf Course 146
38. Twin Ponds Golf Club 149
39. Twining Valley Golf Club 152
40. Upper Perk Golf Course 156
41. Valley Forge Golf Club 159
42. Westover Country Club 162
43. Wood's Golf Center 166

Northampton County

44. Whitetail Golf Club 171

Philadelphia

45. Cobbs Creek Golf Club 175
46. Franklin D. Roosevelt Golf Club 179
47. John F. Byrne Golf Club 184
48. Juniata Golf Club 188
49. Walnut Lane Golf Club 192

York County

50. Springwood Golf Club 196

New Jersey
Atlantic County

51. Blue Heron Pines East 201
52. Harbor Pines Country Club 205
53. Marriott Seaview – Pines Course 209
54. Twisted Dunes Golf Club 213

Burlington County

55. Deerwood Country Club 219
56. Ramblewood Country Club 223
57. Rancocas Golf Club 227

Camden County

58. Pine Hill Golf Club 232
59. Pennsauken Country Club 236

Cape May County

60. Sand Barrens Golf Club 241

Gloucester County

61. Scotland Run 247
62. White Oaks Country Club 252

Mercer County

63. Miry Run Country Club 257
64. Mountain View Golf Club 260
65. Mercer Oaks Golf Course 263

Ocean County

66. Pine Barrens Golf Club 268

Delaware

67. Back Creek Golf Club 274
68. Frog Hollow Golf Club 278
69. Three Little Bakers Country Club 282

Maryland

70. Beechtree Golf Club 286
71. Bulle Rock 290
72. Chesapeake Bay Golf Club at Rising Sun 294
73. Greystone Golf Course 297

Introduction

When a few of us at The Inquirer were kicking around ideas for the new Sunday golf page we were about to launch, I had one regular feature in mind that I was convinced would be popular and appreciated.

"Golf course reviews," I suggested. "Sort of like we review restaurants on the food page."

My thinking was, most golfers around here were probably like me. Unless they were a member of a country club, they had one or two courses — three, if they were lucky — that they returned to time and time again.

In my case, it wasn't loyalty that brought them back time

and time again. It was that the courses were passable, they were reasonably close to home, and they were affordable. But between work and family, who had time to go looking for something better? Why risk wasting your one round of golf a week by driving an hour to play a course a buddy at work had told you about, only to discover it was worse than your regular course? Besides, what else was out there, anyway?

I would make it my business to find out what else was out there. I would throw my clubs in the trunk and roam the region, playing investigative golf, searching relentlessly for the new and different, weeding the good from the bad.

I had no formal credentials to undertake such a mission as self-appointed golf course critic. I had never read a book on golf course design, let alone actually designed a course.

But as a golfer for 35 years, I had done the equivalent of a lot of independent reading. I'd traveled much of North Carolina playing in junior tournaments as a kid, I'd played on my high school team, I'd even played a year of collegiate golf. Living as I had over the years in North and South Carolina, Virginia, Mississippi and Minnesota, I'd also had the chance to play a lot of different kinds of golf courses in different places. I knew what I liked in a golf course, and I thought I had a pretty good sense of what others liked, too.

Just tell them a little about the course, and tell them whether it's worth a try. That was all my goal ever was.

From the very first review on the Sunday that the Golf Report debuted — Limekiln Golf Club, June 30, 1996 — I knew I was onto something. Letters poured in. My voicemail at work filled up. People I knew stopped me on the street. In the years since, my office bookshelf has filled with books on golf course design and the great golf courses of the world. Thanks to my job and the travels that come with it, I have been able to play more than 200 courses, including some of the crown jewels of the game: Augusta National, Pebble Beach, St. Andrews, Pine Valley, Pinehurst No. 2, Merion. I've also found myself on a Wednesday afternoon, alone, in the rain, dragging up the fairway of the saddest, sorriest little municipal courses you've ever seen.

It all comes with the job.

Still, when I go to a course for the first time, I ask myself the same basic questions.   What is my sense of the place just driving into the parking lot?

The clubhouse?   The course?   The cost?   Are the people friendly?   Would I come back?   Would I recommend it to a friend?

Along the way, I've met some terrific people. Occasionally, when a new course is set to open, I'll get a call from a public relations firm asking me to come out.   I'll end up playing with the head pro or maybe the general manager. But more often than not, I arrive unexpected, unannounced and remain undetected; I play with whomever happens to be standing on the first tee.

Along about the 10th or 11th hole, after we've chatted about the weather or the Phillies, the conversation often gets slightly more personal.   You know the kind of conversation I'm talking about.   Who are you?   What do you do for a living?   How can you get away to play golf on a Tuesday morning?

If I tell them the truth, the next question is almost always the same.   Oh, man, they'll say, what a job!   Is it as much fun as it sounds like?

Yes, yes it is.

— Joe Logan

Berks

C O U N T Y

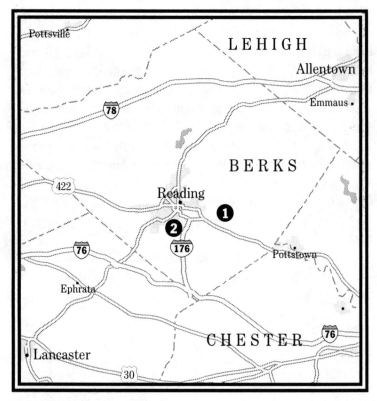

1. Arrowhead Golf Course
2. Flying Hills Golf Course

1. Arrowhead Golf Course

It's a forgiving course — but look out for the trees.

At his father's suggestion 45 years ago, John McLean came home from Texas, where he had settled to farm cotton and tobacco after World War II, to build a golf course on farmland that had been in the family since the 1700s.

Although he had never been a golfer, the idea intrigued the younger McLean. He sold everything in Texas and returned home to Douglassville, just west of Pottstown.

Scorecard

Hole	Yards	Par	HCP
1	470	5	11
2	503	5	9
3	367	4	7
4	155	3	13
5	410	4	3
6	482	5	15
7	407	4	1
8	371	4	5
9	142	3	17
Out	3,302	37	
10	544	5	6
11	127	3	14
12	346	4	12
13	115	3	18
14	346	4	10
15	243	3	4
16	371	4	2
17	313	4	8
18	295	4	16
In	2,700	34	
Total	**6,002**	**71**	

Without so much as reading a book on golf course design, he looked across the family's rolling land and pictured the layout in his mind's eye. Then, with the help of hired hands, he set about clearing trees, tilling the soil and building the greens for what would eventually become the first nine of 27 holes. Today, at age 77, McLean still owns and runs Arrowhead with his wife and daughter.

"I don't know what the big deal is," McLean said the other day, referring to the superstar status of today's top designers. "If you know your hills and the distances and where your wet areas are, it's relatively simple."

Arrowhead is not a great golf course. The 18-hole course,

as they call it, which McLean completed in 1972, is what a golf course architect might call "minimalist."

In an age when most designers force you to fire over water and around vast fairway bunkers, Arrowhead is very forgiving.

There is only one set of tees. There are no fairway bunkers. The few greenside bunkers tend to be small and not very problematic. The greens are flat, round and true. There is no rough to speak of. The fairways, though rolling, tend to be wide and manicured. Other than two small creeks that pose little threat as they cross the first and seventh holes, the only water on Arrowhead is a pond on the eighth that requires a 100-yard carry on your approach shot.

That is not to say there is no trouble on the course. On most every hole, a wayward tee shot will find its way into a line of trees or thick woods that border the fairways on both sides.

And on the 371-yard, par-4 16th, even a dead-center tee shot will likely come to rest on a severe downslope. That's particularly nettlesome for the second shot, which is up a steep hill into a hard-to-hit green.

The 18th, a 295-yard, par-4 dogleg left, is even more curious. Because of the extremely narrow fairway and quick turn no more than 130 yards off the tee, the prudent player must tee off with a short or mid-iron, leaving a longer shot, accurate into a small green. You don't see golf holes like this every day.

Others may find the 15th curious as well. It's also not every day you encounter a 243-yard par 3.

Arrowhead is not a long course (6,002 yards) or particularly difficult. Its above-average slope of 116 is no doubt a result of two par 4s of more than 400 yards on the front side and the 243-yard par 3. More bunkers, which McLean says he has no interest in adding, would surely drive the slope higher.

"Plain Jane, but nice," is one of the comments in Golf Digest's 4,200 Best Places to Play, which gives Arrowhead 2

1/2 stars.

For low handicappers looking for a challenge, Arrowhead won't hold much appeal — it's simply not penal enough to get them sweating. That, of course, is precisely what might attract plenty of mid- and high-handicappers who prefer their good walk not spoiled by the likes of demanding golf shots.

What Arrowhead has going for it are a very reasonable schedule of greens fees, well-kept Kentucky bluegrass fairways and bent greens, and a very comfortable, almost rural, feel to the place. It's not fancy, nor does it aspire to be.

Arrowhead also has one of the more modern conveniences — or inconveniences — of the industry.

When golfers wouldn't stop driving the carts too close to the greens, McLean agreed to be one of the early "guinea pigs" for an electronic system that restricts the carts to the cartpaths. When a cart wanders from the cartpath, an alarm sounds. If it isn't back on the path within 30 seconds, the cart dies on the spot. That, of course, would make for a good ride spoiled.

— Oct. 5, 1997

If You Go

Address: 1539 Weavertown Rd., Douglassville.

Phone: 610-582-4258.

Greens fees: Weekdays, walk for $16, ride for $26. Weekends, walk for $25, ride for $35.

Carts: Walking permitted anytime.

Amenities: Moderately stocked pro shop, driving range, practice green, snack bar, halfway house, pavilion for outings.

Rating: Not difficult, not an inspired layout, but a pleasant country course.

2. Flying Hills Golf Course

A fun series of links sits amid the condos

A little shorter than average, a little tougher than average, a few rolling hills, a spot of water, condos to the left, homes to the right.

That pretty much describes Flying Hills Golf Course in Reading, which wends through the small, comfortable residential and shopping village of the same name.

It's a fun course, if a little condo encroachment here and there doesn't bother you — and if you don't mind riding in a cart. Because of the development, the hike between a few of the holes could be a bit much with a bag slung over your shoulder.

Those caveats aside, Flying Hills makes for a pleasant day on the golf course. It has its share of snoozers, but it also has enough engaging holes to satisfy all but the best golfers. It gets a somewhat generous three stars, or "very good," from *Golf Digest's 4,200 Best Places to Play.*

The most visually arresting hole is easily the 15th, a short par 5 (423 yards from the white tees) that begins from a dramatically elevated tee and plays down to a narrow, tree-lined fairway that resembles a bobsled track. In places, the fairway can't be more than 15 yards wide, but it doesn't matter. All but the wildest tee shot will hit the hill and bound down to the short grass. And because the tee is so elevated, tee shots carry farther, meaning you don't have to be Davis Love 3d to have a go at the green in two.

The 18th, a 152-yard par 3 that's almost all carry over a small lake, is another head turner. It's a terrific hole with one small problem: A street runs right in front of the tee about 20 yards out. You can be lost in concentration, or right in the middle of your swing, only to have your playing partner say,

"Hold it a second."

But neither of those is the toughest hole. That distinction belongs to the second, a long, tight, slightly uphill par 4, with out-of-bounds looming on both sides — trees and a road on the left, condos on the right.

The most curious, yet fun, hole is the third, a short (452 yards) par 5 with a sloping fairway that doglegs hard to the right. What makes the hole curious, however, are the two giant utility poles that sit smack-dab in the middle of the fairway, precisely where a crushed tee shot might land. Even though local rules give you relief, the poles are a bit disconcerting.

From there, Flying Hills features several short and mid-length milder doglegs, most with trees or homes or both bordering the fairways. The best of the bunch is probably the 16th, from an elevated tee over a crest, then onto a large, low

Scorecard

Hole	Blue	White	Red	Par Men's	Ladies'	HCP Men's	Ladies'
1	419	363	343	4	4	11	11
2	415	410	342	4	4	1	5
3	473	452	441	5	5	7	3
4	192	140	131	3	3	15	15
5	431	423	408	4	5	3	7
6	322	301	293	4	4	9	9
7	113	106	92	3	3	17	17
8	529	517	362	5	4	5	1
9	175	166	148	3	3	13	13
Out	3,069	2,878	2,560	35	35		
10	314	305	287	4	4	18	16
11	340	336	326	4	4	16	12
12	351	330	315	4	4	8	8
13	335	328	314	4	4	12	14
14	169	160	144	3	3	10	10
15	461	450	376	5	5	6	6
16	424	371	364	4	4	2	2
17	392	385	371	4	4	4	4
18	168	152	119	3	3	14	18
In	2,954	2,817	2,616	35	35		
Total	**6,023**	**5,695**	**5,176**	**70**	**70**		

green tucked back in the woods.

Despite the carry required at the 18th, the best par 3 may well be the 14th, a 160-yarder from an elevated tee over a ravine onto an elevated green enshrouded by trees.

The course, built in 1970 by local developer Bill Whitman, was one of the early efforts at integrating a golf course and a residential community, according to Whitman's son, Byron, an executive with Flying Hills. Today, there are 130 single-family houses, 650 apartments, and about 600 townhouses.

The course was designed by the late Irv Althouse, a superintendent with a few course layouts to his credit, who stayed on for years to tend the course.

The most interesting anecdote from those days, said the younger Whitman, was the day a very young Tom Fazio showed up at his father's office.

"He was right out of design school and offered to do all our greens for $20,000," Whitman said. "We thought it was too expensive at the time. Now, Tom Fazio won't even look at you for less than $1 million."

Over the years, the Whitmans have added traps, mounds and fairway contouring, and they hope to acquire the land to add a driving range and practice green.

— Sept. 21, 1997

If You Go

Address: 10 Village Center Dr., Reading.

Phone: 610-775-4063.

Greens fees: Weekdays, walk for $21, ride for $22 (must be two people). Weekends, walk for $23, ride for $32.

Amenities: Moderately stocked pro shop, restaurant and bar, halfway house.

Carts: Walking is permitted anytime.

Rating: Fun, well-conditioned, mid-level course.

Bucks

C O U N T Y

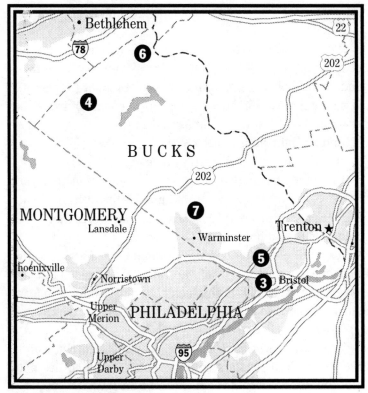

3. Bensalem Country Club
4. Fox Hollow Golf Club
5. Middletown Country Club
6. Northampton Valley Country Club
7. Five Ponds Golf Club

3. Bensalem Country Club

Course offers a whole lot of surprises

I don't know about you, but I'd never heard much of anything, good or bad, about Bensalem Country Club.

I knew it was just beyond the Philadelphia city limits, and I had seen somewhere that it was short (6,131 yards) and pretty easy (119 slope). I assumed it was a lackluster, working stiff's daily-fee track of no particular distinction — hardly worth the trip.

Well, I made that trip and I'm glad I did. Bensalem turned out to be an inviting little course with lots of personality: a good mix of holes, plenty of hills and trees, tight (in places), big subtle greens, some tricky doglegs, a couple of excellent par 4s, and one of the best par 3s in the area.

And it's quite affordable.

"It really is a sleeper," pro Jim Bogan said.

For some reason, Bensalem is not a course that gets a lot of talk. Not that it deserves to be lumped in with the ultra-elite courses in the area. It doesn't, but it deserves more of a reputation than it has.

It's not the least bit fancy or pretentious. ("We aren't into the high-end public thing, definitely not," Bogan said.) But not every golfer is looking for high-end. Some are quite comfortable with the "old shoe" feel, which, if you ask me, pretty much describes Bensalem.

The snack bar/grill room has a VFW-hall feel to it, with a bunch of retired regulars sitting around swapping lies and yelling at whatever game happens to be on TV.

It wasn't always this way. When it opened in 1960, Bensalem was private — Cornwell Golf Club, built on property that was once the estate of a wealthy family, the Hansells.

The designer was William Gordon, a popular and prolific area architect who began his career with the great Toomey and Flynn and went on to lay out or help revise such respected courses as Du Pont Country Club, portions of Saucon Valley's Grace and Weyhill courses, Sunnybrook Country Club, Hawk Valley, Locust Valley, White Manor, Gulph Mills, Manufacturers, Philmont, Radnor Valley, and Saucon's Old Course.

When Ford Hansell died in 1984, the course was bought by developer Al Bader, who took it semiprivate before going daily-fee four years later. Since then, it has been a quiet course serving mostly golfers from the Northeast and the near north suburbs and a few visitors from South Jersey.

If there are raps on Bensalem, they're that it can get crowded, especially during the peak season, and that the lack of a fairway sprinkler system leaves it vulnerable to heat waves.

At least one of those problems should be solved by the spring. According to Bogan, the two big improvements on tap

Scorecard

Hole	Blue	White	Red	Par Men's	Par Ladies'	HCP Men's	HCP Ladies'
1	323	307	291	4	4	16	12
2	346	334	322	4	4	10	6
3	500	488	475	5	5	1	1
4	160	145	130	3	3	13	18
5	315	304	294	4	4	14	13
6	198	183	168	3	3	8	17
7	322	309	295	4	4	18	11
8	372	313	304	4	4	6	5
9	393	355	347	4	4	5	3
Out	2,929	2738	2,626	35	35		
10	372	357	341	4	4	11	10
11	156	144	132	3	3	17	15
12	349	335	326	4	4	15	14
13	400	388	375	4	5	4	16
14	220	210	199	3	4	3	7
15	398	381	361	4	4	12	8
16	515	473	457	5	5	2	2
17	399	376	356	4	4	9	9
18	393	387	381	4	4	7	4
In	3,202	3,051	2,928	35	37		
Total	**6,131**	**5,789**	**5,554**	**70**	**72**		

for the winter are a new irrigation system and a new fleet of badly needed carts.

As for the course, it starts out OK, nothing special, but gets better and better as you go along: a simple starting hole; a straightforward, tree-lined par 5 that's reachable to better players; a short par 4 (315 yards) that's a tough, tight little driving hole with a green that is three clubs deep; a good nine — fairly tight but not overly penal; and not a lot of bunkers or water, either.

But Bensalem really doesn't bare its teeth until the back nine, beginning with the 14th. It's a 220-yard par 3, from an elevated tee, over a crevice, into a large elevated green protected by bunkers and sloping back to front — easily the most memorable hole on the course and, on a windy day, the toughest.

But Gordon is not finished. What had been an ideal walking course until the previous hole is suddenly hilly. The next hole, a par 4, is also from an elevated tee, out of a chute, up an inclined fairway.

The 16th, the only other par 5, while only 515 yards, demands three well-placed shots for any hope at par. To go for the green in 2, you'll want to keep your tee shot left; the green, after all, is tucked behind trees on the right. But if you keep your tee shot left, you're completely blocked out by a huge tree that protrudes into the fairway from the left side.

The finishing hole is also a dandy, not to mention picturesque. It's not overly long, only 393 yards, but it takes a solid, well-placed tee shot to negotiate a fairway that falls off to the left. Short-knockers also get a little weak-kneed dealing with the second shot over the creek and the greenside bunkers.

— Nov. 7, 1999

If You Go

Address: 2000 Brown Ave., Bensalem.

Phone: 215-639-5556.

Greens fees: Weekdays, walk for $25, ride for $38. Weekends, ride for $40.

Carts: No walking on weekends.

Amenities: Well-stocked pro shop; snack bar/grill room; lighted driving range; putting and chipping green; banquet facilities for 250. Outings welcome.

Rating: Overlooked outside the Northeast section of the city, but a fun course and a good layout; suitable for most levels of players.

4. Fox Hollow Golf Club

Good golf, great price

Remember that old radio ad campaign for the furniture outlets in Quakertown: "Drive a little, save a lot"?

Turns out it also applies to golf.

Tucked in a woodsy enclave just south of Quakertown is Fox Hollow Golf Club, a pleasant little course of medium difficulty, with sufficient charm and pricing affordable enough to make it worth the occasional trek.

Price alone would make Fox Hollow a nice find, but it's a decent course, too.

At 6,198 yards and with a 118 slope from the white tees, Fox Hollow is not overly long or penal — you can roll the ball up on most greens, making it manageable for higher handicappers.

Low handicappers can choose to bite off a little more. From the back tees, Fox Hollow plays 6,613 yards to a 123 slope, and only one par 5 is reachable, even for big hitters.

The outward nine is mostly flat but not boring, thanks to the pond on the first hole and three doglegs. The back nine is shorter but a bit hillier and arguably more challenging.

Fox Hollow was built in 1966 as Thunderbird Golf Club by then-owner Al Cirino. In 1986, a group of investors headed by area resident Jack Eckenrode bought the course, infused it with some cash, and renamed it for the den of foxes that lived just off the 11th tee.

Since then, Eckenrode, who plays in the occasional senior pro event, has added a few flourishes to Cirino's design. He added a few fairway bunkers, enlarged the pond on the first, put in another small pond between the fifth and sixth fairways, and reshaped a few greens.

Among Fox Hollow regulars — Eckenrode says there's a steady stream of players from Philadelphia, drawn by the price and the folksy atmosphere — the favorite hole is the first.

That's not surprising. Although it's a fairly short par-4, 354 yards, players see a tree line up the left side, the pond in front of the green, and sizable bunkers left and right of the green. Most courses start off a little easier.

Other quality holes on the front side are the 582-yard, par-5 sixth, where the fairway narrows, then bends left. The 389-yard, par-4 dogleg ninth is another favorite among regulars, requiring a well-placed tee shot.

The most ill-conceived hole is the 10th, a 437-yard dogleg right with a banked fairway and huge collection bunker on the right. So far, so good. But the second shot must be hit straight uphill onto a smallish, blind green that slopes from front to back.

For the first-timer, the par-5 dogleg 12th is also a bit of a puzzle from the tee. A tree line juts halfway across the fairway

Scorecard

Hole	Blue	White	Red	Par	HCP	Red HCP
1	364	354	291	4	5	7
2	366	346	279	4	15	11
3	188	163	114	3	11	17
4	562	552	389	5	5	3
5	392	382	296	4	9	13
6	582	532	397	5	1	1
7	378	349	245	4	17	15
8	180	171	146	3	13	9
9	389	369	307	4	7	5
Out	3,401	3,218	2,464	36		
10	437	421	331	4	4	4
11	149	134	109	3	16	14
12	495	485	391	5	8	6
13	354	316	255	4	12	16
14	155	134	106	3	10	8
15	673	603	525	5	2	2
16	137	128	102	3	18	18
17	372	362	339	4	14	10
18	440	397	356	4	6	12
In	3,212	2,980	2,520	35		
Total	**6,613**	**6,198**	**4,984**	**71**		

from the left, making it almost impossible to cut the corner.

And a golfer who splits the fairway risks carrying the ball into the 50-yard-long bunker that runs along the right side at the turn of the fairway. Still, said Eckenrode, many regulars have figured out the 12th and find it to be their best birdie opportunity.

The 15th is the longest hole — 675 from the blues, 603 from the whites — and the most unusual. It takes two solid, straight shots to get the ball down to a hollow, where the 15th suddenly takes a 90-degree turn right and heads uphill into a bunkered, sloping green. Cutting the corner here is out of the question.

"People either love this hole or hate it," Eckenrode said.

Enough regulars hate it that Eckenrode is considering breaking the 15th into two holes — a 400-yard, straight par 4, then an uphill par 3 that would begin at the bottom of the hollow.

If he does that, Eckenrode would lose the best par 3 on the course, the 16th, a short but picturesque and tricky little hole that would eventually be combined with the straight, par-4 17th to create a par 5. Eckenrode said he plans to decide by October.

Either way, the 18th, another of the fun holes at Fox Hollow, will remain intact. It's a downhill, mild dogleg right into a bunkered green that makes for a respectable finishing hole.

— July 20, 1997

If You Go

Address: 2020 Trumbauersville Rd., Quakertown.

Green fees: $30 weekdays; $40 weekends. (Coupon rate. Coupons are available upon entry).

Phone: 215-538-1920.

Carts: Mandatory weekends and holidays until noon.

Amenities: Moderately stocked pro shop, plus driving range, putting green, snack bar and grill, and banquet facilities (outings welcome).

Rating: Pleasant midlevel loop, folksy atmosphere.

5. Middletown Country Club

Course Is Short Of Being Sweet

If you look up Middletown Country Club in Golf Digest's 4,200 Best Places to Play, the municipal course in the Bucks County suburb of the same name doesn't exactly get a ringing endorsement.

One star, as in "basic golf."

It doesn't fare much better in the player comments: "poor condition," "too short," "some real weak holes" and "very strange layout."

Granted, Middletown will never show up on the short list of potential U.S. Open sites — a Knights of Columbus outing is more likely — but it's not all that bad.

Yes, it's short — only 5,862 yards from the back tees. Par is only 68; the slope from the white tees is only 109. Last week, thanks to no rain and a faulty irrigation system, the fairways were as hard as cart paths. And, yes, you do come across two or three very funky holes. (The 89-yard downhill sixth comes to mind. You stand on the tee wondering whether to hit it or throw it.)

Still, the course does have enough moments and enough redeeming holes to make it a viable loop, especially for golfers not looking for the ultimate test.

"When we're in good shape and the word gets out, we get play from all over," pro Don Beardsley said last week. "In the spring and summer, we had lots of definition from fairway to rough, but it's a shame to see what Mother Nature can do."

For my money, that's the biggest problem at Middletown — conditioning.

Being too short is not the worst thing in the world.

But it's less forgivable when you have to search for grass on the tee, or hit a tee shot that lands in the middle of the fairway, then bounds sideways until it hangs up in the rough under a tree.

For Middletown regulars, then, it should come as good news that the township, which has owned the course since 1986, is considering installing a new sprinkler system.

The course has a bit of an interesting past. The name of the designer was not readily available, but it was owned during the 1950s by George Fazio, a former PGA tour pro and course architect from Norristown. For a time, Gary Player even played out of Middletown CC.

The course was later sold to another local family, the Ciminos, before Middletown Township bought it. It's managed by GolfCorp.

Generally speaking, Middletown is hilly, with only one par 5 and plenty of very short par 4s.

The best of the holes come on the backside, starting with the 10th, a 216-yard par 3 that requires a needle-thread tee

Scorecard

Hole	Blue	White	Men's Par	Men's HCP	Red	Ladies' Par	Ladies' HCP
1	413	391	4	10	370	4	10
2	439	420	4	8	364	4	8
3	236	176	3	6	176	3	6
4	517	501	5	2	486	5	2
5	355	335	4	12	315	4	12
6	111	89	3	18	73	3	18
7	362	342	4	4	342	4	4
8	172	159	3	16	159	3	16
9	297	278	4	14	247	4	14
Out	2,902	2,691	34		2,532	34	
10	223	216	3	7	176	3	7
11	263	239	4	15	220	4	15
12	431	416	4	9	416	4	9
13	410	410	4	5	342	5	5
14	194	174	3	13	162	3	13
15	430	430	4	3	430	5	3
16	448	409	4	1	369	5	1
17	246	226	4	17	226	4	17
18	314	306	4	11	258	4	11
In	2,960	2,826	34		2,599	38	
Total	5,862	5,517	68		5,131	72	

shot through trees onto a tough, elevated green.

The next hole, although a bit quirky, has its share of charm. It's a very short par 4 (239 yards from the whites) that's driveable for some players, assuming they don't top it into the creek or lose it into the trees left and right.

At the 13th, a 410-yard dogleg, you can take the high road left for a mid-iron approach shot downhill and over a pond onto a big, inviting green. Or you can cut the corner and hope you clear the rough and reach the flats in front of the pond for a wedge onto the green.

The 14th — 174 yards, with an elevated tee and large, elevated green — is perhaps the best par 3 on the course. But the toughest and most interesting hole is easily the 16th, a 448-yard dogleg, where the second shot is over water onto a very small, elevated green tucked back in the trees. Nice hole.

— September 14, 1997

If You Go

Address: 420 N. Bellevue Ave., Langhorne.

Phone: 215-757-6953.

Greens fees: Weekdays, walk for $27, ride for $42. Weekends, walk for $32, ride for $47.

Carts: Mandatory weekends until 1pm.

Amenities: Well-stocked pro shop, snack bar, halfway house, putting green, banquet facility. Outings welcome.

Rating: Basic golf, but it could be, and might be, more.

6. Northampton Valley Country Club

A secret worth telling

Sometimes you find intriguing golf courses in places you never expected. That's the case with Northampton Valley Country Club.

A semiprivate track, Northampton is no secret to golfers in and around the Bucks County town of Richboro — at least, not judging from the crowd one afternoon last week. But its reputation doesn't seem to extend down to Philadelphia.

That's a little surprising. Although it's a bit on the short side (6,045 from the white tees), Northampton has just the kind of pleasant, medium-difficulty layout with a decent mix of holes, big and friendly greens, and well-mowed fairways that ought to make it attractive to many mid-handicap golfers.

There's quite a bit to like about Northampton. Maybe it was the children laughing and splashing in the pool near the clubhouse, or the youngsters and women out in force on the course, but the place has a wholesome, family feel to it.

"We have people who play here and then go elsewhere, but they always come back here and say they like it a lot," owner Philip Sklar said.

As for the course — tree-lined, heavily bunkered, with five water holes and huge greens — it's not a stern test for better golfers, but it can be a handful for mid- and high-handicappers.

From the blue tees, Northampton plays 6,302 yards to a 123 slope, right at the national average for length, but a bit above average in difficulty. Golf Digest's 4,200 Best Places to Play gives it 2½ stars, the knock on the course in player comments being "flat, not very inventive" and "lots of similar holes."

That evaluation may be a little outdated. True, the course,

especially on the front side, does suffer a bit from too many short, straight par 4s.

"I wish it were a trifle longer, but for the average golfer, it's enough," Sklar said.

Sklar and his son, Gary, who now runs Northampton, have made and are continuing to make the kind of improvements that could qualify Northampton for three stars.

The most recent improvement was this year's decision to turn the ninth from a very short, forgettable par 4 into the course's signature hole.

To accomplish that feat, the Sklars built a gigantic, tiered green 207 yards out from the blue tees and significantly enlarged a pond that gives a golfer fits. (The pond also extends over to the eighth hole, squeezing the fairway to about 15 yards in the driving area.)

Over the last five or six years, the Sklars have added about 20 bunkers and moved several tees back. More recent-

Scorecard

Hole	Blue	White	Yellow	Red	Par	HCP
1	366	357	315	307	4	9
2	433	415	372	366	4/5	3
3	395	358	295	285	4	7
4	385	362	288	280	4	13
5	545	520	406	400	5	1
6	170	161	156	150	3	17
7	371	362	262	255	4	11
8	349	340	330	325	4	15
9	207	184	148	140	3	5
Out	3,221	3,059	2,572	2,478	35/36	
10	328	316	293	281	4	16
11	338	333	318	306	4	18
12	205	192	162	153	3	8
13	410	398	322	312	4	4
14	185	170	146	138	3	12
15	375	367	300	294	4	10
16	515	500	359	354	5	6
17	410	405	351	344	4	2
18	315	305	260	255	4	14
In	3,081	2,986	2,511	2,437	35	
Total	6,302	6,045	5,083	4,915	70/71	

ly, they added a sizable fairway mound on the short par-4 11th, complicating that tee shot.

In the future, the Sklars plan to move the tees back about 30 yards on the short par-4 third and the par-5 fifth, and add a pond and mounds around the green at the short par-4 fourth.

"We try to do something every year to improve the course," the elder Sklar said.

Even without the improvements, Northampton already has some fine holes. Regulars enjoy the 545-yard fifth, a dogleg up a mild crest, then downhill over a creek. Because it's so well bunkered, even big hitters will have a hard time reaching the green in 2.

On the backside, the narrow, tree-lined par-5 16th can be a nightmare if you're not straight off the tee. And the 18th, despite being only 315 yards from the back tees, is a tricky, cuttable dogleg over a small pond.

Though it wasn't what it is today, Northampton has been around since 1964, when Sklar, then a young stockbroker, took a leave of absence from his firm and persuaded several friends to invest in building a course. The late Ed Ault, the very prolific Washington-area architect, handled the design.

"I got into it on a lark, and it has turned out to be the love of my life," said Sklar, who eventually quit the brokerage business.

— Aug. 17, 1997

If You Go

Address: Route 332 and Newtown Rd., Richboro

Phone: 215-355-2234

Greens fees: Weekdays, walk for $28, ride for $43. Weekends, walk for $36, ride for $51.

Carts: Mon.-Thurs., walking is permitted anytime. On Fridays carts are mandatory until 4 p.m. Sat., Sun., and holidays, carts are mandatory until 1 p.m.

7. Five Ponds Golf Club

Offers plenty of challenges

It's always a pleasure to be pleasantly surprised by a golf course.

That's exactly what happened with a lap around Warminster's township-owned Five Ponds Golf Club, which turned out to have a fun, well-conditioned, moderately priced layout and that's a relatively recent addition to the public-course scene in this area.

It's hard to say why my expectations of Five Ponds were low, other than that it had been around for eight years and I hadn't heard of it until a casual mention by a recent golf partner.

Built on what was once farmland off Street Road in Warminster, Five Ponds is not overly difficult, but it's certainly no pushover, either. With a few ho-hum holes here and several gems there, it plays a respectable 6,760 yards from the blue tees, with a 121 slope. There's enough course to please almost any level of golfer.

"Some people love it, some hate it because they think it's too hard," says recreation director Karen Whitney.

Says course manager Beau McKevitt: "It's a relatively good challenge for a daily-fee course."

More than a few golfers in that neck of the woods must agree. Just this year, readers of the Doylestown Intelligencer/Record voted Five Ponds the best golf course in Bucks and Montgomery Counties.

Designed by Hassentlug and Associates, a Pittsburgh golf-course architectural firm, Five Ponds was a family farm until eight years ago. When Warminster Township took over the property, officials there decided to build a golf course for several reasons: They wanted to provide recreation for the residents, they wanted the land to remain open space and they hoped to generate a little revenue.

The course takes its name from the five small ponds scattered across the layout. Four of those ponds are man-made; the fifth and original pond, ironically, doesn't come into play because it borders the driveway into the clubhouse.

As for the course, Five Ponds sprawls across gently rolling terrain. Some holes have plenty of open space, some have tight, tree-lined fairways.

The front nine is less interesting than the back. Indeed, standing on the first tee — a lazy, wide-open, downhill dogleg left — Five Ponds doesn't look to be much of a challenge.

But it quickly gets better. The third hole is a tasty little 180-yard par 3 over a pond, and the fourth is a fun par 4 over water into something of a peninsula green. The No. 1 handicap hole is the 455-yard, par-4 eighth, where all but the big hitters will come up short in regulation.

Scorecard

Hole	Blue	White	Gold	Red	Par	HCP
1	380	365	345	335	4	15
2	395	375	330	315	4	9
3	180	165	145	135	3	7
4	415	385	360	295	4	3
5	545	540	485	450	5	13
6	375	360	320	305	4	17
7	185	175	155	145	3	11
8	455	435	390	345	4	1
9	400	395	350	320	4	5
Out	3,330	3,195	2,880	2,645	35	
10	390	380	365	330	4	10
11	225	185	165	135	3	6
12	530	520	500	480	5	8
13	370	360	350	295	4	14
14	405	370	330	310	4	16
15	555	535	525	460	5	4
16	440	405	380	345	4	2
17	165	150	140	130	3	12
18	350	340	315	300	4	18
In	3,430	3,245	3,070	2,785	36	
Total	**6,760**	**6,440**	**5,950**	**5,430**	**71**	

The back nine features the more interesting holes. No. 12, a 530-yard par 5, is a very tight, tree-lined hole that's a problem for anybody who can't keep it on the straight and narrow.

The best is reserved for the four finishing holes. No. 15, a 555-yard, par 5, dogleg left, goes down a hill to a creek, then up, then left, into a green guarded by bunkers. This would be a fine hole on any golf course.

Next up is a tricky par 4, the 440-yard, uphill dogleg-right 16th that requires a tee shot to split a narrow chute of trees on the left and right. The hole's length will make you want to hit driver; the trees will make you favor a fairway wood or long iron.

If you manage that hole, you're on to the 165-yard, par-3 17th, which plays from an elevated tee over a pond. If the wind is blowing, or if the pin is tucked behind the tree on the left, take a deep breath and say a prayer before you hit.

The 18th, a slightly uphill, 350-yard, par 4, is not a guaranteed par, either, although it is the most forgiving of the finishing holes.

Five Ponds is not exotic or exclusive. But it's well-conceived and well-maintained. If that appeals to you, you may be pleasantly surprised, too.

— Oct. 13, 1996

If You Go

Address: 1225 W. Street Rd. Warminster

Phone: 215-956-9727

Greens fees: Weekdays; walk for $26, ride for $38. Weekends, walk for $30, ride for $42.

Other Bucks County Courses

Neshaminy Valley Golf Club
Alms House Rd., Jamison.
215-343-6930
$22 weekdays, $28 weekends. Carts are an additional $11.

Oxford Valley Golf Course
141 South Oxford Valley Rd., Fairless Hills.
215-945-8644
$8 weekdays, weekends

Somerton Springs Golf
53 Bustleton Pike. Feasterville.
215-322-8344
$9 weekdays; $12 weekends

Spring Mill Country Club
80 Jacksonville Rd., Ivyland.
215-672-6110
$80 anytime; $60 if accompanied by a member

The Fairways Golf and Country Club
750 Country Club Lane, Warrington.
215- 343-9979
Weekdays, $22 to walk, $30 to ride; weekends $28 to walk, $38 to ride.

Chester

C O U N T Y

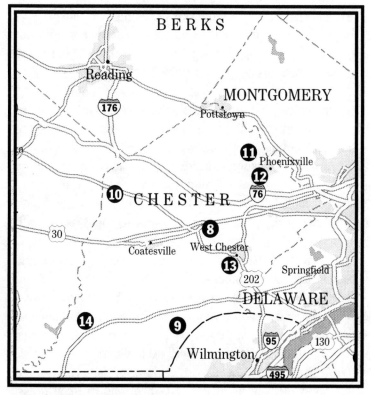

8. Downingtown Country Club
9. Hartefeld National
10. Honeybrook Golf Club
11. Kimberton Golf Club
12. Pickering Valley Golf Club
13. Tattersall Golf Club
14. Wyncote Golf Club

8. Downingtown Country Club

Course that challenges high- and low-handicappers alike

If the boom in golf is responsible for the construction of several new courses in the Philadelphia area, it's also behind the much-needed face-lifts of a few others.

Case in point: Downingtown Country Club.

Don't let the name fool you. Downingtown, an original George Fazio design from the mid-1960s that once was part of the defunct Downingtown Inn Resort, is no members-only enclave. In fact, it's not a country club at all.

It's a daily-fee course that plans to offer "country club" amenities when farmhouse-to-clubhouse renovation is complete in late fall. The clubhouse — an old farmhouse joined to a second building, overlooking the second green — will feature a pro shop, locker room, restaurant and banquet facility.

"We want to be as good as Hartefeld National and Wyncote," said Jeff Broadbelt, Downingtown's director of golf operations, referring to two other recent, top-drawer additions to the local public-course scene.

Time will tell. The redone course, however, is ready and willing to take on all comers.

From the championship tees, Downingtown measures 6,619 yards and boasts a 72.9 course rating and a 132 slope. From the white tees, it measures a more modest 5,771 yards, with a 125 slope. Nothing to sneeze at, in either case.

Indeed, Downingtown, with its mix of flat, rolling and water holes, as well as plenty of bunkers and fescue grass, can be downright cruel to the high-handicapper and a testy challenge for the mid- and low-handicapper.

Two weeks ago, when 73 area seniors descended on Downingtown in hopes of qualifying for one of four spots in this weekend's U.S. Senior Open outside Cleveland, only five golfers broke par (the low score was a 2-under 70) and only three others managed even par.

"The layout is very good, and it was a legitimate challenge," senior tour player Bob Dickson told the local paper, the Daily Local News, at the time. "I thought this course was an appropriate test of golf."

If the course stood tall, it may well have been thanks in considerable measure to last year's redesign work by Broadbelt, a former greens superintendent at Chester Valley Golf Club, and Gil Hanse, a young golf architect from Malvern who helped design Stonewall Golf Club in Chester County.

They added a new irrigation system, trimmed or cut down about 500 unhealthy trees, and added two ponds that come into play on the 13th, 14th and 17th, plus a creek that slices through the picturesque 18th.

But mostly what they did was toughen up the 40-odd

Scorecard

Hole	Black	Blue	White	Red	Par	HCP	Ladies' HCP
1	397	378	361	316	4	11	7
2	369	359	334	302	4	5	5
3	187	169	140	123	3	17	15
4	323	300	289	267	4	15	13
5	361	338	307	286	4	9	17
6	403	382	328	302	4	1	3
7	390	369	350	320	4	3	9
8	498	478	456	412	5	7	1
9	361	345	331	289	4	13	11
Out	3,289	3,118	2,896	2,617	36		
10	331	314	303	268	4	14	16
11	476	431	410	358	4	2	2
12	170	161	139	120	3	16	14
13	497	467	418	372	5	6	8
14	393	372	351	299	4	10	10
15	162	131	114	82	3	18	18
16	531	507	495	434	5	4	4
17	208	172	144	110	3	12	12
18	562	536	501	432	5	8	6
In	3330	3,091	2,875	2,475	36		
Total	**6,619**	**6,209**	**5,771**	**5,092**	**72**		

bunkers, add about 50 — greenside pot bunkers, a British Open-style collection overgrown with fescue — and elongate traps that pinch both sides.

To wit: Broadbelt's favorite hole, the 300-yard, par-4 fourth, a lazy little dogleg to the right. Except that Hanse and Broadbelt, no doubt with fiendish delight, erected a virtual wall of fescue-laden bunkers across much of the fairway, daring golfers to do anything but lay up or stay wide left. Fun hole.

But frankly, even with invigorated bunkers and tall, unfriendly grass, several par 4s on the front nine, ranging from 300 to 378 yards, come off as rather ordinary.

Curiously, the No. 1 handicap hole, the 382-yard, par-4 sixth, with a pond left of the green, was neither the most difficult nor the most interesting hole on the course.

For the low-handicapper, the back nine is much more interesting than the front. It boasts three par 5s (a rarity) and three par 3s (also a rarity), two of them over water.

As for interesting, there are the 12th, a 161-yard, par 3 over water; the uphill, par-5 13th; the 172-yard, pond-protected, par-3 17th, and the 536-yard, par-5 18th.

Downingtown Country Club is a welcome addition to the publinks scene, a place where a high-handicapper and a low-handicapper can share an enjoyable round.

One note: Cart fees are very high, $20 a person. As Broadbelt tells it, it's not because they're trying to gouge the public, but because they want to discourage riding.

"We want you to walk," he said. "We want to have an old-fashioned flavor. It crossed my mind not to have carts at all, but I was worried about shutting out people who need them."

There are no caddies now, but Broadbelt is considering adding them. Pull carts can be rented.

— July 7, 1996

If You Go

Address: 85 Country Club Drive. (Behind the Brandywine Square Shopping Center in Downingtown, off of U.S. Route 30.)

Phone: 610-269-2000.

Greens fees: Friday through Sunday, $63 without cart. Monday through Thursday, $53 without cart.

Carts: Never mandatory. $20 a person.

Rating: Well-conditioned. Practice your sand play. Downingtown can frustrate the high-handicapper, but the low-handicapper can break 80.

9. Hartefeld National

Public course among the elite

Of all the new or redesigned golf courses in the area, the one that has received the most publicity and praise is Hartefeld National, south of Avondale, Chester County, near Wilmington.

After playing a round, it's easy to see why. Public golf courses don't come much better than this.

Designed by Tom Fazio, whom Golf Digest calls the premier course architect in the world today, the 16-month-old Hartefeld National already has cracked Golf magazine's elite list of top-10 public tracks in the country. No surprise, also, that it's in the running for the Golf Digest selection as best

Scorecard

Hole	Fazio	Back	Middle	Front	Par	HCP	Ladies HCP
1	579	539	505	411	5	7	5
2	162	143	121	101	3	17	17
3	410	397	376	306	4	5	7
4	450	423	392	337	4	3	3
5	534	507	486	445	5	11	1
6	198	174	153	116	3	15	13
7	406	360	333	289	4	9	11
8	472	443	379	296	4	1	9
9	223	202	156	115	3	13	15
Out	3,434	3,188	2,901	2,416	35		
10	425	392	365	349	4	10	12
11	186	181	155	125	3	18	16
12	346	324	313	238	4	16	14
13	581	543	507	463	5	4	2
14	198	174	151	107	3	14	18
15	392	366	346	296	4	12	6
16	552	510	458	383	5	2	10
17	447	418	395	367	4	8	4
18	409	374	345	321	4	6	8
In	3,535	3,282	3,085	2,649	36		
Total	6,969	6,470	5,936	5,065	71		

new course of 1996.

What makes Hartefeld so special?

Three key ingredients: a wonderful, rolling piece of rural real estate that's wooded in some areas and wide-open links style in others; the most celebrated designer on the scene today; and an owner — Wilmington restaurateur and 2-handicapper Davis Sezna — who knows how to cater to customers.

"When you have Tom Fazio, all you do is introduce him to a great piece of property," said Sezna, whose 1492 Hospitality Group in Wilmington owns the Columbus Inn, Klondike Kate's and Kid Sheleen's.

"My only prerequisite was a course that could be enjoyed by everybody, but be able to set up for championship play if I wanted to."

Fazio, who also designed the lavishly praised Galloway National at the Shore, certainly accomplished that. On perhaps a half-dozen holes, you may find yourself standing on the tee marveling at what lies before you and muttering: "Wow."

And yet Hartefeld is not a backbreaker. From the championship tees, it's long — 6,969 yards — and plays to a 73.2 rating and a 131 slope. But from the middle tees, the Hartefeld course measures only 5,936 yards and carries a 68.3 rating and a 123 slope.

There's water on only one hole, the sixth, a medium-length par 3. And even from the back tees, the half-dozen or so holes that require carries over ravines are not overwhelming.

The strength of Hartefeld National — and the source of its beauty and uniqueness — is the contour of the land, which was once part of the estate of a wealthy Delaware family, the Robinsons. Scarcely a single hole is flat — they roll and pitch, or slash across ravines — giving Hartefeld National a distinctly different feel from almost any other course in the area.

Take the 15th through the 18th, for example, as picturesque and terrific a sequence of four holes as you could hope to find.

Fifteen, a 392-yard par 4 from the championship tees, begins from an elevated tee and requires a drive over a 150-yard ravine into an elevated, uphill fairway, framed by trees on the right and far left, as well as bunkers. The 16th, a 552-yard par 5, is all uphill, punctuated by nasty bunkers, into a treacherous, sloping green. The 17th, a 447-yard par 4, takes you back down the hill, with a large, hungry bunker pinching the fairway from the left. And the 18th, a 409-yard par 4, starts from another elevated tee, over a ravine, into an uphill, dogleg-right fairway.

A personal favorite is the 5th, a 534-yard par 5 from the championship tees that slopes downhill to a small ravine that gobbles up long tee shots, before heading uphill again, dog-legging left as it goes, into an elevated green.

What's most interesting about the hole is the approach shot into the green. Because the fifth plays 507 or less from the shorter tees, many players will be tempted to go for the green in 2. But the green is guarded by a small army of ghastly bunkers that have "snowman" written all over them.

What's Sezna's favorite hole?

"That's like asking me which is my favorite son," he said.

Greens fees at Hartefeld National are not cheap, $110 weekends and weekdays, including mandatory cart fees. Nor is Hartefeld — located between Interstate 95 and U.S. Route 1 — easily accessible for many Philadelphia area golfers. But the trek is worth it, at least once or twice a year.

And because Sezna is a veteran of the hospitality industry, he has devoted probably as much attention to the service from the staff, the clubhouse, the restaurant and the grill, called the Walker Cup Room, honoring the nation's finest amateurs. It has all paid off in a state-of-the-art public facility.

— Sept. 15, 1995

If You Go

Address: Route 7, near the intersection with Route 41, Avondale.

Phone: 610-268-8800.

Greens fees: Weekdays and weekends, $110, including cart. No pull-carts allowed.

Carts: Walking permitted anytime, but cart fees are included.

Amenities: First-class restaurant, grill room and pub; well-stocked pro shop; driving range.

Rating: Hartefeld National is this area's premier daily-fee golf course.

10. Honeybrook Golf Club

A work in progress, but full of promise

Once again, farming's loss is golf's gain. This time, it's in the form of Honeybrook Golf Club, a very pleasant, reasonably priced, daily-fee course in the farthest reaches of Chester County.

Open for just a week, Honeybrook is anything but another entry in that growing market of 7,000-yard, top-dollar, country-clubs-for-a-day affairs designed by a big-name architect.

Rather, it's the latest addition to another growing category: good quality, mid-priced layouts that hope to appeal to the players who want more than a run-down, $25 public course but can't afford or justify the $100 greens fees at the upscale publics.

The result at Honeybrook is a homey, unpretentious facility, where the clubhouse is being fashioned from an old barn, and the 6,341-yard course is first-rate but not awesome.

Whom to thank? The Piersol siblings: Tom, the general manager; Ted, the assistant superintendent; and sister Donna Horvath, who doubles as the business manager and chief hot-dog saleswoman.

"It was risky, but we looked at it as something we all could do," Tom Piersol said last week, recalling the decision to give up years of dairy farming to enter an uncertain business they knew little or nothing about. (None of them plays golf.) "And we're all in our 40s, so we decided we could take a couple of bad years in the beginning, if we had to. We plan to be in this for the long haul."

The rolling 165-acre tract, which is about 10 miles from Downingtown, had been in the Piersol family since the 1930s. Tom and Ted, both with degrees in biology from Lycoming College, had spent the last 15 years running the farm, while Donna was the office manager for their father, a veterinarian in New Holland.

By 1994, the brothers realized the farm couldn't generate enough income for their families, but it was too much for just one of them to run. What to do? Sell out to real estate developers and get killed by taxes, or keep the land and build a golf course?

If the crowd there on Thursday — only the fourth day of operation — was any indication, the Piersols made a smart move.

Honeybrook is still very much a work in progress. Renovations on the barn-turned-clubhouse won't be finished for another three or four weeks. For now, the pro shop and snack bar operate out of humble, temporary quarters. But Honeybrook has real promise.

For a course that has been open just a matter of days, it is in commendable shape. The tees, fairways and greens are

Scorecard

Hole	Blue	White	Yellow	Red	Par	HCP	Ladies HCP
1	367	361	334	323	4	13	9
2	367	359	351	330	4	9	7
3	185	180	167	151	3	17	17
4	552	546	514	437	5	3	3
5	417	413	397	333	4	1	1
6	397	392	382	353	4	5	5
7	336	329	321	265	4	15	13
8	212	187	181	142	3	11	15
9	403	366	362	277	4	4	11
Out	3,236	3,133	3,009	2,611	35		
10	227	192	182	146	3	10	14
11	423	410	397	325	4	2	6
12	561	551	533	454	4	6	5
13	168	158	150	125	3	18	16
14	314	276	260	211	5	8	10
15	545	532	518	446	5	4	5
16	280	268	258	242	4	14	4
17	185	156	146	121	3	16	18
18	402	355	351	280	4	12	12
In	3,105	2,898	2795	2350	35		
Total	**6,341**	**6,031**	**5,804**	**4,961**	**70**		

already grown in. The rough is still gnarly and uncultivated, but that's understandable.

As for the layout, architect Jim Blaukovitch starts you out slow and easy, then works up to the good stuff. The first and second holes are simple, up-and-back par 4s that reveal little of the twists and turns to come.

Although the front nine has its moments — the fifth, a tough par 4 with a blind tee shot and long approach shot over water, is the signature hole — the best Honeybrook has to offer comes late in the outward nine and over much of the back side.

Given the terrain, it's hard to find a hole that doesn't offer some kind of elevation change, which more often than not complicates either the tee shot or the approach. The seventh, for example, plays just 336 yards from the back tee, but it's all downhill, and the short approach shot is over wild grass into a sunken, bowlike green that is virtually blind — even after a bomb off the tee.

Blaukovitch makes the most of another short par 4 on the back, the 314-yard 14th. From the back tees, you're looking at a very tight shot because of trees right and left, and a 200-yard carry over wild grass into a decidedly small landing area. Once you have negotiated all that, the 100-yard second shot is a cinch.

There are a couple of forgettable holes as well, but Blaukovitch makes up for them with strong par 3s, ranging from 168 to 227 yards from the tips. He also doesn't short-change you on any of the three par 5s, which all go in the 550-yard range and are not reachable by the likes of me.

There's not much water at Honeybrook. The little ponds on Nos. 1 and 2 shouldn't give most people any problem, although the water guarding the fifth green is another story entirely. Can you carry a second shot close to 200 yards?

Like so many farms converted into courses, Honeybrook's front and back nines are quite different as the course makes its way from nearly treeless, rolling pasture on the front into wooded wetlands on the back. Put it all together, and it adds up to a slope of 128 from the back tees.

At some point during the round, you'll probably also realize just how far out in the country you are. The day I played, just as I settled in over my putt at the fifth green, a young Amish woman in a buggy came clippity-clopping down the nearby road. Then, at the 15th and 16th, it was impossible not to get a snootful of the rich and unmistakable aroma of a dairy farm next door. Whew.

"A number of people have commented on that," head pro Michael Spease said. "I'm a little anxious to see what that's going to smell like in summer."

— April 23, 2000

If You Go

Address: 1422 Cambridge Rd., Honey Brook.

Phone: 610-273-0207.

Greens fees: Monday through Thursday $32 to walk, $45 to ride. Friday through Sunday, $59 including cart.

Carts: Walking permitted anytime.

Amenities: Clubhouse with pro shop and snack bar (under construction); grass driving range; putting green; casual outdoor banquet facility for 180. Outings welcome.

Rating: Great addition to the mid-price market. Solid layout; good condition; friendly, unpretentious atmosphere.

11. Kimberton Golf Club

A shot-and-beer kind of course

In a world where most of the new courses these days seem to be those country-club-for-a-day affairs, there's still plenty of room for the working stiff's golf course.

Just ask Bob Hays.

"We don't have any illusions about what we are or any pretensions to compete with the upscale courses," Hays, the head professional, general manager and co-owner of Kimberton Golf Club near Phoenixville, said last week.

"We know what we are and we're comfortable with it — we're playable, affordable, and we have a friendly, almost family atmosphere."

Make no mistake: If you're a golfer who favors the upscale side of the game, Kimberton is probably not for you.

While the course, like Waynesborough Country Club, is a George Fazio design, it's never going to be a candidate for a PGA stop. And all you need to know about the clubhouse, such as it is, is that it has Old Milwaukee beer on tap.

But Hays, whose family has owned Kimberton since it was opened in 1962, is not about to apologize. If anything, he believes the "everyman" atmosphere goes a long way toward explaining Kimberton's success over four decades.

"The proliferation of upscale courses is great, but they're not affordable to the vast majority of people," Hays said. "There's real need for a facility like this to get people interested and to grow the game."

Kimberton, named for the small town nearby, was built on what was once Hays family farmland. Hays' father, Bob Sr., was behind the project, rounding up several investors. When word got out that they were building a course, they were approached by Fazio, a Norristown native and former tour professional who was trying to carve out a career as a golf-course architect.

"He had designed one other course at the time, but he hadn't been paid for it," Hays said. "We were the first to pay him."

Fazio's nephew, Tom, now the kingpin in the world of golf-course design, was still in high school, but he pitched in to help his uncle.

Bob Jr. was 12 at the time, but he, too, went to work at the course. After college, he never thought of working anywhere else. When his father retired in 1986, he took over as head professional and general manager. Today, he owns Kimberton with Elizabeth Palmer, whose late husband was one of the original investors.

"This has been my life's work," Hays said.

Everything about Kimberton is meat and potatoes, sort of golf's equivalent of a beer-and-a-shot bar. The combination

Scorecard

Hole	Blue	White	Gold	Red	Par	Red Par	HCP	Red HCP
1	394	378	370	364	4	4	11	3
2	416	403	392	333	4	4	9	7
3	390	374	363	296	4	4	1	1
4	192	182	166	139	3	3	13	13
5	419	407	394	312	4	4	7	1
6	176	164	150	88	3	3	15	15
7	540	508	506	448	5	5	5	5
8	389	374	364	302	4	4	3	9
9	143	120	118	116	3	3	17	17
Out	3,059	2,910	2,822	2,398	34	34		
10	314	308	304	302	4	4	14	8
11	465	445	432	421	4	5	2	4
12	364	350	338	260	4	4	4	6
13	365	354	346	248	4	4	10	14
14	208	199	194	190	3	3	12	10
15	516	489	475	398	5	5	8	12
16	159	136	130	122	3	3	18	18
17	510	494	484	423	5	5	6	2
18	344	331	320	258	4	4	16	16
In	3,245	3,106	3,023	2,612	36	37		
Total	6,304	6,016	5,845	5,010	70	71		

pro shop and snack bar is casual. The course, while generally flat and heavy on short par 4s, does offer enough in the way of gentle hills, doglegs and water hazards to warrant an above-average 123 slope from the back tees. A glance at the score-card suggests Kimberton is short — 6,304 yards — but that's mostly because it has only three par 5s.

First-timers looking for a test might be a little concerned after the first two holes. They are both short, flat, ho-hum par 4s. But it picks up at the third with a 390-yard dogleg that can give you fits if you miss the fairway and a second shot over water. The eighth, a rolling par 4 with a pond lurking on the right, can also be devilish if players are not careful.

On the inward nine, Hays favors the 465-yard 11th, a par 5 converted to a par 4, partly because it's the one hole many players can't reach in regulation. It's a good hole, as is the 14th, the longest par 3 at 208 yards.

But the vote for best hole would probably go to the 15th, a 516-yard par 5 that plays from an elevated tee, through trees, onto a sloping fairway, then around to a green tucked into the trees. With very little effort at all, you can walk away here with a double bogey.

The other par 5 on the back, the 17th, also presents many players with the dilemma of laying up safely in front of the pond or going for broke in 2.

When I played, it wasn't the layout that caused concern, it was the course's condition. The rough was way up, the fair-ways looked as if they hadn't been cut in days, and even the tees were overgrown.

That, Hays said, is unusual for Kimberton. But like most every course in the area, Kimberton was hit hard by this sum-mer's drought. Groundskeepers lost all the fairways, then spent all the time and energy reseeding and fertilizing while also trying to keep the greens from going south. The result was that the staff got a little behind in mowing.

"Normally, we try to keep everything cut down pretty low," Hays said.

Good. I was glad to hear that, and I'm sure the regulars at Kimberton will be, too.

— Sept. 26, 1999

If You Go

Address: Route 23, about three miles west of Phoenixville.

Phone: 610-933-8836.

Greens fees: Weekdays, $23 to walk, $34 to ride. Weekends, $33 to walk, $44 to ride.

Carts: Walking permitted anytime.

Amenities: Well-stocked pro shop. Putting green. No driving range, though there is a range next door. Snack bar. Outings and leagues welcome.

Rating: Midlevel layout. Affordable, casual, friendly. Good course for beginners, seniors, and middle-to-high handicappers.

12. Pickering Valley Golf Club

Six brothers weave tale of two courses

If the economy of the '80s was disastrous for farmers, it was nothing short of fabulous for golfers — especially public-course golfers.

Area courses built in the past decade on what was once farmland include Royal Oaks in Lebanon, Wyncote in Oxford — both terrific courses — and the quite decent municipal track in Warminster, Five Ponds.

Now add to that daily-fee list Pickering Valley Golf Club near Phoenixville, which the six Thompson brothers have transformed over the last decade from a dairy farm to a no-frills, mid-level public track.

"We were in the same situation as other family farms, fighting to stay aboveboard," said Jerry Thompson, Pickering Valley's greens superintendent, who with his brothers grew up on the 200-acre spread.

"In the '80s, when the prime rate went to 22 percent, we didn't want to let the land go, so we turned it into a golf course," he said.

The Thompsons, who had dabbled at golf, didn't have a big developer's deep pockets to bring in a top-name designer, so brother John got the nod. (He has gone on to participate in designing several other area courses, including Moccasin Run, Fox Chase and Spring Hollow.)

These days, all the Thompson brothers — Jerry, Ben, John, Steve, Jim and Tom, ages 38 to 52 — live with their families on or adjacent to the property, and they work at Pickering Valley.

Tom, the oldest, runs the pro shop. The rest work "outside," according to Jerry. "It's a pretty enjoyable situation," he said.

Pickering Valley's front side — wide-open pasture that's

hilly in places — opened in 1985. The back nine — also hilly, but tighter and more challenging, thanks to trees — opened the following year.

The course is delightful in places, confounding in others. Because the Thompsons didn't have millions for giant earth-movers, Pickering Valley pretty much adheres to the terrain as laid out by nature and interpreted by John Thompson.

The most boring hole on the course without question is No. 1, a wide-open, straight-away, uphill par 4 that measures 295 yards from the white tees. Trudging up that fairway is enough to make you wonder why you came in the first place.

But Pickering Valley quickly redeems itself. The second hole, a long par 3 from a wooded, elevated tee over a pond into a green set among trees, is perhaps the most picturesque hole on the course.

Scorecard

Hole	Blue	White	Red	Par	HCP
1	311	295	285	4	10
2	216	183	143	3	12
3	361	346	283	4	2
4	472	455	386	5	16
5	446	421	302	4	4
6	215	208	191	3	18
7	408	354	324	4	6
8	488	465	380	5	14
9	367	332	314	4	8
Out	3,284	3,059	2,608	36	
10	186	149	103	3	17
11	363	346	304	4	3
12	322	306	249	4	11
13	381	367	332	4	5
14	487	464	420	5	7
15	356	336	320	4	13
16	180	158	103	3	9
17	558	515	420	5	15
18	413	398	276	4	1
In	3,246	3,039	2,527	36	
Total	**6,530**	**6,098**	**5,135**	**72**	

The next few holes are forgettable until you come to No. 8, a 465-yard, 90-degree dogleg left that confronts the golfer with a sloping fairway and two small ponds.

It also confronts the golfer with a small sign on the tee unlike any other I've seen in more than 35 years of golf. It says: "No cutting corners: 2-stroke penalty."

The reason, said Jerry Thompson, is that the dogleg on the eight is severe enough that some golfers try to cut the corner by hitting a blind tee shot over the crest on the left, chewing the hole in half. Because of the danger posed to the group in front, the Thompsons decided they had to do something.

"That's the luxury of local rules," he said. "There's the danger of a ball hitting somebody on the head."

For my money, the back side is better. The 10th is a fun little downhill par 3 over a pond. The 12th, at only 322 yards from the blue tees, is a short, downhill par 4, but the tree-lined fairway is tighter than a corridor. The 13th is not a bad little dogleg-right par 4.

And then you come to the 14th, a 487-yard par 5, which struck me as a metaphor for all that is right — and wrong — with Pickering Valley.

You play two or three holes that are fun and challenging, and you start to think it's a fun course. Then suddenly you hit a hole like the 14th, where there's no green in sight, no clue where to aim a tee shot, and you're left shaking your head in dismay. It's a cycle that repeats itself several times over the course of a round at Pickering Valley.

For regulars, that's not a problem. But for first-time golfers, ouch.

Whether or not you become a regular at Pickering Valley, one thing is for sure: Somewhere out there, one of the six Thompson brothers is probably watching, so for goodness sakes be sure to fix that ball mark and replace that divot.

— Oct. 27, 1996

If You Go

Address: 450 S. Whitehorse Rd., Phoenixville.

Phone: 610-933-2223

Greens fees: Weekdays, $24 to walk, $36 to ride; $45 weekends.

Carts: Carts are mandatory on weekends.

13. Tattersall Golf Club

Pricey course is well worth a try when it finally opens

Magazine and newspaper ads have been running for weeks. In certain golf circles, anticipation is running high. But so far, Tattersall Golf Club, the new upscale daily-fee course near West Chester, has yet to open, and it won't for another week, maybe three.

The folks at Tattersall themselves don't seem to know exactly when. It all depends on how quickly a subcontractor can finish last-minute touch-up work so that the course complies with government regulations.

When it does officially open, here's betting you will like it.

Tattersall, one of a dozen new courses developed around the country by Meadowbrook Golf Group Inc., the company that manages the Philadelphia city courses, should eventually stand toe-to-toe with the other pricey country-clubs-for-a-day in the Chester County neighborhood, namely Hartefeld National and Wyncote.

It could be spring, however, before Tattersall is completely in operation. The 6,826-yard course, designed by Rees Jones, is ready, waiting and looking good. But the clubhouse, which is being converted from a 17th-century farmhouse on the property, is still in the early stages of restoration.

The plan, naturally, is to establish Tattersall as part of the "rota" of fancy, daily-fee courses in Chester County. The hope is that golfers who can afford $100 greens fees will play Hartefeld National one week, Wyncote the next, then Tattersall.

"Our experience with this kind of customer is that about 20 percent become regulars and view it as their country club, and 80 percent have it in their rotation of courses or play it on special occasions," Mike Rippey, vice president of

Meadowbrook, said the other day.

For the upscale crowd, that would make for an interesting mix of courses. After a recent round there, I came away thinking Tattersall can play in that league, although it is very different from both Hartefeld, which can play long and demanding, and Wyncote, which is largely wide-open and rolling.

Tattersall, while not brutally difficult, can also be demanding, playing to a 73 rating and 132 slope from the tips.

Scorecard

Hole	Tattersall	Bordley	Broad Run	Brandywine	Par
1	498	479	456	425	5
2	415	393	385	337	4
3	379	348	309	285	4
4	387	342	299	242	4
5	318	298	280	250	4
6	414	399	377	314	4
7	429	412	388	347	4
8	152	137	123	104	3
9	401	381	366	310	4
Out	3393	3189	2983	2614	36
10	205	169	154	124	3
11	386	363	345	307	4
12	528	505	473	458	5
13	197	171	147	126	3
14	425	403	381	292	4
15	549	520	495	442	5
16	399	381	367	311	4
17	193	160	145	129	3
18	551	535	521	483	5
In	3433	3207	3028	2672	36
Total	**6,826**	**6,396**	**6,011**	**5,286**	**72**

It rolls across the hills, down into the valleys and, in places, through the woodlands of Chester County. In several places, you'll find yourself pausing to have a look at the commanding view. In other places, it can be downright tight, fraught with danger for the wayward shot.

What good golfers will immediately like about Tattersall is the need for shot-making. Jones, son of the late Robert Trent Jones and Golf World magazine's architect of the year in 1995, doesn't build tricked-up golf courses, although his layouts also aren't forgiving of the truly lousy shot. Jones builds substantial courses — he designed Lookaway in Bucks County, too — and he makes you work for par on most every hole.

That becomes evident right away at Tattersall with an opening par 5 that flows down toward a waste area, then back up a hill to a mostly blind green. If you're not careful, you can make a double bogey before you get your shoes tied.

From there, Jones slashes across hillsides, carving out a string of six long to mid-length par 4s (only one par 5 and one par 3 are on the front) that don't give you much chance to relax. Every chance he gets, Jones likes to confront you with a shot that's dramatic in appearance — often with a change in elevation — and also makes you wonder if the yardage is correct.

The 429-yard seventh is the brute of the front, for my money. It's fairly long but also narrow, with a wooded hillside on the left and a right side that plummets down toward very bad things.

The stars of the back nine are the 12th, a sweeping 528-yard dogleg par 5 that begins from an elevated tee and works its way around and back uphill; and the 13th, a 197-yard downhill par 3 that boasts a green bigger than a lot of townships in Chester County.

The most curious hole on the course is the par-3 17th, with its 100-foot drop down to the green. Out of curiosity, I hit two balls there, one from the tips (193 yards) and one from the front tees (129 yards). Go figure — I hit the green from the back and missed it from the front.

At 551 yards, the par-5 18th is the longest hole on the course and a terrific closing hole. It would also be one of the most attractive holes at Tattersall, if there were not an obtrusive series of giant electrical towers that spoil the sight. Oh, well.

All in all, Tattersall is a winner. Just be sure to pack your credit cards along with your A game.

— Aug. 6, 2000

If You Go

Address: 1520 Tattersall Way, West Chester.
Phone: 610-738-4410.

Web site: www.tattersallgolfclub.com

Greens fees: Weekdays $88. Weekends $108. Includes cart fee.

Carts: Walking permitted anytime, although cart fees are included.

Amenities: Driving range and putting green. Corporate outings welcome.

Rating: Top-of-the-line daily-fee facility. It won't make you forget Hartefeld or Wyncote, but it stands on its own. Tough course from the tips, even for low-handicappers. Could present problems for high-handicappers and beginners. Definitely worth sampling by the well-traveled player.

14. Wyncote Golf Club

A course with a difference

In politics, there are Democrats and there are Republicans. In golf, there are those who will travel to England and Scotland just to play links-style courses and there are those who can't stay far enough away from them.

Do you know which kind of golfer you are?

Before you plunk down money for that plane ticket abroad, you might want to find out. It's possible with a trip to southern Chester County, to a three-year-old, upscale daily-fee course called Wyncote Golf Club.

"We are a very different kind of golf course," said Wyncote's general manager, Bruce Einstein. "But we wanted to be different. We wanted to offer golfers a different option to the traditional East Coast course."

Different it is.

Fashioned from what was once rolling farmland and environmentally protected marshland, the topography at Wyncote ("windy cottage") has dictated a sprawling, wide-open layout, where holes weave up and down, back and forth, and where you can wave to other golfers four fairways away. Certainly no trees obscure your view.

"Four trees on the front side, four on the back," the starter joked recently on the first tee. He must have counted the tall bushes.

Of course, just because you won't find your ball stymied behind a tree doesn't mean Wyncote is easy — not by a long shot. Playing a whopping 7,012 yards from the back tees, Wyncote sports a 73.8 course rating and a 128 slope, making it well above average in difficulty. From the red tees, Wyncote plays a much more manageable 5,454 yards.

The course has already won two significant awards in its short existence: In 1993, Golf Digest named it the third-best new public course in the country. Last year, the magazine deemed it the best public course in Pennsylvania.

Because of the lack of trees, the wind can whip across the 180-acre layout as if it were a Kansas wheat field, leaving you flapping like that mean old woman pedaling her bicycle up the road in The Wizard of Oz.

It also means you can find yourself hitting two clubs more, two clubs less, or, if it's a crosswind, aiming at the wrong green. If you have ever watched a British Open on television, you know what we're talking about.

The topography, combined with the raw elements of Mother Nature, also affects course conditions. The bent-grass fairways and greens tend to be dry and hard to hold.

Just like in the British Open, hitting short and rolling the ball onto the green is often the best option, which is why designer Brian Ault built very few traps directly in front of

Scorecard

Hole	Black	Blue	White	Red	Par	HCP	Red HCP
1	5,777	521	480	443	5	7	5
2	460	426	407	358	4	3	1
3	356	342	306	275	4	11	9
4	401	364	334	329	4	1	3
5	188	163	147	130	3	17	15
6	348	342	309	286	4	15	13
7	417	408	378	343	4	5	7
8	222	180	147	128	3	13	17
9	529	487	452	422	5	9	11
Out	3,498	3,233	2,960	2,714	36		
10	568	517	477	429	5	8	8
11	196	185	159	135	3	16	16
12	361	348	323	287	4	12	10
13	456	444	416	377	4	2	4
14	363	351	340	294	4	10	12
15	187	172	157	119	3	18	18
16	424	391	374	341	4	6	6
17	379	369	334	284	4	14	14
18	580	566	534	474	5	4	2
In	5,414	3,343	3,114	2,740	36		
Total	**7,012**	**6,576**	**6,074**	**5,454**	**72**		

the greens. It's also why the sprinkler heads offer three distance measurements: front, center and back of the green.

Technically, Einstein points out, Wyncote is not a links course, it's a heathland course. Links courses are oceanside; heathland courses, a common design early in the century, are inland.

Either way, there are several memorable holes. Nos. 1 and 10, side-by-side, mirror-image par 5s separated by wild grass and a pond fronting the sprawling double green, were originally considered the "signature" holes.

But Einstein says Wyncote regulars also particularly enjoy two other holes, the third and fourth.

The third, at 356 yards from the back tees, is a dogleg left that runs alongside marshland that cuts across in front of the green. A small pond also protects the green, which is elevated. The fourth, at 401 yards from the back tees, is straight, with marshland to the left, a road to the right, and a two-tiered fairway. Both are very tough holes.

If you have never played a links or heathland course, Wyncote might be worth a look just for a change of pace. Chances are you will either love it or hate it.

A few other things you need to know about Wyncote: It's a bit pricey at $75 on weekends. For riders, it's cart paths only. If you choose to walk, be forewarned it's a hike from some greens to the next tee. It's also in a dry township, although Einstein says complicated local laws make "wet" outings and gatherings permissible.

— July 28, 1996

If You Go

Address: 50 Wyncote Drive, Oxford.

Phone: 610-932-8900

Greens fees: Weekdays, walk for $55, ride for $75. Weekends, $88, includes cart.

Carts: Walking permitted anytime. Cart fees are included weekends and holidays.

Other Chester County Courses

Ingleside Golf Club
104 Horseshoe Drive, Thorndale.
610-384-9128
Weekdays, $22 to walk, $30 to ride;
weekends, $30 to walk, $44 to ride.

Loch Nairn Golf Course
514 McCue Rd., Avondale.
610-268-2234
Weekdays, $25 to walk, $37 to ride;
weekends, $36 to walk, $48 to ride.

Meadow Brook Golf Club
1416 State Rd., Phoenixville
610-933-2929
$16 weekdays; $21 weekends. Carts are $7 per nine holes single,
$5.50 each additional person.

Moccasin Run Golf Course
402 Schoff Rd., Atglen.
610-593-2600
$23 weekdays; $35 weekends. Carts are $12 per person.

Spring Hollow Golf Course
3350 Schuylkill Rd., Spring City.
610-948-5566
Weekdays, $23 to walk, $37 to ride; weekends $28 to walk, $42 to
ride. Carts are mandatory until noon on weekends.

Delaware

C O U N T Y

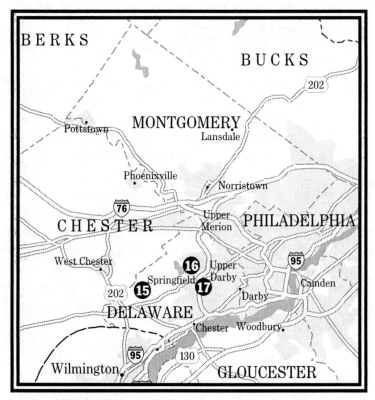

15. Golf Course at Glen Mills
16. Paxon Hollow
17. Springfield Country Club

15. Golf Course at Glen Mills

A good challenge, perhaps too good

In golf circles, the talk about the Golf Course at Glen Mills School has been going on for more than a year.

It's understandable. Glen Mills, after all, is no ordinary school. Its 900-plus students — boys, ages 14 to 18 — arrive as troubled youths, sent by court systems in 28 states after one too many brushes with the law.

"It's invitation only," one administrator described the school last week.

And the Golf Course at Glen Mills, which opened last weekend?

It's good, very good. It's beautiful as it carves its way through the hillsides and rich forests of rural Delaware County. It's also tough and demanding, almost unfair at times with its extremely tight, rolling fairways, brutal knee-high wild-grass rough, and dicey greens.

For Glen Mills, the new golf course is a novel and perhaps brilliant idea. Money generated from the course will be funneled into the nonprofit school's college scholarship fund so disadvantaged graduates can continue their education. Meanwhile, the boys who work around the golf course's pro shop and on the maintenance crew will eventually leave the school with one more marketable skill.

"We've already placed three boys," said Glen Mills board member Ron Pilot.

For golfers, the question is: What is the place like? Is it a quality track? And do the boys, who range from onetime petty thieves to former gang members who have robbed banks and been involved in killings, pose any threat? Will you feel safe and comfortable?

After one visit, I don't presume to be able to answer all these questions with authority and for all time. But I can tell you that, yes, while it's pricey, the Golf Course at Glen Mills is worth a visit.

And, no, I didn't feel threatened or unsafe, not in the least, not at any time. Not at the bag drop, where you first encounter students, not in the pro shop, where they work behind the counter, and not out on the course, where they mow, water and sprinkle sand in divots.

School officials know well the fears and stereotypes they are up against in making the course a success.

"One mistake, one problem, is all it will take," Pilot said. "We know that."

As he spoke, a Glen Mills student, all smiles and pleasantries, was not 20 feet away, chatting up a golfer. What could such a delightful kid possibly have done?

"Bank robbery," Pilot said. "Went in with a toy gun."

If you're comfortable with the concept, which is admitted-

Scorecard

Hole	Scratch	Director	Middle	Preferred	Forward	Par	HCP	Ladies' HCP
1	374	357	325	308	265	4	18	18
2	431	416	378	339	304	4	6	6
3	394	376	359	331	277	4	11	11
4	572	548	524	505	441	5	7	7
5	181	171	162	136	101	3	17	17
6	547	528	511	476	415	5	15	15
7	221	208	191	151	129	3	3	3
8	325	313	307	273	244	4	13	13
9	433	376	366	318	301	4	4	4
Out	3,478	3,293	3,123	2,837	2,477	36		
10	207	195	181	144	111	3	12	2
11	376	364	349	314	281	4	2	4
12	339	329	318	282	234	4	9	9
13	443	421	399	335	308	4	5	5
14	161	154	144	126	98	3	14	14
15	529	513	491	465	403	5	16	16
16	156	146	134	121	89	3	8	8
17	483	472	468	435	381	5	10	1
18	464	427	404	371	321	4	1	3
In	3,158	3,021	2,888	2,593	2,226	35		
Total	6,636	6,314	6,011	5,430	4,703	71		

ly a departure from a hoity-toity country club, the Golf Course at Glen Mills is very much worth a try.

It was designed by Bobby Weed, a Florida architect who has laid out a couple of the PGA Tour's TPC courses, and it is no pushover. It is, in fact, more than many high-handicappers and beginners might want to tackle.

Weed has taken a terrific and generous piece of land on the sprawling 800-acre Glen Mills property and created a course that can give the average golfer fits of frustration.

He gives golfers blind tee shots, doglegs, water holes, forced carries, sloped fairways, changes of elevation from tee to green, and time and time again, narrow, hard-to-hit fairways that are lined by ball-eating rough.

If Glen Mills is going to have a motto, it might well be: "You'll never find it in there."

From the tips, Glen Mills measures 6,636 yards, which surprised me, because I would have guessed it was closer to 10 miles. Weed has provided five sets of tees, however, so players can back it down to as little as 4,703 yards.

The course doesn't yet have a rating or a slope. I'm guessing it will come in with some serious numbers, maybe 135 for a slope. That's a day's work.

You realize early on that Weed is not out to make your day easy. Take the 572-yard fourth hole, for example, a double-dogleg par 5 that plays right, then left, then right again — unless of course you decide to test your long-ball with an approach shot over what must be 220 yards of sand and other mess into a green that doesn't want to be hit from that far away.

There's also the par-5 sixth, another dogleg, albeit it gentler, that grows narrower and narrower as players approach the green, until foursomes are pretty much walking single file.

The par-3 10th is one of the more curious and intimidating holes on the course. The tee is elevated, and the green is huge and rectangular. It measures 207 from the back tees, and everything from tee to green is gnarly mess that will swallow up golf balls forever.

If I were to quibble with Weed, my main criticism would be over the width of his fairways. Maybe pros can hit a tee shot 250 yards and land it in a space no more than 20 yards wide, but not a 17-handicapper, especially when the rough is so unforgiving.

There are also a couple of greens that are suspect, to my way of thinking. I can't imagine what he was thinking at the 221-yard seventh, a long, uphill par 3 with a huge green that looks as if it has a herd of elephants buried beneath it.

All in all, however, I'd go back. I might leave my driver in the trunk next time, and I'd surely pack an extra sleeve of balls, but I'd definitely go back.

The final hurdle Glen Mills must clear is the price. For the rest of the season, the green fees are going to be $65 weekdays and weekends, with cart. That is a fair price.

But come springtime, the weekend rate (Friday through Sunday), is going up to $90, which will push Glen Mills into the category of "special occasion" golf for many golfers. I hope they reconsider.

— Sept. 3, 2000

If You Go

Address: 221 Glen Mills Rd., Glen Mills.

Phone: 610-558-2142 or 2143.

Green fees: Weekdays, $65. Weekends, $85. All fees include cart.

Carts: Walk anytime; carts are included in greens fee.

Amenities: Clubhouse, driving range and putting green. Snack bar.

Rating: Tough but beautiful golf course. Hilly, narrow fairways, nasty rough, tricky greens. Condition good for a brand new course. Should be a treat in another year or so. Unpretentious facility, staffed in part by students at Glen Mills School.

16. Paxon Hollow

Short in size, but long in pleasure

"Good things come in small packages" can apply to golf courses, too. Paxon Hollow Country Club is a fine example.

Though the name suggests a private club, Paxon Hollow is a municipal track owned and operated by Marple Township, which bought the 70-year-old course in 1967. Before that, it had several incarnations as a private club.

Terrific golf holes abound — doglegs, sloping fairways, elevated tees and greens — and it's considerably more picturesque and manicured than your run-of-the-mill muni track.

But Paxon Hollow is short — too short for some golfers. Even from the back tees, it measures a mere 5,641 yards, far below the national average of 6,300 yards, with a slope of 116. From the whites (5,407) and the reds (4,935), it's inching toward "executive" course range.

To a lot of players, the skimpy length is no problem. But for low-handicappers or big to moderate hitters, a round at Paxon Hollow means admiring the look of a hole from the tee, then finding yourself again hitting driver and wedge.

Case in point: The 10th hole, a 277-yard, dogleg-right. What a gorgeous little golf hole. You stand there on a well-elevated tee, looking down on a slightly sloping fairway that bends to the right and a creek that cuts across the fairway just off the tee, then runs up the right side.

During a recent round, my playing partners all hit decent drives, leaving them with lob-wedges and chips into the green. Smelling an easy birdie, I managed to hit my worst tee shot of the day — fat and ugly — that by rights ought to have spelled trouble. But no, I still had nothing more than a wedge into the green. I felt foolish walking away with par.

Nevertheless, Paxon Hollow is a very pleasurable golf course. It is mature, dating to the 1920s, and it serves up more than a few fun, challenging holes, short or not.

Cases in point: the fifth and sixth holes. The fifth is a 326-yard, mild dogleg-left with trouble in the form of a ravine and tall grass along the left side. The prudent player stays far right of that, leaving a mid- to short-iron into a green protected by bunkers on the right and left front. On a windy day, which it was when I was there, it was no easy par.

The sixth, a 308-yard par 4, has an elevated tee from which the fairway drops and then gradually rises as it reaches the green. The wrinkle on this hole is not so much the woods up the left side as it is the stands of huge trees about 200 yards out that pinch the fairway down to about 20 yards.

More than a few players probably toy with the idea of hitting driver before finally playing it safe off the tee with a fairway wood or long iron.

On the back side, there's the 10th, of course, but I also

Scorecard

Hole	Blue	White	Red	Par	Ladies' Par	HCP	Red HCP
1	330	319	290	4	4	12	10
2	128	119	113	3	3	17	18
3	495	480	341	5	5	9	6
4	146	135	125	3	3	15	16
5	326	317	309	4	4	13	8
6	308	299	265	4	4	8	4
7	453	441	437	5	5	11	2
8	169	158	147	3	3	5	12
9	377	363	283	4	4	3	14
Out	2,732	2,631	2,309	35	35		
10	277	250	238	4	4	16	13
11	436	407	393	5	5	7	3
12	356	350	345	4	4	6	7
13	343	323	303	4	4	1	5
14	381	370	359	4	5	4	15
15	163	150	140	3	3	10	9
16	302	292	281	4	4	14	11
17	116	115	95	3	3	18	17
18	535	519	472	5	5	2	1
In	2,909	2,776	2,626	36	37		
Total	**5,641**	**5,407**	**4,935**	**71**	**72**		

liked the 12th, 13th, 17th and 18th.

The 12th, only 356 yards, requires a second shot over a ravine into a tricky, elevated green. The 13th, a 343-yard dog-leg-left with trouble all up the left side, is the No. 1 handicap hole, thanks to tough tee-shot placement and a nail-biter second shot into a partially hidden green. The 17th, at 116 yards, is a wedge shot for almost everyone because it's straight down from the tee.

The best hole is the 18th, the longest par 5 at Paxon Hollow at 535 yards. From the tee, the fairway is framed by woods on the right and a creek running up the left side, before it cuts across the fairway about midway up the hole.

The second shot can be dicey because it's over the creek and uphill into a fairway that throws most everything right — often behind a big sycamore tree that could give you fits on your third shot into the green.

If you like your golf courses long, Paxon Hollow is not for you. For all others, it's a gem worth trying.

— May 25, 1997

If You Go

Address: 850 Paxon Hollow Rd., Broomall.

Phone: 610-353-0220.

Greens fees: Nonresidents, weekends, $50 to ride, $35 to walk; weekdays, $47 and 32. Marple Township residents, weekends, $42 to ride, $27 to walk; weekdays, $39 and $24; seniors, weekday, $18 to walk.

Carts: Mandatory until 2 p.m. on weekends and holidays.

Amenities: Moderately stocked pro shop, snack bar, banquet facilities. Outings welcome. No driving range.

Rating: Short, but sweet.

17. Springfield Country Club

Short on challenges, long on promise

Springfield Country Club, the municipal loop in the Delaware County township, isn't long, particularly tough or all that fancy.

But if an award is ever given for golf courses trying to improve, Springfield could easily walk away with a ribbon.

For the past two years (and for two more years to come) Springfield has been teeming with bulldozers and grounds crews recasting the course from a short but sweet 5,546-yard hill-and-dale into a longer, lusher and, ultimately, tougher test of golf.

By project's end, Springfield will measure 6,000 yards, and par will be increased from 69 to 70. In addition, virtually every green will be moved and rebuilt, several holes will be lengthened or redirected, the weakest par 3 is likely to be replaced by a signature-hole par 3, and, if the township commissioners approve, there will be a new clubhouse.

Eventually, the sequence of several holes also will be changed and the front and back nines will be flip-flopped.

Got all that?

Don't even try. Just remember that a very pleasant little track should be even better.

"We're accomplishing it little by little," said Springfield director Bob Giannini. "We want to end up with a longer, more interesting course."

Springfield Township has operated the course since 1956 and owned it since 1964. But the transformation didn't begin until a couple of years ago when then-superintendent David Myers, who died this past winter, informed the township that there was no way to improve the condition of the old, badly designed greens without completely rebuilding them. Township officials said go ahead.

Once that project was under way, everybody involved wondered, why stop there? Why not tackle the course's other shortcomings as well? Why not tackle the biggest shortcoming of all, the fact that the course was simply too short for better golfers?

Because of space limitations, there was only so much lengthening and rerouting they could do. But they have tried to make the most of the acreage they do have, adding about 500 yards and a few twists and turns.

"Where we can't challenge big hitters with length, we're trying to challenge them with a dogleg or something else," Giannini said.

Specifically, the weakest par 3 at Springfield (the 18th) will be closed to make room for a new, picturesque par 3 (the fifth hole) that will play 220 yards from the back tees and demand a shot over a sizable ravine and creek.

Scorecard

Hole	Blue	White	Red	Par	Red Par	HCP	Red HCP
1	353	344	314	4	4	6	2
2	505	490	314	5	5	10	18
3	187	160	145	3	3	14	14
4	293	276	261	4	4	18	16
5	277	261	252	4	4	16	10
6	281	274	266	4	4	12	6
7	193	186	145	3	3	8	12
8	308	301	288	4	4	4	8
9	371	354	288	4	4	2	4
Out	2,646	2,768	2,327	35	35		
10	410	398	376	4	5	1	3
11	385	376	364	4	5	3	15
12	325	315	308	4	4	9	7
13	374	365	342	4	5	7	17
14	169	156	122	3	3	15	11
15	431	425	419	5	4	5	1
16	187	176	144	3	3	13	9
17	350	343	313	4	4	11	5
18	147	143	137	3	3	17	13
In	2,667	2,756	2,524	34	37		
Total	**5,313**	**5,524**	**4,851**	**69**	**72**		

From there, the old No. 5 becomes the new No. 6, along with a makeover from a short, ordinary par 4 into a 500-yard par 5 back over that same ravine, sans the creek.

Other changes also are in the works, but they're far too complicated to go into here, except for the possibility of a new clubhouse that would sit on what is now the 18th.

"We're doing feasibility studies," Giannini said. "The commissioners will probably decide something by the fall."

Even as it is, Springfield, with its hills and mix of holes, is a fun round of golf. Much like neighboring Paxon Hollow, what it lacks in length, it makes up for with variety.

Perhaps the two best holes on the course are the ninth and 10th, 371 and 410 yards, respectively. The ninth, a mild dogleg, plays from an elevated tee into a gently sloping fairway with trees up the right side. Aside from being the No. 4 handicap hole, it's also one of the prettier holes on the course.

There's no rest for the weary, however. After a soda and a hotdog at the halfway house, you face the 10th, the No. 3 handicap hole and the only par 4 on the course that will likely find better golfers with a long iron in their hands for their second shots. That assumes they've hit a good enough tee shot for their approach shot to be able to carry over a ravine that fronts the elevated green. Tough hole for any golfer.

Other than a long, hard-to-hit par 3 (the seventh) and a too-short par 5 (the 15th, 431 yards), Springfield's personality is mostly made up of short but testy little dogleg par 4s. Big hitters are looking at a lot of driver-9-irons, but short hitters will find those holes much more challenging.

Overall, the course plays about average in terms of difficulty — 114 slope from the back tees, 108 from the whites. Those figures will likely go up.

Like most municipal courses, Springfield is busy — about 48,000 rounds a year — and doesn't have the feel of an exclusive country club, but it does have a bit more upscale ambience than many municipal courses.

— September 7, 1997

If You Go

Address: 400 W. Sproul Rd., Springfield.

Phone: 610-543-9860

Greens fees: Weekdays, walk for $32, ride for $47. Weekends, ride for $41, ride for $56.

Carts: Walking permitted anytime

Other Delaware County Course

Clayton Park Golf Course
Box 85 Conchester Highway (Rt. 322), Glen Mills.
610-459-4510
$9 weekdays; $10 weekends

Olde Masters Golf Club
4600 West Chester Pike, Newtown Square.
610-356-7606
$12 weekdays. $13 weekends. Carts are $8.50 per person.

Dauphin
C O U N T Y

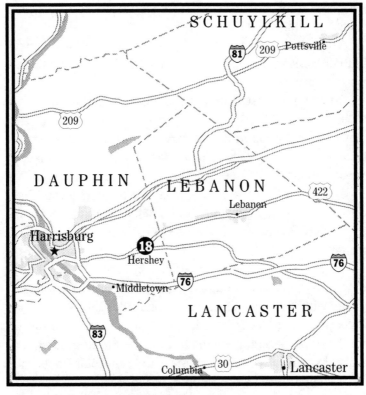

18. Country Club of Hershey

18. Country Club of Hershey

Hershey South is mostly sweet

Planning a weekend trip to HersheyPark with the family anytime soon?

If you are, and if there's any chance you can squeeze in a round of golf during your stay, most definitely throw your clubs into the trunk. In the proverbial shadow of the theme park, there are three fine, fine golf courses — two semi-privates, one daily-fee — all worth the effort.

They are the West, East and South Courses of the Country Club of Hershey, but don't let the name fool you — no memberships are required here.

To play the West Course, a four-star track that's the best of the bunch, you'll have to purchase one of the golf packages that include a room at the country club, or be a guest at the Hotel Hershey or Hershey Lodge. Same for the East Course, a 3½-star loop that's a slight cut below but a strong course.

But to play the South Course, also a 3½-star layout that was known as Parkview until May 1994, all you need to do is pay a daily greens fee. There are worse ways to spend your money.

The West Course, once home to the LPGA's Lady Keystone Open, stands out among the three. At almost 6,900 yards, with a 131 slope, it's an absolute delight — hills and wide, sweeping tree-lined fairways, not to mention a tough par 3 that plays right up to the front yard of Milton Hershey's old mansion and benefits from the waft of chocolate in the air. It's a course in the best tradition of old East Coast country clubs.

The East Course adjoins the West, and if it didn't, it would probably get more of the attention it deserves. On the East, just when you hit a stretch of two or three holes that don't quite measure up to the West, you suddenly come across another two or three that make you wonder why the West gets all the attention.

But because of the restrictions on play on those two courses, it's the South Course — a separate place about a mile away — that will get our attention.

Granted, when you pull into the parking lot at the South Course, with its public-course-looking clubhouse and rubber-mat driving range, it appears to pale in comparison to the country-club scene over at the East and West.

So what? A clubhouse is not always a true indicator of the golf course that lies beyond. If the South Course were in the suburbs of Philadelphia, it would be an immediate favorite among area golfers.

The South Course, opened in 1927, was designed by the same man responsible for the West: Maurice McCarthy, an Irish immigrant and teaching pro who was a friend of Milton

East Course

Hole	Blue	White	Red	Par	Ladies' Par	HCP	Ladies' HCP
1	500	478	444	5	5	11	3
2	193	170	118	3	3	15	17
3	448	421	386	4	4	1	7
4	437	371	345	4	4	17	13
5	356	336	323	4	4	17	13
6	554	515	461	5	5	9	1
7	458	382	358	4	4	7	9
8	224	202	168	3	3	5	15
9	420	394	359	4	4	3	5
Out							
10	393	376	346	4	4	10	6
11	420	372	341	4	4	12	8
12	414	387	309	4	4	8	14
13	187	160	120	3	3	18	18
14	540	481	443	5	5	4	2
15	467	407	343	4	4	2	12
16	215	170	133	3	3	14	16
17	379	362	346	4	4	16	4
18	456	379	302	4	4	6	10
In	3,471	3,094	2,683	35	35		
Total	**7,061**	**6,363**	**5,645**	**71**	**71**		

Hershey.

Just as at the West Course, McCarthy took full advantage of the foliage, hills and creeks that will give any golfer fits on at least two holes.

At its best, the South Course can hold its head almost as high as the West. At its worst, the South Course is inconsistent, even unfair, in a couple of places. But the two or three sore spots don't sour its overall quality.

The South Course plays only 6,204 yards, with a 121 slope from the blue tees, but that seems misleading. It plays longer and tougher, more like a 128 slope. Head professional Steve Krall said the USGA has been asked to reevaluate the course.

Good golf holes come at you early on at the South Course. The second hole is a downhill par 3 over a creek that looks innocent enough from the tee, but proves deceptive and very difficult to par.

West Course

Hole	Blue	White	Red	Par	Ladies' Par	HCP	Ladies' HCP
1	437	424	407	4	5	1	7
2	568	542	531	5	5	5	1
3	354	305	291	4	4	13	11
4	307	279	238	4	4	15	13
5	176	164	153	3	3	17	15
6	345	335	272	4	4	11	9
7	550	519	500	5	5	7	3
8	232	209	171	3	3	9	17
9	389	368	349	4	4	3	5
Out	3,358	3,145	2,912	36	37		
10	422	406	369	4	5	6	10
11	354	338	324	4	4	12	12
12	180	169	159	3	3	16	16
13	568	537	382	5	5	2	6
14	354	329	307	4	4	14	14
15	501	488	476	5	5	8	2
16	517	500	427	5	5	10	4
17	182	157	153	3	3	18	18
18	424	411	399	4	5	4	8
In	3,502	3,335	2,996	37	39		
Total	**6,860**	**6,480**	**5,908**	**73**	**76**		

That's quickly followed by the fourth, a 305-yard par 4 that's a personal favorite. Though short, the hole looks ominous from the tee, thanks to a wide creek that runs up the left side of the hole, then veers right and drastically squeezes the fairway to about 15 yards at just about the spot your tee shot might land. This hole can be either an easy par or a nasty double bogey.

Then comes a par 3 that seems short on the scorecard — only 140 from the blues — but it's a blind shot up a nearly vertical hill, made even more difficult when the wind is swirling.

South Course regulars say the course doesn't really show its colors until you hit the 8-9-10 stretch.

The eigth is a long, straight 450-yard par 4 that's complicated by OB on the left, OB on the right, a fairway with a left-to-right slope, and a swale that can leave even a good tee shot with a blind, long-iron approach into a distant, uphill green.

South Course

Hole	Blue	White	Red	Par	Forward Par	HCP	Forward HCP
1	367	355	284	4	4	8	8
2	218	177	153	3	3	6	6
3	351	310	301	4	4	12	12
4	305	280	270	4	4	10	10
5	140	130	125	3	3	14	14
6	367	339	223	4	4	16	16
7	397	376	287	4	4	18	18
8	450	412	338	4	5	2	2
9	476	463	422	5	5	4	4
Out	3,071	2,842	2,403	35	36		
10	419	409	256	4	4	1	1
11	177	136	103	3	3	11	11
12	360	342	243	4	4	7	7
13	361	350	295	4	4	5	5
14	323	311	299	4	4	17	17
15	455	425	410	5	5	9	9
16	323	289	270	4	4	13	13
17	425	418	316	4	4	3	3
18	290	276	261	4	4	15	15
In	3,133	2,956	2,453	36	36		
Total	**6,204**	**5,798**	**4,856**	**71**	**72**		

Then comes the ninth, a treacherous downhill, dogleg-left par 5 that features a blind tee shot and a zigzagging creek that creates an island fairway/landing area for your second shot. The first time you play this hole, you'll cuss it as unfair; the second time, you'll love its nuances.

The toughest hole — and the favorite among regulars — is the 10th, a devilish, tree-lined, uphill 419-yard par 4 that's as pretty as any hole around. From the well-elevated tee, the green looks to be about two miles away.

But it's also at the 10th that the South Course needs some work.

Even if you hit a career tee shot, you face an uphill mid- or long-iron into a huge green that's banked like a turn at Charlotte Motor Speedway, and tiered in a fashion that makes even a terrific second shot seem inadequate. If the pin is on the top tier, a bogey will seem like an accomplishment.

My only other complaint about the South Course is the 15th, a 455-yard, dogleg-right par 5 that demands a blind tee shot and blind uphill second shot. Two blind shots in a row seem a bit much, even if you know the course.

Even so, the pluses of the South Course far outweigh the minuses. Play here once, and chances are you'll find yourself saying to the kids, "Hey, what do you think about a trip to HersheyPark?"

— May 11, 1997

If You Go

Address: 600 W. Derry Rd., Hershey.

Phone: 717-534-3450.

Greens fees: Weekdays, $50. Weekends, $65.

Carts: Mandatory at all times.

Amenities: Moderately stocked pro shop, bar and grill, driving range, outings and leagues welcome.

Lancaster

C O U N T Y

19. Hawk Valley Golf Club
20. Pilgrim's Oak Golf Course

19. Hawk Valley Golf Club

Beware the unforgiving greens

They call Hawk Valley Golf Club "The Hawk" for short, but "The Mean Green" probably is more accurate.

We're talking some cruel, cruel greens — oil-slicked Indy 500 kind of greens.

You might know the type. You barely touch that eight-foot birdie putt, just enough to get it rolling. But by the time it finally stops, you're slack-jawed over the 12-footer you now have coming back for par. Don't even mention the tricky three-footer just to save face and bogey.

"The strength of the course is definitely the fast, undulating greens," said head pro Kevin Donnachie.

There's nothing at all wrong with the rest of the course, which is only five minutes off Exit 21 of the Pennsylvania Turnpike, in tiny Denver, Lancaster County.

Golf Digest's 4,200 Best Places to Play gives it three stars in the latest edition, citing player comments such as "supersonic putting surfaces," "good shape" and "good test, challenging but not a killer."

Hawk Valley is not a killer. It's a good, solid, well-maintained, mid-level course that has the potential to appeal to almost every level of golfer. It's a bit flat and a bit short, unless you play from the back tees. But it has a healthy enough mix of tight holes, open holes, doglegs and water holes to make it a workout for most players.

From the back tees, the Hawk measures 6,743 yards and plays to a 132 slope, which is no easy test. From the whites, it's considerably shorter at 6,189 yards, but still holds to a 127 slope, well above the national average of 113.

It's also far enough out in the country to have a much folksier, less-hectic feel than so many of the public courses in and around Philadelphia. That, too, can be quite appealing.

For my money, the biggest disappointment about Hawk Valley was the par 3s — all are rather ho-hum shots with no water, wetlands or even looming trees to negotiate. But Donnachie pointed out that the par 3s get considerably tougher from the back tees, from which they suddenly stretch to 187, 205, 168 and 195 yards.

Hawk Valley, which opened in 1971, was designed by the prolific son-and-father duo of David and the late William Gordon, who also laid out the courses at Locust Valley Country Club, White Manor Country Club, and DuPont Country Club, to name a few.

The elder Gordon also had a hand in remodeling Gulph Mills Country Club, Manufacturers Golf and Country Club, Philmont Country Club, Radnor Valley Country Club, and Saucon Valley Country Club's Old Course.

Six years after it opened, Jim and Dot Fricke, who live on

Scorecard

Hole	Blue	White	Gold	Red	Par	HCP	Ladies' HCP
1	440/400	380	345	340	4	1	5
2	430/392	372	320	312	4	15	15
3	495	480	440	435	5	9	3
4	187	160	152	145	3	17	17
5	382	360	292	286	4	11	11
6	535/506	490	460	456	5	3	7
7	205	159	155	152	3	7	9
8	350	335	294	288	4	13	13
9	370	355	311	306	4	5	1
Out	3394/3287	3091	2769	2720	36		
10	485	470	410	405	5	2	4
11	168	143	120	114	3	18	18
12	362	347	310	302	4	8	8
13	442/402	380	365	305	4	12	10
14	382/355	320	305	300	4	14	14
15	505	490	430	425	5	6	6
16	410	395	365	360	4	4	2
17	195	168	150	146/108	3	16	16
18	400	385	354	345	4	10	12
In	3349/3282	3098	2809	2702/2665	36		
Total	**6743/6569**	**6189**	**5578**	**5422/5385**	**72**		

the property, bought the Hawk from its original developers. They have made a number of changes over the years, adding back tees on several holes and redoing the bunkers for the first 14 holes last year. The bunkers on holes 15 to 18 are scheduled for renovation in late fall.

The Hawk starts you off with the No. 1-handicap hole, a 380-yard, mild dogleg right that looks more ominous from the tee than it is.

A far more interesting hole is the par-5 No. 3, a slight dog-leg left with out of bounds all along the right side, trees up the left, and a green that's slick and well-protected by a nasty, yawning bunker on the left front.

The other par 5 on the front, the sixth, is only 490 yards from the white tees, but it may be the testiest hole going out. It's tight, with trees lining both sides of the fairway, and it's over a crest, then downhill into a well-bunkered green. It's easy to birdie, easy to bogey.

From the tee, the eigth looks to be an easy birdie hole. It's a downhill, short par 4, 335 yards, which means a short iron onto the green for most players. But No. 8 is one of those user-friendly greens, where a six-foot birdie putt quickly can become a three-foot bogey putt.

The most unusual hole is the 10th, an almost horseshoe-shaped double dogleg par 5 that's quite tight. Big hitters will be tempted to blow their tee shots over the trees and cut the first corner; all others play it up the left side, then up the left side again for a short iron to a green guarded by bunkers and trees on the right.

Another favorite among Hawk Valley regulars is the 14th — perhaps the most picturesque hole — a short but sweeping dogleg right that's choked by six bunkers at the turn and around the green. Again, the 14th is 3-putt country.

Don't say you haven't been warned.

— Aug. 3, 1997

If You Go

Address: Crestview Drive, Denver.

Phone: 717-445-5445.

Greens fees: Weekends, $42 to ride, $30 to walk (after 2 p.m.). Weekdays, $30 to ride, $22 to walk.

Carts: Mandatory Friday, Saturday, and Sunday until 2 p.m.

Amenities: Well-stocked pro shop, snack bar, putting green, banquet facilities. Outings welcome.

20. Pilgrim's Oak Golf Course

Solid, challenging

Another dairy farm bites the dust, and up comes another quality, upscale, public place to play golf.

This one is the year-old Pilgrim's Oak Golf Course in southern Lancaster County, in the same neck of the woods as Hartefeld National and Wyncote Golf Club.

Few oaks and no pilgrims were in evidence on a recent day, but if you like links-style courses, there's little else to quibble about.

"Every hole out here, you get a different look," said Pilgrim's Oak's director of golf, Jeff Bell. "You'll hit every club in your bag, and I think it's playable for everyone from scratch to 36 handicap."

Scorecard

Hole	Pro.	Champ.	Tourn.	Inter.	Rec.	Par	HCP
1	424	377	366	345	321	4	11
2	419	397	384	377	322	4	5
3	435	408	371	339	310	4	9
4	129	129	115	98	88	3	17
5	352	338	322	303	282	4	15
6	535	510	490	457	401	5	13
7	432	391	367	350	311	4	3
8	206	180	164	133	120	3	7
9	551	528	509	437	414	5	1
Out	3,483	3,258	3,088	2,839	2,569	36	
10	426	386	378	360	333	4	16
11	391	363	341	325	290	4	4
12	223	196	178	134	95	3	6
13	382	370	350	326	303	4	8
14	558	520	499	471	412	5	12
15	439	413	392	372	346	4	10
16	395	358	333	300	278	4	18
17	186	172	157	111	106	3	14
18	560	495	469	422	332	5/4	2
In	3,560	3,273	3,097	2,821	2,495	36/35	
Total	**7,043**	**6,531**	**6,185**	**5,660**	**5,064**	**72/71**	

Except for four or five pretty ordinary holes — mostly on the front side — Pilgrim's Oak is a pleasant, challenging, well-conditioned course that should have a decent shot at joining Hartefeld and Wyncote as one of the region's handful of courses rated four stars by *Golf Digest's Places to Play*.

The front side is the sort of wide-open, links-style layout you find at Wyncote; the back nine, though still the same rolling topography, is tighter and more tree-lined, like Hartefeld. Of the seven holes with water, four have ponds or small lakes that can be a problem.

The more prevailing characteristics are the openness on the front, which won't brutalize a wayward driver unless you reach the wild, knee-high fescue; the considerable mounding throughout; a general paucity of greenside bunkers; and the greens themselves — small greens, in some cases roughly the size of a bathroom throw rug.

"Since he made the greens so small, he didn't want to penalize you for missing them," Bell said of course designer Michael Hurdzan, whose work includes the new Sand Barrens in Cape May County with partner Dana Fry, as well as Jericho National, now being built in Bucks County.

Hurdzan may not penalize golfers with many bunkers, but on a couple of holes — the long par-3 eighth and the par-5 15th come to mind — the tiny greens themselves struck me as penalty enough.

Thanks to five sets of tees, Pilgrim's Oak can play as long or as short as you like, from a low of 5,064 yards from the front tees to 7,043 from the tips. No matter which set of tees suits your game, it's going to play tough — from the front tees, the slope is 129; from the back tees, it's 138.

Easily the best stretch of holes is the 11th through the 14th. The 11th — Bell's favorite — is a downhill, dogleg, 363-yard par 4 into an angled fairway, then up to an elevated green. Actually, it's prettier than it is tough.

The 12th is the most picturesque and among the toughest holes on the course — a 196-yard par 3 that's all carry over water and wetlands. The green looks to be carved out of the side of a hill. Short, left or long here is a goodbye ball; bogey, maybe even double bogey, should be a good score. Come to think of it, how often do you see a par 3 as the No. 6 handicap hole on a course?

The 13th, one of the few tree-lined holes, is a narrow, leisurely dogleg with mounds up the right side and a view of farmland and silos in the distance that can't help but remind you this is not Philadelphia.

The finishing hole is also quite nice — a 495-yard par 5 from an elevated tee, with water on the left and more to the right front of the green. Go for this green in 2 and you're flirting with trouble.

The bottom line on Pilgrim's Oak: Every time I came across a stretch of two or three ho-hum holes, Hurdzan came back with a treat. If you don't mind the drive — two to three hours from Center City, depending — it's definitely worth a try.

— June 29, 1997

If You Go

Address: 1107 Pilgrim's Pathway, Peach Bottom.

Phone: 717-548-3011

Greens fees: Weekends, $56 to ride, $32 to walk. Weekdays, $44 to ride, $32 to walk.

Carts: Walking permitted anytime. Cart fees included after 2 p.m. weekends.

Web site: www.pilgrimsoak.com

Amenities: New facility with well-stocked pro shop, driving range, putting and chipping green, snack bar with light fare, outing pavilion for 250, outings welcome.

Rating: Fine course, a cross between Hartefeld National and Wyncote.

Lebanon
C O U N T Y

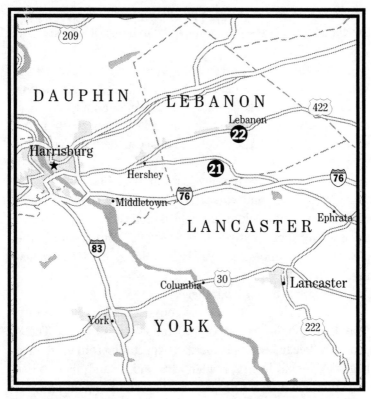

21. Iron Valley Golf Club
22. Royal Oaks Golf Club

21. Iron Valley Golf Club

A very pleasant surprise

When a golf course has a name like Iron Valley, you, as I was, might be inclined to dismiss it as probably too far away to be given much thought. You would be mistaken.

If you like courses that are hilly, demanding, reasonably priced and different from anything else in these parts, you would also be mistaken not to pile your favorite foursome into the car and head west on the turnpike to Lebanon County. You won't regret the trip.

From the moment I stepped onto the first tee at Iron Valley Golf Club last week, I knew I was in for an interesting round of golf. Most golf courses start you out slow and easy, maybe a simple and forgiving par 4 that allows you to make up for that warm-up bucket of balls you didn't have quite enough time to hit.

Not Iron Valley. From the tips, you're looking at 469 yards worth of fairway that cuts a swath through woods left and woods right as it tumbles downward then veers right. Even in the unlikely event that you hammer your first tee shot of the day, you're looking at 200 yards into the green. Good morning!

It only gets better from there.

I've got to say that of all the courses I've played recently, Iron Valley came as the biggest and best surprise. That's probably because I had no real expectations other than a heads-up e-mail from a reader who said he and his buddies had stumbled across this great new course. I'm glad I gave it a try.

What I think will attract Philadelphia-area golfers is that Iron Valley is so utterly different from most everything we have around here.

Designed by P.B. Dye, younger son of the legendary Pete

Dye, Iron Valley's front nine is carved out of the Rexmont Mountain, a slab of beautiful tree-filled real estate that sits atop a labyrinth of now-closed mine shafts that once produced iron ore for cannon shot during the Revolutionary War.

Hole after hole is a treat. There are dramatic par 3s. There is a short par 4 that is complicated by a yawning chasm on the second shot.

And then there's the fourth, a 588-yard par 5 that tumbles down, down, down and around a small lake created by a mine shaft that was deliberately caved-in years ago. You stand there over your second shot, drinking in the view, saying to yourself, "Wow."

They will let you walk Iron Valley if you want. Good luck. I wouldn't try it unless I had the stamina of a 19-year-old with a backpack full of water bottles and Power Bars.

Scorecard

Hole	Pro.	Champ.	Regular	Forward	Par
1	469	423	384	344	4
2	356	340	312	255	4
3	177	138	125	113	3
4	588	542	500	442	5
5	383	360	315	262	4
6	456	422	387	335	4
7	494	471	425	405	5
8	181	165	145	121	3
9	427	389	374	284	4
Out	3,531	3,250	2,967	2,562	36
10	435	380	351	290	4
11	373	343	327	233	4
12	511	472	422	390	5
13	448	428	410	305	4
14	124	116	95	85	3
15	473	427	385	289	4
16	535	497	456	372	5
17	201	173	155	110	3
18	395	367	310	269	4
In	3,495	3,202	2,911	2,343	36
Total	**7,026**	**6,452**	**5,878**	**4,905**	**72**

The back nine at Iron Valley couldn't be more different than the tree-lined front, but it's no less interesting. That's because the front, aptly called the "mine nine," is where they dug ore until 1973. The back nine, dubbed the "tailings nine," is where they deposited the leftover silt. It's almost eerie.

"First time I saw this, I thought it looked like moonscape," general manager George Schneiter, one of nine area investors who own the course, said as we stood on the elevated 10th tee.

To your right, the back nine fans out across part of a gray valley of tailings, interrupted only by the sight of marshes, a man-made lake and lush green fairways made possible by tons of topsoil that was trucked in.

The more dramatic site is to the left, however, where the 10th fairway runs along the crest of the mountain's edge of tailings, which created what was once the largest man-made earthen dam in the country. The commanding view of the Lebanon Valley below is spectacular.

The sign at the 10th tee is imposing. "EXTREME SLOPE. ABSOLUTELY, POSITIVELY, NO ATTEMPT TO RETRIEVE BALL FROM BEYOND DAM BREAST."

Deeper into the back nine, Dye couldn't resist the temptation to create a hole with an island green, much like his father did with the notorious 17th at TPC Sawgrass. Iron Valley's green is smaller, but the hole is shorter, only 124 yards. Still, if the wind whips up, you've got problems.

My favorite holes on the back, however, are the 15th and 16th, a long, uphill par 4 into a treacherous green followed by a narrow, hilly par 5 that wraps around water. Great couple of holes.

It's impossible to come away from Iron Valley without a smile on your face. Open only since May, it hasn't been rated yet, but my guess is the slope will come in around 130, maybe even a little higher.

With the water, the hills, a few forced carries and the difficulty of some second shots, Iron Valley could be a struggle for higher handicappers. Better players will welcome the challenge. Any player will enjoy the scenery.

— July 9, 2000

If You Go

Address: Route 322, Cornwall.

Phone: 717-279-7409

Greens fees: Weekdays, $44 to ride, $32 to walk. Weekends, $56 until 2 p.m. After 2 p.m., $44 to ride, $32 to walk.

Carts: Walking is permitted anytime.

Web site: www.ironvalley.com

Amenities: Well-stocked pro shop, snack bar, open-air facility for outings, driving range, and putting greens. Plans call for a clubhouse to be built in the next year or two.

Rating: Must-play. Different from anything around Philadelphia. Challenging, well-run, comfortable and unpretentious. Excellent value. Terrific addition to the daily-fee golf scene.

22. Royal Oaks Golf Club

Makes the trip worthwhile

Conventional wisdom has it that two hours is about as far as most golfers will drive to play a round of golf — and it had better be a special course.

Royal Oaks Golf Club in Lebanon, 15 miles east of Hershey, just barely makes it under the two-hour wire for most golfers in the Philadelphia area.

As for being special, Golf Digest magazine in January ranked Royal Oaks as the fifth-best public course in Pennsylvania. More recently, in that magazine's Places to Play book, the four-year-old links-style course was one of only four within two hours of Billy Penn's hat that rated four stars for "outstanding."

"Best-kept secret in eastern Pennsylvania," says one player comment in Places to Play. "Excellent value," says another. "Still needs to mature," says another.

All three are true. Because it's so far off the beaten path — in the "boonies," head professional Stu Hanford Jr. readily concedes — Royal Oaks isn't exactly Topic A among Philadelphia golfers. But given the paucity of top-drawer public courses in this area, if it were closer, weekends would find Royal Oaks as crowded as the restrooms in the third quarter of an Eagles game.

As for maturity, true again. For a mere babe of a golf course, Royal Oaks' fairways and greens are well on the way to excellence. But the course is built on a former cattle farm — i.e., few trees — and the many saplings planted to enhance the layout have yet to fully develop.

Because the course is wide-open and windblown in places, it has a definite links-style feel, especially on the front side, akin to Wyncote Golf Club.

Indeed, a common piece of advice to newcomers at Royal

Oaks is, "Aim for that silo off in the distance."

But on other holes — particularly on the back nine — several creeks and ponds give Royal Oaks a look and feel more like a course in Myrtle Beach, S.C.

If you can keep the ball on the short grass, Royal Oaks is not a killer. It is relatively flat overall, although it does feature a few holes with rolling terrain. The fairways are generous for the most part, and the greens sizable, though not as big as those on many new courses. From the blue tees, it measures 6,555 yards, and has a slope rating of 121 and a par rating of 71.4.

But on almost every hole, a golfer confronts a problem and a risk/reward decision. And that really is the essence of Royal Oaks. There are no holes that are so breathtaking that you're left standing on the tee, marveling. But there also are no boring or tricked-up holes — the kind that leave you shaking your head in dismay while walking off a green. It is a mod-

Scorecard

Hole	Black	Blue	White	Gold	Red	Par	HCP
1	564	544	518	467	414	5	5
2	317	314	287	260	235	4	13
3	217	170	145	126	97	3	15
4	461	461/435	415/400	370	328	4	1
5	214	211	168	148	125	3	7
6	419	392	365	324	288	4	9
7	550	549	506	474	441	5	3
8	178	153	132	118	100	3	17
9	526	511	474	443	389	5	11
Out	3,446	3,305	3,110	2,730	2,417	36	
10	412	394	370	323	283	4	14
11	169	149	110	101	95	3	18
12	421	396	358	313	264	4	12
13	498	496	477/436	409	361	5	10
14	453	423	397	350	313	4	4
15	194	191	174/151	128	109	3	8
16	385	382	334	293	257	4	16
17	414	411	367	293	257	4	16
18	436	408	396/367	336	293	4	6
In	3,382	3,250	2,983	2,584	2,270	35	
Total	**6,828**	**6,555**	**6,093**	**5,314**	**4,687**	**71**	

ern and well-designed golf course.

Consider the first hole, a 544-yard, par-5 double dogleg. On your second shot, do you play it safe up the left side to avoid the three fairway bunkers on the right? Or are you enough of a gambler to go for the birdie by trying to chew off the second half of the dogleg?

Then there's the 496-yard, par-5 12th, where you lay up to a creek, then face the choice of powering it 230 yards over a small lake onto the green for the 2-putt birdie or taking the conservative route up the right side.

Until a few years ago, Royal Oaks — named for its location at the intersection of Royal Road and Oak Street — was just a rolling pasture that was home to the Hanford family's cattle and horse farm.

Stu Hanford was a pretty fair golfer, as were his sons, especially Stu Jr. They both honed their games across the street at Lebanon Country Club. When farming eventually lost its appeal, the elder Hanford decided to build a golf course.

He brought in the bank, then architect Ron Forse, a devotee of the Donald Ross school. Now, with Stu Jr., 26, as head pro and manager, they're bringing in golfers from all over eastern Pennsylvania.

— Oct. 20, 1996

If You Go

Address: 3350 West Oak St., Lebanon.

Phone: 717-274-5406

Greens fees: Weekends, $49 to ride, $38 to walk. Weekdays, $35 to ride, $28 to walk.

Carts: Walking is permitted anytime.

Web: www.gothamgolf.com

Lehigh

C O U N T Y

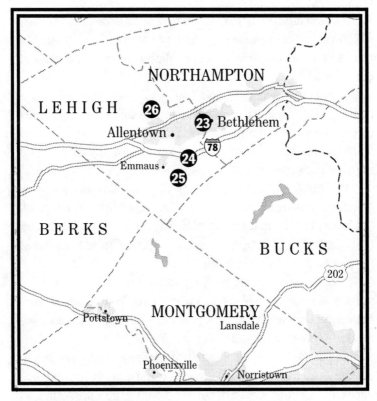

23. Bethlehem Golf Club
24. Center Valley Club
25. Locust Valley Golf Course
26. Olde Homestead Golf Course

23. Bethlehem Golf Club

This municipal course is a secret no longer

Golfers in Bethlehem probably won't appreciate my revealing their little secret, but they have one heck of a first-rate, dirt-cheap municipal course up there that you ought to know about.

It's called Bethlehem Golf Club, and it's owned by the city, which means there's nothing fancy or pretentious about the pro shop or the clubhouse. We're talking "muni" facility here, but so what?

You won't care much as you play your way around a course that is long (7,017 yards), plenty tough (73.6 rating, 127 slope), well-maintained, and has a kind of large-scale sweep to the holes that you won't find on any of the city-owned municipal courses in and around Philadelphia.

Just how good Bethlehem Golf Club is came as a surprise to me. I had heard of it, even heard some talk that it was good, but it was hardly on my must-play list. But as I was headed up there last week, I happened to talk to a golf buddy who used to spend a lot of time in Bethlehem.

"Great course, man. You're going to love it," he said. "And nobody down here knows about it." This from a single-digit handicapper, who these days plays the finest private courses around Philadelphia and is not given to fawning.

As I stood on tee after tee the other day, facing yet another par 4 of more than 400 yards (nine par 4s exceed 400 yards), I suddenly knew what he meant. The course boasts one solid hole after another and big, sweeping, rolling fairways that run toward well-bunkered, undulating greens that often slope away from you.

It has uphill holes, downhill holes, and holes with sloping fairways. It has short, lazy doglegs and long par 5s. It has a couple of par 3s that stack up against some of the best in the region. It's just a fun, playable course that tests most every aspect of your game.

The whole time I was playing, I was trying to think of how best to describe Bethlehem Golf Club. I kept coming back to the term "poor man's major-championship course."

I don't mean that as a slap at the course or at the people who play it. It's just that Bethlehem struck me as the kind of large-scale course demanded by a U.S. Open or a PGA Championship, minus all the trappings of wealth and privilege you find at a Congressional Country Club or a Pebble Beach.

Hole for hole, Bethlehem can hold its head high. It's not just me who thinks so. In the just-released edition of Golf Digest's Places to Play, Bethlehem GC got bumped up from 2$1/2$ stars to 3$1/2$. If you ask me, it's better than several of the

Scorecard

Hole	Blue	White	Gold	Red	Par	HCP	Red HCP
1	403	380	349	314	4	8	1
2	536	517	484	438	5	12	11
3	449	427	410	344	4	2	5
4	192	176	153	141	3	10	10
5	446	423	407	304	4	4	6
6	565	544	505	452	5	6	2
7	350	328	302	291	4	18	16
8	175	160	150		3	16	17
9	417	397	368	315	4	14	14
Out	3,533	3,352	3,128	2735	36		
10	430	418	398	363	4	1	4
11	367	349	311	226	4	17	18
12	443	426	402	322	4	11	12
13	422	403	363	293	4	5	9
14	186	173	160	150	3	13	7
15	543	520	487	435	5	15	15
16	208	188	163	146	3	7	3
17	430	413	375	296	4	9	8
18	455	432	403	296	4	3	13
In	3,284	3,322	3,062	2,527	35		
Total	**7,017**	**6,674**	**6,190**	**5,262**	**71**		

courses in the area that rate four stars.

There's not a drop of water on the course, nor are there any long, forced carries that so intimidate high-handicappers. In fact, the fairways tend to be wide and accommodating. But if you play from either the back tees (7,017 yards) or the second tees (6,674), you had better be prepared to hit some quality, long iron shots into the greens.

That said, Bethlehem isn't overly penal. It's not one of those courses on which the slightly errant approach shot quickly spells doom and an 8 on your card. Indeed, it's straightforward and fair. Recovery shots are possible. Catastrophe is avoidable.

The course has been open since 1956. It was designed by father and son William and David Gordon, who also did Hawk Valley, Locust Valley and Saucon Valley's Grace course. Bethlehem has never hosted a big-deal tournament, although you will find that many local club pros respect the course. So do daily-fee golfers around town who swarm the 18-hole "Monocacy" course and the nine-hole sister track just across the street. (I didn't play the nine-hole course, but I have heard good things about it.)

If I have a reservation in recommending Bethlehem, it's that it's packed from cheek to jowl on weekends. I played on an overcast Wednesday afternoon, when the course was nearly empty. Unless you have time to kill, the smart move might be to sneak up for a midweek round.

— May 21, 2000

If You Go

Address: 400 Illicks Mill Rd., Bethlehem.

Phone: 610-691-9393.

Greens fees: Weekends, $36 to ride, $25 to walk. Weekdays, $29 to ride, $18 to walk. (Rates slightly lower for Bethlehem residents).

Carts: Walking permitted anytime.

Amenities: Well-stocked pro shop, driving range, three practice putting greens, casual restaurant and snack bar, small locker-room facility. Outings welcome.

Rating: First-rate municipal facility. Terrific course that is well-kept, long and demanding, without being too much for the high-handicapper. Unpretentious, low-key atmosphere. A must-play for anybody seeking to sample the region's quality daily-fee courses.

24. Center Valley Club

Nearly lives up to its advance billing

The list of public-access courses in the Philadelphia region that Golf Digest has awarded four stars — the coveted "outstanding" rating — is not long.

Wyncote in Oxford, near Wilmington. Hartefeld National, near Avondale in southern Chester County, will surely make the list in future editions of Places to Play.

If you're willing to drive 90 minutes, there's also Royal Oaks, east of Harrisburg, in Lebanon. And Blue Heron Pines at the Jersey Shore.

So, when the magazine recently bestowed four stars on another nearby course south of Allentown, the four-year-old Center Valley Club, a quick shot up Route 309 or the Northeast Extension of the Pennsylvania Turnpike, it seemed worth checking out.

To be honest, based on a round last weekend, Golf Digest's rating for Center Valley seemed a little generous, but not by much. Many area golfers will likely find it worth the trek.

Beyond the course itself, Center Valley is a welcoming and well-run facility — clean, accommodating and full of cheerful staffers.

Name another course where the starter announces the names of each golfer over a loudspeaker at the first tee, as though you were contestants in a tournament.

And name another area course where pace of play is enough of a priority that four very visible clocks have been placed around the course, or where rangers constantly monitor your progress. (In the pro shop last Sunday, a walkie-talkie crackled with one ranger asking another to please go advise one foursome that if the golfers couldn't keep up, then perhaps Center Valley was not the course for them.)

The course itself, built atop an old zinc mine now filled
with water, is first-rate. It measures 6,904 yards from the
championship tees and carries a 74.1 rating and a 135 slope.
From the whites, it's a considerably shorter 5,951 yards, with
a 68.8 rating and a 124 slope for men, 74.8 and 135 for women.

The front side is links-style, with few trees and heavy on
the now-popular mounds that serve to create a bobsled-
course effect on several holes. The back side, with several
tree-lined fairways, is the more traditional parkland-style,
and the more interesting of the two nines.

Eleven of the 18 holes confront the player with some
degree of dogleg. Water comes into play on 11 holes — mere
creeks on four holes, more ominous ponds or small lakes on
the rest.

"The large lake by Nos. 13 and 14 are connected to the
mines," said Larry Wise, director of golf at Center Valley. "We

Scorecard

Hole	Champ	Pine	Oak	Cedar	Willow	Par	HCP
1	396	366	348	338	289	4	11
2	162	139	115	107	89	3	17
3	550	522	501	420	404	5	7
4	377	342	307	297	280	4	13
5	397	361	352	327	300	4	5
6	514	501	486	460	434	5	9
7	450	394	336	328	306	4	1
8	168	154	134	114	97	3	15
9	438	412	377	312	294	4	3
Out	3,452	3,191	2,956	2,703	2,493	36	
10	360	334	290	276	236	4	6
11	594	553	529	454	421	5	8
12	419	402	345	341	304	4	4
13	153	139	133	122	100	3	18
14	368	348	327	294	262	4	16
15	393	358	330	276	252	4	14
16	233	218	208	151	123	3	12
17	485	458	443	405	385	5	10
18	447	405	390	373	356	4	2
In	3,452	3,215	2,995	2,692	2,439	36	
Total	**6,904**	**6,406**	**5,951**	**5,395**	**4,932**	**72**	

don't hunt for balls in there. We don't know how deep it is."

Center Valley — designed by Jeffrey Cornish, a Massachusetts architect who is a past president of the Golf Course Architects of America — opened in June 1992 and is part of the Stabler Center business and residential development.

On the front nine, you might feel in places that Cornish got carried away with his Scottish theme of high mounds encasing the fairways. Except for the par-3 second and eighth holes, both delicate little shots over ponds, almost the entire front side involves standing on a tee and gazing up a tunnel-like fairway. Sail a shot over the mounds and you've got a problem. Some golfers find that appealing, some don't.

The back nine is more interesting. The 10th is a 360-yard, par-4 dogleg right that requires a tee shot over a creek and marsh, into a fairway with water on the left, with more water guarding the green.

The 14th, a 368-yard par 4 with a stand of menacing trees front and center in the fairway, was the only aggravating hole on the course. On the tee, you have three choices: Hit a medium-to-long iron over a lake to a small landing area, leaving a short iron into the green; bust a tee shot over the landing area, as well as over a set of bunkers beyond it, for a short pitch into the green; or play it safe by staying right of the trees into a much more abundant fairway on the right side.

That seemed the prudent thing to do to minimize the risk of taking a double bogey. Wham — tee shot of the day, right up the heart of the right side, where the ball came to rest behind a tree that was out of view from the tee. Result: bogey.

Among Center Valley regulars, Wise said, the most controversial hole is the 17th, a 485-yard, par-5 dogleg right.

The tee shot must first clear marsh, which is hard enough for many golfers, but it must also avoid a small wetland farther ahead, right at the bend, where slicers lose it and long hitters try to cut the corner. More than a few players would like to bulldoze that hazard.

"We can't fill it because of [environmental] regulations," Wise said. "Besides, without it, number 17 is just a hard par 4."

— Sept. 22, 1996

If You Go

Address: Part of the Stabler Center business and residential development, south of Allentown off Saucon Valley Road, near Route 309.

Greens fees: Weekends, $70 to ride, $70 to walk. Weekdays, $70 to ride, $70 to walk.

Carts: Walking is permitted anytime, although cart fees are included.

Web: www.centervalleygolfclub.com

Amenities: Reasonably stocked pro shop; men and women's locker rooms without showers; pub and grill with outdoor patio. Outings welcome.

Rating: Fine course, pleasant atmosphere and staff.

25. Locust Valley Golf Club

For quality, no slouch

Mention golf courses in the Allentown-Bethlehem area, and the first place that comes to mind is Saucon Valley Country Club, which hosted the U.S. Senior Open in 1992 and is scheduled to do so again in 2000.

There's also plenty to be said for the four-star public course south of Allentown, Center Valley Club.

But daily-fee players on the lookout for another quality track should also consider Locust Valley Golf Club in Coopersburg, over the Lehigh County line near Route 309.

Locust Valley — a one-time private club rescued from bankruptcy a dozen years ago by four local businessmen — is no Saucon Valley, nor is it on a par with Center Valley, but that still leaves plenty of room for quality.

A no-frills operation to be sure, Locust Valley is a mature, tree-lined course, where narrow fairways and small, bunkered greens will test the accuracy of your driver and irons.

Designed by William Gordon, who laid out Saucon Valley's celebrated Grace course, Locust Valley doesn't aspire to greatness. But it offers picturesque and demanding holes, and fully deserves its three-star rating from Golf Digest's Places to Play. Some of the comments in Places to Play are right on the money: "old-time feel . . . tree-lined slicer's nightmare . . . good variety of holes . . . shotmaker's course . . . used to be private club and has seen better days."

Indeed, any golfer wrestling with a wayward driver faces quite the conundrum at Locust Valley. At 6,503 yards from the back tees, with a slope of 132, the course is long enough to tempt you to reach for the big stick time and time again. Yet, with virtually every fairway lined by trees on one or both sides, you can frequently find yourself punching out from under a limb or peering around at the green from behind a towering oak.

"The third [406 yards] and fourth holes [434] are famous among regulars because they are so tight and long," said Rick Schwab, who owns the course along with his father, Carl; local businessman Don Stahley; and head professional Jim Kuehner.

Famous holes, maybe, but certainly not favorites among the regulars. That status is reserved for the ninth, a downhill wedge plop (120 yards) over a pond, and for the 18th, a 385-yard downhill dogleg that dares you to cut the corner over two ponds for a better shot into the small, slightly elevated green. (The 18th is also easily the most picture-perfect hole on the course.)

Even though mountains are visible in the distance, Locust Valley is, save for a handful of holes, flat. The only water on

Scorecard

Hole	Black	Blue	White	Red	Par	HCP	Red HCP
1	486	482	450	416	5	7	1
2	350	331	292	286	4	13	13
3	406	396	349	343	4	3	7
4	434	428	374	367	4	1	5
5	363	351	321	316	4	11	9
6	188	179	152	146	3	15	15
7	513	495	475	423	5	9	3
8	374	317	297	287	4	5	11
9	120	100	80	78	3	17	17
Out	3,234	3,079	2,790	2,662	36		
10	336	324	307	303	4	18	14
11	351	337	317	282	4	12	18
12	379	369	357	319	4	8	6
13	150	137	125	120	3	16	16
14	510	501	433	427	5	4	2
15	421	409	312	307	4	2	8
16	539	497	478	428	5	14	4
17	198	186	173	153	3	10	10
18	385	353	321	309	4	6	12
In	3,269	3,113	2,823	2,648	36		
Total	**6,503**	**6,192**	**5,613**	**5,310**	**72**		

the course is on Nos. 9 and 18.

Gordon — who also designed Bethlehem Municipal, Bucks Country Golf Club, Sunnybrook Country Club and White Manor Country Club — laid out the first nine at what was then Locust Valley Country Club in 1954. He returned the next year to complete the 18th, then did considerable redesign work in 1963.

In 1985, with the club facing serious money woes, Schwab and his partners stepped in and made it public.

Anyone who hasn't played the course in several years might notice a difference — an irrigation system installed last year will keep the fairways from burning out in July and August.

A survey last year indicated that 40 percent of the patrons come from Montgomery and Bucks Counties.

— June 1, 1997

If You Go

Address: 5525 Locust Valley Rd., Coopersburg, Pa.

Phone: 610-282-4711.

Greens fees: Weekends, $46 to ride, $46 to walk. Weekdays, $36 to ride, $23 to walk.

Carts: Walking is permitted anytime. Cart fees are included weekends before noon.

Amenities: Moderately stocked pro shop, outdoor snack bar, indoor and outdoor banquet facilities, no driving range.

Rating: Tight, well-conditioned, good loop.

26. Olde Homestead Golf Club

A pleasant, small-town feel

Once again, family farming's loss is golf's gain.

This time, the piece of property in question is 15 miles north of Allentown, a 230-acre slab of rolling countryside that for generations was the Snyder family potato farm. Now, thanks to the threat of inheritance taxes and advances in modern earthmoving equipment, we have instead Olde Homestead Golf Club, a pleasant, scenic, aptly named links-style loop.

Is it the second coming of Wyncote Golf Club, the four-star links course in lower Chester County? No. Is it a refreshing departure from many of the mediocre public layouts closer to Philadelphia? Yes.

Golf course aside, there's something inviting about Olde Homestead. Maybe it's the quaint, refurbished clubhouse that was the Snyder homestead for the better part of 100 years. Maybe it's the family-oriented, small-town feel of the whole place — people actually smile and say, "Hello."

Or maybe it's simply the knowledge that Olde Homestead was born as a labor of love, a family enterprise that was the best way the next generation of Snyders could think of to keep the land in the family rather than sell it off to pay estate taxes.

"There weren't a lot of options," said general manager Glen Smith, a former Bell Laboratories engineer, who, with his wife, Sally, a Snyder heir, owns and runs Olde Homestead.

"We could have sold it for housing for a lot of money, but that would have defeated the purpose."

Instead, the Smiths threw caution to the wind. Borrowing against the value of the land, Smith left his job of almost 20 years, as did Sally, a schoolteacher, and they set about developing.

Open three years, Olde Homestead is slowly but surely taking shape. But the Smiths wince every time another big expense comes down the pike.

Just last week, for example, the place was abuzz because a local kid who mowed fairways there last summer got drafted by the New York Mets. His sister still works in the pro shop. His brother still mows fairways at Olde Homestead.

Indeed, even as Smith was playing a round with me, the newest Met's brother drove by on a fine piece of equipment. Smith waved at the kid, then turned and said, "A mower like that — $38,000."

You could feel his pain.

Because of realities like that, you almost feel guilty quibbling that a fairway landing area at Olde Homestead could have been a little flatter here or 10 yards wider there. You

Scorecard

Hole	Trailblazer	Pioneer	Home-steader	Settler	Front-iersman	Par	HCP
1	514	497	482	416	409	5	4
2	417	403	336	314	258	4	12
3	455	448	420	402	308	4	6
4	436	426	400	388	341	4	8
5	423	393	382	342	333	4	10
6	178	160	149	138	105	3	16
7	363	351	329	319	272	4	14
8	548	540	487	477	426	5	2
9	190	178	171	154	135	3	18
Out	3,524	3,396	3,156	2,950	2,587	36	
10	365	350	310	285	225	4	11
11	350	325	310	285	225	4	9
12	540	520	485	465	420	5	3
13	195	180	170	155	120	3	17
14	390	375	340	315	285	4	3
15	365	350	340	315	275	4	7
16	550	530	500	475	455	5	1
17	231	222	167	133	106	3	15
18	390	370	355	335	275	4	5
In	3,376	3,222	2,997	2,773	2,426	36	
Total	**6,900**	**6,618**	**6,153**	**5,723**	**5,013**	**72**	

know that to Smith, those 10 extra yards would have meant hiring two guys on bulldozers for three more days at a time when the construction budget was pretty much depleted.

Not that Smith, or architect Jim Blaukovitch, needs to apologize. Given the budget and the topography that climbs upward, then falls off dramatically, then wends through trees on a few holes, they've come up with a playable, pleasurable course.

There are two or three holes that evoke a shrug, but Olde Homestead also boasts four or five very fine holes. Of course, nobody knows the strengths and weaknesses of the course better than Smith himself, and he is constantly toying with what they can do to make it better. Eventually, if money permits, they'd like to add another 18.

As it is, from the tips, Olde Homestead plays 6,900 yards to a testy 132 slope. From the shortest of its five sets of tees, the course goes 5,013 yards and 115 slope. Golf's Digest's Places to Play gives Olde Homestead 3½ stars.

In general, it's a wide-open links-style course that rolls up and down across pastureland, in addition to the added mounding. But trees do come into play on four or five holes, and creeks and ponds can give you fits on four or five others.

Olde Homestead tests you right out of the parking lot. Where most golf courses begin with a rather-benign, straight par 4 to let you warm up, here you are faced right away with a good double-bogey opportunity.

It comes in the form of a par 5, with a small landing area between trees and a creek on the left and a hillside on the right. Because of a small, tiered green protected by trees, traps and a creek in front, only John Daly will be thinking of going for it. Be advised to hit a bucket of balls before starting.

The third, fourth and fifth holes are all long, straight par 4s. The sixth, however, is quite a change of pace — a 160-yard par 3 that goes from way up high, down through trees on either side to a gigantic, elongated green.

The seventh, a 351-yard par 4, is a complete departure

from the rest of the course. From tee to green, it is enshrouded by trees, with a creek and protected marshland slashing across the fairway to test the accuracy of tee shots.

On the backside, the 10th and 11th — both short par 4s — wrap around a small lake and provide ample opportunity to get into trouble. The middle of the back, just like the middle of the front, is meat-and-potatoes golf across hill and dale.

The 16th, a par 5, is the No. 1 and most picturesque hole. From high atop a bluff, the tee shot is over scruff and marsh to a fairway far below. From there, the hole turns left and works its way back uphill.

If you hate to ride in carts, Olde Homestead may not be a course for you. This is the foot of Blue Mountain we're talking about, and it's quite a hike across some serious elevation changes.

But if you like to get out of the city, if you like a warmer, small-town, wholesome feel, Olde Homestead is worth a try.

— June 7, 1998

If You Go

Address: 6598 Route 309, New Tripoli.

Phone: 610-298-4653.

Greens fees: Weekends, $55 to ride, $55 to walk. Weekdays, $43 to ride, $43 to walk.

Carts: Carts mandatory weekends before twilight.

Web site: www.oldehomesteadgolfclub.com

Montgomery

C O U N T Y

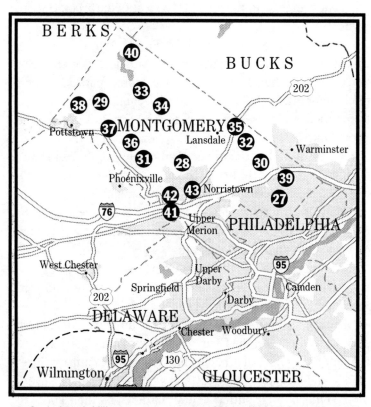

27. Cedarbrook Hills
28. Center Square Golf Club
29. Hickory Valley Golf Club
30. Horsham Valley Golf Club
31. Jeffersonville Golf Club
32. Limekiln Golf Club
33. Macoby Run Golf Course
34. Mainland Golf Course
35. PineCrest Golf Club
36. Skippack Golf Course
37. Turtle Creek Golf Course
38. Twin Ponds Golf Club
39. Twining Valley Golf Club
40. Upper Perk Golf Course
41. Valley Forge Golf Club
42. Westover Country Club
43. Wood's Golf Center

27. Cedarbrook Hills: Short Course

For the young and old, a gem

If the world needs another fabulous, 7,000-yard championship layout, what it may need even more are decent courses that embrace kids and senior citizens.

That brings us to the Short Course at Cedarbrook Hills in Wyncote.

Granted, in golf parlance, the Short Course is a par-3 course. Somehow, that seems an almost pejorative term. But don't confuse the Short Course with some patchy, two-bit pitch-and-putt. With its mix of quality, challenging holes, not to mention manicured, bent-grass fairways and greens, the Short Course is a small-scale gem, plain and simple.

Recast from the remnants of an original A.W. Tillinghast design from the early 1920s, the Short Course is a fun little test. Yes, there's an 85-yard hole like you might find at a pitch-and-putt. But there are also a 240-yard beast and a slew of respectable 115-to-185-yard par 3s that will test the iron play of even single-digit handicappers.

Perhaps best of all, the Short Course is a terrific, welcoming environment for youngsters learning the game and seniors who no longer seek the wrath of a full-blown golf course.

During a round last week, I teed it up with a delightful, spry, retired couple, the Chaneys, for whom the Short Course is plenty of golf. Bill Chaney has had double hip replacements, and he and Peg Chaney had suction-cup ball removers on the ends of their putters. They got down on their knees to mark their balls on the greens. They were having a blast.

In front of us was a foursome of boys who couldn't have been older than 13. They were banging balls left and right and smiling every step of the way. Behind us were four more kids. Not a grown-up in the group.

That said, the Short Course is not simply a place to drop off your kids. It's also an ideal place to play a family round or to introduce a child to the game. So welcoming is the place that it has a separate scorecard for children that reads: "The Short Course: Where Junior Golf Rules."

Why a separate card? A 185-yard hole, such as the 12th, may be a par 3 for you, but not for a 10-year-old boy. For that youngster, 13 of the holes at the Short Course play as par 4s, and two of them as par 5s, for a total par of 71. Girls have their own par of 75.

"We believe the biggest draw is going to be from families, juniors and intermediates," said Richard Fahey of Matrix Development Corp., which took over management of the Short Course last year.

Scorecard

Hole	Blue	Red	Par	HCP	Red HCP
1	119	95	3	17	17
2	162	142	3	5	11
3	170	118	3	3	1
4	116	109	3	15	7
5	129	101	3	13	3
6	167	114	3	1	5
7	140	127	3	11	9
8	143	97	3	9	15
9	148	102	3	7	13
Out	1,294	1,005	27		
10	181	166	3	6	8
11	177	157	3	16	12
12	185	169	3	8	6
13	85	77	3	18	18
14	173	144	3	14	16
15	159	150	3	10	14
16	166	154	3	12	10
17	240	186	3	2	2
18	210	191	3	4	4
In	1,576	1,394	27		
Total	**2,870**	**2,399**	**54**		

In addition, Fahey said they are seeing some play from better golfers looking to work on their iron play or short game, or simply slip in a quick round (average round: 2 hours, 15 minutes).

"Even good players don't eat the place up," said Fahey, referring to the challenge.

Designed by Tillinghast as the original Cedarbrook Country Club 18-hole layout, the Short Course was the site of some championship golf in the 1930s and '40s. Fahey says Ben Hogan won a tournament there in the '40s.

In the '60s, with Cedarbrook Country Club moving to Blue Bell, a big chunk of the course was used to build what are now the adjoining Cedarbrook Apartments. At the time, George Fazio, uncle of the famed Tom Fazio, was brought in to turn the remaining real estate into a par-3 course for residents of the apartment complex — sort of the ultimate in then-suburban living.

Only one Tillinghast hole — the original 10th, now the fifth at the Short Course — remains intact, and it's arguably the best on the property. But Fazio did keep about half a dozen of Tillinghast's original green complexes.

Fazio fashioned a few easy holes without bunkers, and a few more difficult shots from elevated tees, sloping fairways and well-protected greens.

Over the years, as the residents of Cedarbrook Apartments aged, the course saw fewer and fewer rounds, reaching a low of about 3,000 two years ago. Last year, the current owner, Roseland Management of New Jersey, brought in Matrix to revitalize and manage the place.

Matrix hired a new superintendent, Mike Farina, who has done a commendable job, and threw open the doors to the public, particularly children and seniors.

The result is not another top-dollar championship course. It's a fun, wholesome, well-run, reasonably priced place to learn and enjoy the game.

— July 5, 1998

If You Go

Address: Limekiln Pike and Ogontz Avenue, Wyncote.

Phone: 215-881-6890.

Green fees: Weekdays, walk for $16, ride for $26; Weekends, walk for $20, ride for $30.

Carts: Walking permitted anytime.

Amenities: Moderately stocked pro shop, snack bar, putting green, banquet facilities. No driving range.

Rating: Terrific for youngsters, seniors and all level of players wanting to work on their iron game.

28. Center Square Golf Club

Plays middle of the road

If letters and phone calls are any indication, golfers want to read about the newest and best courses in the area. But they also want help in finding mid-priced, mid-level tracks that they can play for a little variety.

There's a ton of them out there, many of which you've probably never heard of. Case in point: Center Square Golf Club in Montgomery County.

Center Square, on Route 73 a few miles west of Route 202, is good enough to have hosted the USGA's Women's Public Links Championship in 1980 — and the tournament will return there next June — but it has never cut a high profile among area courses.

Though the front side is decidedly ho-hum, the back side is tight and hilly enough to provide an overall challenge for most levels of golfers.

Golf Digest's "Places to Play" guide rates Center Square two stars — "good, not great, but not a rip-off either" — and offers a mixed bag of comments from golfers ranging from "good layout for a short course" to "challenging course but too wide open."

Longtime Center Square head professional John Trullinger agrees. "The front nine is fairly wide-open and flat," he said. "The back is more challenging, tighter, more hills, more trees."

At only 6,342 yards from the blue tees, with a slope of 116, Center Square is not going to blow anybody away. But unless you're a low-handicapper looking for a fight, it probably won't bore you, either.

There's water on only one hole (the medium-length, par-3 18th), and the longest of the three par-5s is only 531 yards from the back tees. There are two longish par-3s (the third,

200 yards, and the 14th, 206 yards), but both holes are fairly forgiving of a lousy tee shot.

More than anything, Center Square is characterized by its abundance of short- to medium-length par-4s, which will suit plenty of golfers just fine. What better way to pile up the pars than a tee shot and an 8-iron or pitching wedge into the green?

That's not to say the short par-4s are all a snap. The fifth, a 365-yard dogleg left, requires a substantial and well-placed tee shot for a decent go at the green. The second, at only 317 yards, can give you fits if you leave your tee shot in the woods to the right or left. And the 15th and 16th holes — 379 and 313 yards, respectively — are hilly and tight enough to make many golfers reach for the 3-wood off the tee.

For better golfers, the most interesting holes will be the two par-5s on the back nine. At the 521-yard 12th, large stands

Scorecard

Hole	Blue	White	Red	Par	Ladies' Par	HCP	Ladies' HCP
1	389	376	363	4	4	4	6
2	317	305	294	4	4	14	12
3	212	200	155	3	3	6	16
4	332	326	320	4	4	16	8
5	364	351	302	4	4	12	10
6	515	497	434	5	5	10	4
7	166	154	146	3	3	18	18
8	419	403	388	4	5	2	2
9	380	369	359	4	4	8	14
Out	3,094	2,981	2,761	35	36		
10	397	380	371	4	4	3	5
11	326	316	306	4	4	15	7
12	521	507	424	5	5	7	13
13	416	405	395	4	5	1	1
14	206	190	182	3	3	9	17
15	379	310	297	4	4	13	9
16	313	303	293	4	4	11	15
17	531	524	498	5	5	5	3
18	159	132	121	3	3	17	11
In	3,248	3,067	2,887	36	37		
Total	**6,342**	**6,048**	**5,648**	**71**	**73**		

of trees pinch the fairway from the left and right, at about the spot where a well-hit tee shot should come to rest. From there, it's a blind second shot up and over a crest, down a long, sloping fairway, into a green with bunkers left, right and rear.

At the 531-yard 17th, it's up and over a crest, with a stand of trees on the left and trees lining the fairway down the right side. Hang it out too far to the right and you've got real problems. A nasty bunker in front of the green will make you think twice about trying to get home in two strokes. A wiser shot would be something high and soft.

Designed in the early '60s by Ed Ault, an architect of some note from the Washington-Baltimore area, Center Square has been owned for the last eight years by brothers Fran and Butch Pietrini, who are in the construction business.

"They've put quite a bit of money into it," said Trullinger, who has been at Center Square since the beginning. "We're going to put in cart paths eventually. We just want to keep improving it."

— Nov. 3, 1996

If You Go

Address: 2026 Skippack Pike & Whitehall Rd., Center Square.

Phone: 610- 584-5700.

Greens fees: Monday-Thursday, $26 to walk, $39 to ride; Friday-Sunday $40 to walk after 1 p.m., $53 to ride.

Carts: Weekdays, walking permitted anytime. Weekends, walking is permitted after 1 p.m.

29. Hickory Valley Golf Club

Two for the price of one

Half old, half new. Half trees, half fescue. That's perhaps the best way to describe the newly opened Presidential Course, aimed at the upscale daily-fee player, at Hickory Valley Golf Club in Gilbertsville.

If you like your golf courses wide open, with huge, undulating greens and laden with tons of unruly fescue grass to snare errant shots, the front side of the Presidential may be for you.

If you like a more traditional design, with smaller, flatter greens and narrow, corridor-style fairways walled by tall oak trees, you'll probably favor the Presidential's back nine.

Sound like a golf course with something of a split personality? You got it.

The Presidential, which opened on June 27, is yet another new area course going after the daily-fee golfer looking for something of a private-course feel.

As at Downingtown Country Club, a new clubhouse and pro shop are in the long-range plans. For now, the Presidential shares an adequate pro shop/snack bar with the Ambassador Course, its less difficult (and less expensive) sister layout.

As for the Presidential Course, it is a marriage of old and new — specifically, of nine holes from Hickory Valley's old 27-hole layout and a new nine from architect Ron Prichard, who also designed TPC Avenel in Nashville and, closer to home, PineCrest in Montgomeryville.

Some might argue the Presidential's is sort of a forced marriage.

Prichard's nine — actually holes 2 through 10 — has a contemporary look and feel, being heavily bunkered and winding through an environmentally protected area. Most anything off the fairway is lost to the fescue. Seven of Prichard's holes are doglegs, including the par-5, double-dogleg fourth. Because of the undulations and tiers on the sprawling greens, pin placements can radically change the level of difficulty of most holes.

By contrast, the old Red nine — No. 1, then 11 through 18 — was designed in 1968 and tends to be straight, with manageable rough. Rather than fescue, the threat to errant shots tends to be towering trees that squeeze some fairway landing areas to as little as 18 yards. (Yikes!) The small, flat greens may be the Red nine's biggest liability.

Does the difference in styles cause the marriage to feel, well, a bit forced?

"We were concerned about that," said Michael Storti, Hickory Valley's director of golf. "But the comment from people so far is that they like it. We haven't had one complaint."

Presidential Course

Hole	Championship	Tournament	Players	Forward	Par	HCP
1	359	348	340	333	4	16
2	412	388	359	341	4	10
3	369	354	312	299	4	9
4	540	524	494	471	5	3
5	165	138	104	471	3	17
6	486	463	429	410	5	5
7	166	144	128	108	3	15
8	396	375	352	314	4	12
9	374	342	317	294	4	11
Out	3,267	3,076	2,836	2,650	36	
10	441	424	396	366	4	2
11	194	185	140	135	3	14
12	371	357	307	303	4	7
13	459	369	314	307	4	4
14	540	528	476	460	5	6
15	125	111	104	97	3	18
16	480	422	405	400	5	8
17	446	378	316	302	4	1
18	352	336	256	251	4	13
In	3,409	3,110	2,714	2,621	36	
Total	**6,676**	**6,186**	**5,549**	**5,271**	**72**	

Ambassador Course

Hole	Championship	Tournament	Players	Forward	Par	HCP
1	486	469	411	401	5	1
2	342	322	294	288	4	5
3	183	168	163	153	3	17
4	568	454	419	412	5	3
5	377	368	311	306	4	7
6	269	258	253	249	4	13
7	174	164	139	132	3	15
8	386	378	348	338	4	9
9	375	365	317	309	4	11
Out	3,160	2,946	2,655	2,588	36	
10	530	467	417	409	5	4
11	365	349	297	281	4	6
12	133	120	103	89	3	18
13	331	317	229	219	4	12
14	167	160	139	123	3	16
15	379	349	306	301	4	8
16	402	388	320	314	4	10
17	366	354	286	280	4	14
18	609	519	461	454	5	2
In	3,282	3,023	2,558	2,470	36	
Total	**6,442**	**5,969**	**5,213**	**5,058**	**72**	

The plan, Storti said, is to bring Prichard back, probably after the season, for a little marriage counseling — for instance, to add bunkers and mounds to the old Red nine.

Even with its split personality, the Presidential can be a pleasant, challenging loop. From the back tees, it plays 6,676 yards and boasts a course rating of 72.8 and a slope of 133 — respectable by every measure.

With all the fescue on the front side, as well as water on seven of the 18 holes, the Presidential can be a multiple-lost-ball experience for the high- and low-handicapper alike. Pack an extra sleeve.

Two other things about the course: First, it has something of a rural, open-space look and feel because it's in the country. (Gilbertsville is just north of Pottstown.) Second, Storti and his rangers are fighting to keep it from becoming too clogged. Tee times are staggered by 10 minutes, as recommended by the USGA, and play is limited to 120 people per day.

"It's a young course," Storti said. "We don't want to wear it out in three months and suffer the effects for years to come."

— July 21, 1996

If You Go

Address: 1921 Ludwig Road. Gilbertsville

Phone: 610-754 9862

Greens fees: Presidential. Weekdays, walk for $28, ride for $40. Weekends, $55, cart included.

Ambassador. Weekdays, walk for $19, ride for $31. Weekends, $40, cart included.

Carts: Walk Anytime. Cart fees included on weekends.

30. Horsham Valley Golf Club

A short, solid course with homey appeal

Just as Cheers was a neighborhood tavern, Horsham Valley Golf Club in Ambler is a neighborhood golf course.

Short at only 5,115 yards from the back tees, Horsham Valley will never be mistaken for a championship layout — not with seven par 3s, a slope of only 102, and a par of 66.

But so what?

On any given day, Horsham Valley is brimming with as many happy golfers as any swanky country club in the area. For plenty of golfers, Horsham Valley fits like a comfy old shoe.

While it won't present much challenge to low-handicappers, Horsham Valley is a reasonable test for mid-level players working on their games, it's ideal for juniors and seniors, and it's a great place to sneak in that quick, after-work round.

For the cost-conscious, Horsham Valley's best selling points may be its walk-anytime policy and greens-fee schedule — twilight rates as low as $15.

"You don't have to hit it long, but you have to be straight," said head pro Harry Barbin, who owns Horsham Valley with his father, Harry Barbin Sr., and their business partner, David Koch. "And because we have small greens, you have to be very precise with your irons."

That's a fair assessment.

Of Horsham Valley's 10 par 4s, only one is longer than 400 yards. Most measure 300 to 365 yards, and a couple are even under 300. Hole after hole is a short, straight par 4 into a small green with one bunker or no bunkers. There's only one par 5, the 18th, and it's less than 500 yards.

There's not a truly tough hole on the course — until you hit the middle of the back nine, where things suddenly get dicey at Horsham Valley's version of Amen Corner.

It starts at the 13th hole, the 403-yard dogleg, where most players try to lay up with a fairway wood or long iron in front of a creek. Mature trees surrounding the small green can be a challenge.

The par-4 14th hole, while slightly shorter, is complicated by a large, overgrown, weed-filled waste bunker in the center of the fairway. Only big hitters can toy with the idea of carrying this bunker.

Scorecard

Hole	Regular	Forward	Par	HCP	Forward HCP
1	364	324	4	2	2
2	356	315	4	6	16
3	315	283	4	12	14
4	127	116	3	10	10
5	387	357	4	4	4
6	168	158	3	8	6
7	336	305	4	14	18
8	122	112	3	18	12
9	361	331	4	16	8
Out	2,536	2,301	33		
10	171	142	3	7	9
11	296	267	4	17	15
12	179	162	3	13	11
13	403	301	4	3	3
14	386	277	4	11	5
15	184	152	3	1	1
16	283	242	4	15	17
17	184	142	3	5	7
18	493	444	5	9	13
In	2,579	2,129	33		
Total	**5,115**	**4,430**	**66**		

The 15th hole, a 184-yard par 3, has by far the toughest tee shot on the course, and is the signature hole. The biggest problem is a creek that slashes across the fairway, then wraps around the right side. Trees on the left preclude a bailout area, and bunkers await a shot that's too long.

The tee shot at the 16th hole, a 283-yard dogleg left, is the only complaint you'll get here. Overhanging trees make for a chute off the tee that's so narrow, it's a wonder anybody ever hits the fairway.

The course opened in 1957 as a nine-hole course, designed by owner Doug Melville and his father, Jock Melville, who also designed what is now Twining Valley. Over the next decade, another nine holes were added. Barbin and his partners bought the course in 1980.

Since then, there has been a series of improvements. An irrigation system was added, bunkers were recast, and eight new tees have been built over the last three years.

Barbin and Horsham Valley do their parts for junior golf. It's the home course for the Hatboro-Horsham High School golf team, and Wissahickon High practices there.

Horsham Valley is not always aggravation-free. With upward of 40,000 rounds a year played there — many by youngsters and beginners — play can be slow, especially on weekends.

Still, for a lot of golfers, that's a small price to pay, especially if the fairways are full and mowed, the snack bar is stocked with cheap hot dogs and cold drinks, and the staff is cordial.

— Aug. 16, 1998

If You Go

Address: 500 Babylon Rd., Ambler.

Phone: 215-646-4707.

Greens fees: Weekends, $30 to walk, $40 to ride; weekdays $23 to walk, $35 to ride.

Carts: Walking permitted anytime.

Amenities: Well-stocked pro shop; range and putting green; snack bar. Leagues and outings welcome.

Rating: Fun loop for mid-level player, juniors and seniors. Great walking course.

31. Jeffersonville Golf Club

Real 'muni' reduces game to its basics

If a graduate student in golf-course management wanted to write a paper on the municipal course in America, a good place to start would be Jeffersonville Golf Club in West Norriton Township.

Long lines at the first tee, lots of golfers with mismatched clubs and no head covers on their woods, too many holes too close together, the constant sound of "Fore!" in the air — and yet it's the home course for plenty of golfers who come back week after week.

For whatever their faults, there is almost a certain charm to "munis" — those courses owned and operated by town or counties often on shoestring budgets, for the enjoyment and recreation of taxpayers and other interested parties.

Jeffersonville is no different from many. The pro shop has no pro, only a guy taking greens fees in a room barren of any merchandise other than balls and gloves.

Twenty steps away is the snack bar, another no-frills operation, where working-stiff patrons can review their rounds while they scarf hot dogs, throw back cold ones, and keep their eyes peeled on the college football game or golf tournament on the TV in the corner.

Make your way to the first tee and you find a line of carts that's longer than Ringling Brothers pulling out of town. Few logo golf shirts here.

The players on the tee are more likely to be wearing T-shirts and tennis shoes, swinging drivers that came out of the knock-off barrel at the neighborhood sporting goods store.

None of this is said to poke fun at Jeffersonville. It may be a far cry from the fancy country clubs that are the image of golf in this country, but courses like Jeffersonville are actually the far more common experience for most people. It's golf stripped of all pretense.

Tim DeWan, the township employee who manages Jeffersonville, doesn't know who designed the course. He only knows it opened in 1931 as a privately owned public course under the same name and that West Norriton Township bought it in 1973. Last year, it did a very considerable 46,000 rounds.

It's not a difficult course, with a slope rating of only 105 from the white tees, below the national average of 113. It also plays short — only 5,800 yards from the white tees, 6,122 from the blues.

The holes run the gamut from boring to not bad at all. In general, the course doesn't penalize a golfer too much. It has forgiving fairways and rough, and it has no wide chasms or water requiring long shots. And there's not much in the way of yawning bunkers. There are, however, enough trees to

Scorecard

Hole	Blue	White	Red	Par	Ladies' Par	HCP	Ladies' HCP
1	449	442	397	5	5	4	4
2	347	323	270	4	4	16	10
3	289	274	254	4	4	10	12
4	131	117	96	3	3	18	18
5	380	361	273	4	4	6	8
6	543	536	431	5	5	2	2
7	300	292	257	4	4	14	16
8	202	170	131	3	3	12	14
9	359	350	251	4	4	8	6
Out	3,000	2,865	2,360	36	36		
10	345	333	237	4	4	11	13
11	415	405	322	4	5	1	3
12	317	274	213	4	4	15	15
13	209	175	158	3	3	9	9
14	383	351	278	4	4	13	7
15	386	370	279	4	4	7	5
16	504	493	400	5	5	3	1
17	374	367	336	4	5	5	11
18	189	167	123	3	3	17	17
In	3,122	2,935	2,346	35	37		
Total	**6,122**	**5,800**	**4,706**	**71**	**73**		

stymie the wayward tee shot, and the greens tend to be rather small.

"The course is playable for every level of golfer, especially seniors, because we keep the rough so low," DeWan said. "I'm noticing a lot of young players coming out now, too."

That's not surprising. Because Jefferson is user-friendly, it is a good track on which juniors can learn the game and seniors can get around without having to pull off power shots.

Among regulars, DeWan said, one of the favorite holes is the fourth, a 117-yard par 3 with a green flanked by two of the tougher bunkers on the course. Also, the 11th, a 405-yard par 4 dogleg right over a creek into an angled fairway, then up to a slightly elevated green tucked into trees.

The signature hole, as such, is the 16th, the 493-yard double dogleg that demands two solid pokes just to reach the final turn for the uphill approach into perhaps the trickiest, most undulating green on the course.

Jeffersonville does suffer an affliction common to many wide-open muni courses. Because it is wide-open and the holes are so close together, it's not uncommon for wayward balls to come flying your way several times during a round. Forewarned is forearmed.

— Aug. 31, 1997

If You Go

Address: 2400 W. Main St., Norristown.

Phone: 610-539-0422.

Greens fees: $14 to walk, $24 to ride, (everyday).

Carts: Walking permitted anytime.

Amenities: Minimally stocked pro shop, plus snack bar, putting green and banquet facilities. No driving range. Outings welcome.

Rating: Busy muni.

32. Limekiln Golf Club

While short, it's also challenging

For the typical public-course player in search of a new, reasonably challenging, well-maintained layout, Limekiln Golf Club in Ambler is definitely worth a look.

Short and relatively flat, with water on a half-dozen of its 27 holes, Limekiln is neither a cream puff for low- and mid-handicappers nor too much of a struggle for high-handicappers and seniors. A lap around Limekiln can make for a pleasant round of golf — if it's not too crowded.

"It's basically a nice, sporting, public golf course," said Curt Simmons, a Phillies pitcher from 1947 to 1960, whose assessment rang fair and true even though he does manage and co-own Limekiln. "You can use all the clubs in your bag, but it's not backbreaking."

Simmons and former Phils teammate Robin Roberts (1948-1961) together own 55 percent of Limekiln; four investors own the rest.

Limekiln will never be confused with any of the area's top-notch private courses, but it's stronger than more than a few other public courses in the area — no names, please.

Of the three nines — Red, White and Blue — the Blue course, at 3,197 yards from the back tees, is the favorite among Limekiln regulars. The Blue features what Simmons agrees is the closest he has to a signature hole — the 398-yard third, a testy dogleg left that's the No. 1 handicap hole on the nine.

On this hole, anything but a straight drive presents a problem. A hook is in the woods. A pushed or sliced tee shot leaves a treacherous long iron or fairway wood that must avoid a creek, a tree on the right, and a pond that runs along the right side. Long-ball hitters can find the small front-and-center lake off the tee.

The White course, the second-favorite among Limekiln

regulars, plays 3,237 yards from the back tees. The Red course measures 3,003 from the back tees. No matter what combination you play, 18 holes at Limekiln measures just over 6,200 yards, for a par 70.

Each nine offers one par 5. The longest, the 545-yard second

Red Course

Hole	Back	Middle	Front	Par	Ladies' Par	HCP	Front HCP
1	369	338	310	4	4	6	6
2	165	150	138	3	3	8	8
3	358	323	275	4	4	2	2
4	494	475	394	5	5	4	4
5	438	418	370	4	5	1	1
6	130	105	91	3	3	9	9
7	338	318	288	4	4	7	7
8	352	332	292	4	4	5	5
9	359	342	275	4	4	3	3
Out	3,003	2,801	2,433	35	36		

White Course

1	195	185	165	3	3	5	5
2	545	523	455	5	5	2	2
3	366	343	333	4	4	6	6
4	395	385	352	4	4	1	1
5	355	348	321	4	4	9	9
6	382	370	335	4	4	7	7
7	203	183	163	3	3	4	4
8	375	351	325	4	4	8	8
9	359	342	275	4	4	3	3
Out	3,237	3,089	5,227	35	35		

Blue Course

1	407	384	342	4	4	4	4
2	375	349	335	4	4	5	5
3	398	388	372	4	5	1	1
4	392	380	361	4	4	3	3
5	170	158	138	3	3	8	8
6	349	339	320	4	4	9	9
7	397	387	368	4	4	2	2
8	192	185	162	3	3	6	6
9	517	510	451	5	5	7	7
Out	3,197	3,080	2,849	35	36		

on the White course, is generally not reachable except by the biggest hitters. The other two — the 494-yard fourth on the Red and the 517-yard ninth on the Blue — are more likely birdie holes.

As for the rest, Limekiln offers a nice helping of doglegs and rolling par 4s and a mixed bag of par 3s, from the 130-yard sixth on the Red to the 203-yard seventh on the White.

The toughest combination, Blue/White, has earned a 68.7 rating and a 114 slope, making it a tougher test than all but Cobbs Creek — its approximate equal — among the Philadelphia-area public courses.

Simmons and Roberts bought what is now Limekiln in 1965, when it was an abandoned 18-hole course once known as Oak Park. In 1988, after acquiring enough adjacent farmland, Simmons and Roberts added another nine, designed by Al Janis.

What is now the Red course was the original front nine of Oak Park. Janis' holes have been integrated into the old back nine to create the Blue and White courses.

"We're tentatively planning on redoing some of the holes this fall, mostly to help the drainage on a few greens," said Simmons, a familiar figure around Limekiln whose home abuts the White second fairway. (Roberts lives in Tampa, Fla.) "The architect is working up the bids now."

As for shortcomings, Limekiln's greens and fairways can get harder than a cart path during the hot, dry summer months. And as is the case at many courses these days, a five-hour-plus round is not uncommon during peak hours.

— June 30, 1996

If You Go

Address: 1176 Limekiln Pike, Ambler.

Phone: 215-643-0643.

Web site: www.limegolf.com

Greens fees: Weekdays, $26 to walk, $37 to ride. Weekends, $47, cart included.

33. Macoby Run Golf Course

A course that is being kept in the family

If you favor the informality and personal attention that are often found in family-run shops and restaurants and other small businesses, you'll like the charm and comfort at Macoby Run, a family-run golf course.

About 30 minutes up the Northeast Extension of the Pennsylvania Turnpike and Route 63 in Green Lane, Montgomery County, the Hersh family six years ago turned their former dairy farm into a pleasant loop that rolls across pastureland, climbs hill and dale, and carves its way through enough wooded areas to add spice and variety to several holes.

That Macoby Run is a golf course today is testament to the determination of the Hershes.

There was the financial temptation to sell the scenic property to real estate developers. But the patriarch of the family, Lloyd Hersh, had dreamed of turning the land into a golf course for almost 40 years. Once he began to pursue his dream, he ran headlong into wetlands regulations. The Department of Environmental Resources and the Army Corps of Engineers held off final approval for several years.

After getting the go-ahead, the Hershes brought in landscape architect David Horn of Architerra P.C. in Allentown. By 1991, Macoby Run Golf Course, with its clubhouse looking much like the farm building it once was, was open for business.

"My father was born and raised here in the house, between the second and third holes," said Sheila Hersh-Schaffer, 31, who, with her sister Michele Peart, 30, now runs Macoby Run. "He still lives there today."

The youngest sister, Penelope, 27, works as a ranger on

weekends. Michele's husband, Michael, is the superintendent. Mother Joanne Hersh does most of the baking for the restaurant, while minding a total of four children who belong to Sheila and Michele. Lloyd Hersh has turned things over to the daughters, but he pitches in and chats up the golfers.

But you're probably wondering whether the course at Macoby Run is worth the trip.

The course, which measures 6,238 yards from the white tees and plays to a 118 slope, has its strengths and its weaknesses.

Scorecard

Hole	White	Red	Par	HCP
1	396	299	4	5
2	327	289	4	16
3	466	386	5	1
4	137	120	3	11
5	345	259	4	10
6	467	360	5	6
7	323	268	4	15
8	377	285	4	9
9	222	184	3	8
Out	3,060	2,450	36	
10	388	261	4	4
11	180	159	3	12
12	384	285	4	2
13	512	452	5	3
14	338	277	4	17
15	105	84	3	18
16	513	376	5	13
17	352	284	4	14
18	406	311	4	7
In	3,178	2,489	36	
Total	**6,238**	**4,938**	**72**	

Its strengths — several challenging holes and spectacular vistas — come courtesy of the naturally rolling and hilly terrain. Its weaknesses — there are only two sets of tees, and there is a noticeable lack of bunkers and traps that could shore up its defenses against low-handicappers — are a direct result of the Hershes, instead of a deep-pockets corporation, owning it.

"Traps are very expensive, because sand is so expensive to haul in," Hersh-Schaffer said. "We built some mounds on 16, 17 and 18, and we want to put in some traps, because those holes are a little boring."

(This year, anyway, what money the Hershes can afford to sink into the course must go toward building a sewage treatment plant.)

But the Hershes and Macoby Run owe no apologies. Just

when you think the course is getting ho-hum or too wide-open, it throws a decent golf hole at you.

Golf Digest gives Macoby Run two stars out of four, which is a fair assessment. With a few more years of maturity and a healthy smattering of fairway bunkers and greenside traps, the course would be more challenging and have a higher rating.

The opening three holes alone will have you breathing hard. The first, a 396-yard straightaway par 4, is all uphill. The second, a 327-yard par 4, is all downhill. Then comes the No. 1 handicap hole, a 466-yard par 5 that is almost flat for the tee shot. Then comes a second shot over Macoby Creek and a third shot that's like playing up the side of the Empire State Building.

Thankfully, the fourth is a flip-wedge downhill par 3 that allows you to catch your breath.

As you make your way around the front side, it's almost impossible not to pause in several places and marvel at the wonder of nature. The view is hardly typical for a Philadelphia-area course.

The back nine at Macoby Run is, for the most part, as wide-open and flat as the front side is tight and hilly. There — especially on 13, 14, 16 and 18 — is where the course could benefit significantly from bunkers and traps.

— May 4, 1997

If You Go

Address: 5275 McLean Station Rd., Green Lane.

Phone: 215-541-0161.

Greens fees: Weekends, $27 to walk, $36 to ride. Weekdays, $15 to walk, $24 to ride.

Carts: Walking permitted anytime.

Amenities: Driving range, restaurant, bar and grill, moderately stocked pro shop (no clubs), 200-seat outdoor banquet facility. Outings and leagues welcome.

34. Mainland Golf Course

Thrives off the beaten path

Mainland Golf Course, named for the town just up the Northeast Extension, is a delightful little loop that, frankly, doesn't get the attention it deserves.

It's a safe bet that you won't find a lot of public golf courses in the area in better condition, thanks to superintendent Mike Falcone, a steal from the Philadelphia Cricket Club.

Earlier this week, when even some of the more exclusive country clubs in the area were burned and browned by the heat and drought, Mainland was as green and soft as a politician's slush fund.

It's another safe bet that you won't find many facilities — the course, the bar and grill, the staff — more inviting. Of course, maybe that's just because it's far enough off the beaten path to retain a certain amount of civility.

For the average golfer, Mainland is a course to remember.

Perhaps it won't put up much of a fight for the big hitter or low handicapper — it's only a shade more than 6,000 yards, and its slope is 117. But those rather average figures belie the charm of the Montgomery County course.

Mainland has several short but very interesting holes. It has decent doglegs (one of them quite unusual), a couple of fun par 5s, and three par-3 holes that are as good as you'll find almost anywhere.

"It's a diamond in the rough," said head pro Wayne Morris. "The only drawback to the course is the shortness — you probably won't get to hit every club in your bag. But it can still beat you up."

That's a fair assessment. If you hit your driver 250 yards or more, you're looking at a 9-iron and lob wedges into the greens.

But if you don't mind that, or if you're a shot-knocker, or a senior or junior or woman who doesn't exactly thrive on 430-yard par 4s, Mainland could be perfect for you.

The course, originally called Twin Lakes, opened about 35 years ago as a four-hole track, then went to nine holes and finally 18. It originally was owned by a local family, according to Morris.

"They were doing OK, but I don't think they strove for much publicity," said Morris, who at the time worked up the road at Indian Valley Country Club. "It was extremely average."

Then, three years ago, Sal and Mario Lapio, whose family is in the construction business around Mainland, bought the course and began to infuse it with their money.

Morris, who had taught Sal Lapio to play the game at Indian Valley, was brought on as head pro. Falcone, an assistant superintendent at the Cricket Club, was hired to whip the course into shape.

Back then, as now, the chief weakness was its length — it was only 5,500 yards. So they began moving back the tees where they could. They added a couple of ponds and fairway bunkers, and rebuilt one hole.

More work is planned, but Mainland already is a fun course. Like Paxon Hollow in Delaware County, it's short on yardage but long on quality.

Mainland starts you off with a straightaway, downhill par

Scorecard

Hole	Yards	Par	Ladies' Par	HCP
1	400	4	5	3
2	500	5	5	5
3	358	4	4	9
4	223	3	4	1
5	282	4	4	15
6	312	4	4	11
7	288	4	4	17
8	341	4	4	7
9	127	3	3	13
Out		35	37	
10	281	4	4	18
11	348	4	4	4
12	248	4	4	14
13	306	4	4	12
14	500	5	5	2
15	372	4	4	6
16	171	3	3	8
17	155	3	3	16
18	327	4	4	10
In		35	35	
Total	5,547	70	72	

4 that's a decent and somewhat forgiving opening hole. But very quickly, at No. 2, you're faced with one of the trickier holes on the course, a 524-yard par-5 dogleg-right. Yes, you can cut the corner to go for birdie.

The unique hole on the front side has to be the 349-yard dogleg fifth, which is very narrow and tree-lined. The tee faces one direction, the fairway goes another — in other words, you've got to cut your tee shot right or you're in the sixth fairway. As you get closer to the green, there are a pond and bunkers.

The best hole on the front side, and probably the toughest, is easily the par-3 ninth. It's only 134 yards, but there are out-of-bounds left and OB behind the green, and there's a pond all along the right side. It's pretty from the tee, and tough to walk away from with a par.

The back side consists of ho-hummish par 4s until you hit the 12th, a 308-yard par-4 hole. From the tee, the hole looks tempting but ghoulish. Frankly, it plays shorter — a 60-year-old in the group almost drove the green. But there are wetlands off the tee to be negotiated, plus a lake and trees up the left side.

The par-5 14th is the next truly fun hole. It's a dogleg-right, 529 yards, that no doubt yields its share of birdies and double bogeys. Even with a good tee shot, the turn is way off in the distance, and the green is tucked in the trees behind a pond and a huge bunker. Very nice.

But the best of the back nine may be the three finishing holes. The 16th is a 186-yard par 3, which means most golfers are looking at a long iron or a fairway wood. The problem is, there are trees on the right, woods on the left, a sloping fairway, and bunkers at the greens. Good luck.

The 17th is a shorter, downhill par 3, but matters are complicated by a big tree crowding the right side of the green and a bunker on the left front. Another nice hole.

The course ends with a short par-4 dogleg-left over a creek, with trees guarding the left side and a huge collection bunker up the right side. Even if you hit a well-placed tee shot, another big tree is nestled against the right side of the green, just waiting for you. A fun finishing hole.

— July 27, 1997

If You Go

Address:2250 Rittenhouse Rd., Mainland.

Phone: 215-256-9548.

Greens fees: Mon., $20 to walk, $30 to ride; Tues.-Thurs. $25 to walk, $35 to ride; Fri., $38 to ride. Sat.-Sun., $45 to ride.

Carts: Carts are mandatory until 2 p.m. weekends and holidays.

Amenities: Moderately stocked pro shop, driving range, putting green, bar/restaurant, banquet facilities; outings welcome.

Rating: Short but sweet.

35. PineCrest Golf Club

Challenge to the average golfer

Different people look for different attributes in a golf course.

Some golfers demand a high-slope track that forces them to hit every club in their bag, fashion exacting shots, and constantly strategize.

Others aren't looking for a backbreaker. They tend to judge a course by whether it's well-maintained, or close to home, or where they can usually squeeze in a late-afternoon round, or arrive as a single and almost always get paired up with somebody interesting on the first tee.

For a lot of folks in and around Montgomeryville, that latter set of standards describes a fun little daily-fee course called PineCrest Golf Club.

At 6,331 yards from the blue tees, with a slope of 122, PineCrest is not the ultimate test for the scratch golfer. But it can make for an enjoyable round of golf for most mid- and high-handicappers, seniors, women and young people.

Though straight, relatively short par 4s abound, most every hole at PineCrest offers some kind of defense, whether it's out-of-bounds, trees, water or traps, or a combination thereof.

Take the 350-yard, par-4 fourth hole, for instance. Hardly anybody hits a driver there — fairway woods or long irons are the norm — because two small ponds squeeze the fairway to about 15 yards and guard a small, flat green that can be tough to hold. More than a few golf balls must be at the bottom of those ponds.

And then there's the 10th, a 335-yard par 4, mildly sloping, slight dogleg right. Again, a fairway wood and short iron will get the job done, but there's a trap if you miss right and a creek if you miss long.

On three of the par 3s — the second, 11th and 15th — the distances are short, but they all carry over water.

Until five years ago, PineCrest was known as the Montgomeryville Golf Course. That's when the Klein Co. real-estate developers bought it and began building single-family homes and condos in and around the course. In places, they're a little intrusive.

The developers also brought in golf course architect Ron Prichard, the same designer who reworked Hickory Valley Golf Club. He lengthened several holes, added water and traps in places, and did a good job of giving the course different looks from the various tees.

Somebody must be doing something right at PineCrest. It's almost always loaded with golfers, though they do a pretty good job of keeping play moving. And it always seems to be hosting an outing or a nearby high school golf team.

Should you drive 45 minutes to play PineCrest? Probably

Scorecard

Hole	Blue	White	Red	Par	Red Par	HCP	Red HCP
1	350	345	29	4	4	14	14
2	170	155	111	3	3	12	12
3	537	523	464	5	5	8	8
4	350	340	301	4	4	16	16
5	191	175	142	3	3	10	10
6	408	395	322	4	4	6	6
7	402	395	322	4	4	4	4
8	333	315	283	4	4	18	18
9	426	415	360	4	4	2	2
Out	3,167	3,058	2,635	35	35		
10	160	150	120	3	3	13	13
12	390	380	339	4	4	5	5
13	534	525	466	5	5	9	9
14	432	420	361	4	4	3	3
15	127	127	120	3	3	17	17
16	330	318	277	4	4	15	15
17	422	395	350	4	4	7	7
18	434	415	346	4	4	1	1
In	3,164	3,054	2,649	35	35		
Total	**6,331**	**6,112**	**5,284**	**70**	**70**		

not. But if you live nearby and you're looking for a mid-range course that's well-kept and well-managed, PineCrest might be for you.

— Aug. 18, 1996

If You Go

Address: Route 202 Montgomeryville, Pa. 18936.

Phone: 215-855-6112. Greens Fees: $26 Mon.-Thurs. to walk, $40 to ride; $46 Fri. to ride; $50 Sat.-Sun. to ride Carts: Carts are mandatory Fri.-Sun.

36. Skippack Golf Course

Don't let front nine fool you

Skippack Golf Course is not the most challenging track around or the most exclusive. But daily-fee players in the northern suburbs looking for another mid-level, reasonably priced municipal course for a little variety may find Skippack worth a look.

Skippack, off Route 73 in the Montgomery County town of the same name, is fairly wide-open and forgiving for much of the front nine. There are, after all, only 16 bunkers on the whole course.

But the back nine, with water or tree-lined fairways on nearly every hole, can be tight, stingy, and a bit more challenging.

Skippack has enough hills and doglegs to make most golfers work, yet, except for a few holes on the back nine, it takes a truly errant shot to put you in a wicked situation. The course plays as high as a 120 slope from the back tees — the national average is 113 — or as little as a 110 slope from the front tees.

"It's not like any other course around here," head pro Wes Hollis said. "And if somebody hasn't played here for 10 years, they will be very pleased and surprised when they come back."

The reason is that in 1990, the state park system, which owns and had managed the course, leased it to American Golf Corp., the giant golf-course management company. American spent $1 million refurbishing the clubhouse, added a new sprinkler system, cart paths and a driving range, and did extensive work on the traps.

Last fall, the company rebuilt the front tees, and now it has added a third set of back tees that lengthen the course from its previous 5,734 yards to just over 6,000. That's still a bit short, but the course plays longer because of the rolling terrain.

In coming seasons, Hollis said, mounding will be added to several holes, and the number of bunkers will be increased to about 40, with most on the front side.

It's a wonder the course exists at all. According to Hollis, the state bought the property a number of years ago, intending to flood it to create a reservoir. But local residents voted down the idea, preferring to keep the land as a golf course. Eventually, the state called in American Golf Corp.

"It was pretty much a cow pasture when we took it over," said Hollis, who grew up playing Skippack and is doing most of the design work himself. "We have a master plan."

Indeed, the front side could benefit from enhancements.

For the first few holes, Skippack has a kind of wide-open, typical "muni" look and feel that doesn't really get the juices flowing.

The first hole, a 360-yard par 4 with a slight dogleg, is rather ho-hum. And the second, a 521-yard par 5, although it

Scorecard

Hole	Tourn.	White	Red	Par	HCP	Red HCP
1	323	317	305	4	8	10
2	515	503	368	5	2	2
3	150	146	140	3	16	16
4	444	437	302	4	4	4
5	160	155	140	3	18	18
6	450	445	333	5	10	8
7	198	188	188	3	14	14
8	380	372	307	4	6	6
9	340	329	317	4	12	12
Out	2,960	2,892	2,400	35		
10	330	322	305	4	9	11
11	160	158	140	3	15	15
12	515	504	439	5	3	3
13	420	410	310	4	1	1
14	465	450	437	5	5	5
15	205	196	170	3	13	13
16	310	301	380	4	11	9
17	350	344	302	4	7	7
18	123	120	105	3	17	17
In	2,878	2,805	2,488	35		
Total						

is reachable only by big hitters, doesn't offer much fight.

But things pick up on the latter half of the front side, thanks to the 423-yard, par-4 sixth, which has a huge trap in front of the green, and the 213-yard, downhill, par-3 seventh.

The real challenge at Skippack doesn't come until the back side, however. There, the tree-lined fairways tighten, and Zacharias Creek, which slashes across the course, comes into play on three holes.

Among Skippack regulars, the favorite hole is the 13th, a 450-yard, tight, downhill par 4. It's easy to see why. The hole, the No. 1 handicap hole, is picturesque and tough, requiring a well-placed tee shot onto a shelf and a long approach shot over Zacharias Creek.

Actually, No. 13 is in the midst of what might be called Skippack's version of Amen Corner. The 11th hole is a fun, 173-yard par 3 over a creek and into a green surrounded by trees. The 12th, uphill with trees lining the right side of the fairway, is probably the best par 5 on the course. And the 14th, a tight, uphill par 5, can also spell trouble for the golfer with a wayward driver.

Designed in the 1950s by Harris Smith and Bob Benabia, Skippack was redone in 1988 by X.G. Hassenplug, who also designed Five Ponds in Warminster and Radnor Valley Country Club.

— May 13, 1997

If You Go

Address: Stump Hall and Cedears Roads, off Route 73, in Skippack.

Phone: 610-584-4226.

Greens fees: Weekends, $45 to ride, $24 to walk; Weekdays, $35 to ride, $24 to walk.

Carts: Walking permitted any time; cart fees included before noon weekends and holidays.

Amenities: Reasonably well-stocked pro shop; driving range; snack bar; picnic area; private lessons and clinics. Outings welcome.

Rating: Mid-range muni.

37. Turtle Creek Golf Course

Not a garden-variety midlevel course

Add Turtle Creek Golf Course in Limerick to the growing list of new, midprice, medium-difficulty layouts that are probably best described as "American farm courses."

In the past, for lack of a better term, I've referred to these courses sprouting up in surrounding counties on onetime family farms as "links-style." That's because they are generally wide open and rolling, possessed of few trees and, as a result, often windswept.

But not long ago, while playing just such a course with a friend who is a veteran of golf in Scotland, he looked beyond the out-of-bounds fence at the crops growing on a hillside and at the silo in the distance and suggested a more apt description may be "American farm course."

I immediately agreed. American farm course. It had a certain, well, truth in advertising.

That said, there's no better example of the growing phenomenon than the year-old Turtle Creek.

Like several others in the region, Turtle Creek was for generations a working family farm — in this case a cattle farm, and then a turf farm since the 1960s. It is relatively flat and windswept, and seven of the nine ponds are man-made.

Even more telling, it was not built on a grand scale by developers with deep pockets, but rather by a family — the Waltzes — who went into debt up to their eyeballs because they wanted to keep the land in the family.

"It was scary — it's still scary," said Bill Waltz, who owns and runs Turtle Creek with his wife, Bobbie; his brother Ray; and the offspring from both families (Sandy, Ray Jr., et al.).

Scary — and risky — yes. But the Waltzes, who also own the neighboring driving range and pitch-and-putt, have known this was what they wanted to do with the land for most of the last three decades.

One of the great ironies, Bobbie Waltz said last week, was how hard they worked to get the land flat for turf farming.

"They worked 30 years to get it flat," she said.

And then, when the golf course was suddenly a go, they wanted hills and mounds and all the other topographical features that make for interesting golf layouts.

The job of making the most of the topography fell to South Carolina-based architect Ed Beidel. He incorporated the two existing ponds on the property, and dug seven more. The dirt he amassed from digging the ponds was used to create the mounds that now frame almost every fairway at Turtle Creek.

One thing Beidle didn't come up with was the name. The Waltzes' daughter, Lisa, a television actress in Hollywood, suggested Turtle Creek after dining in a restaurant by the same name in Texas.

Scorecard

Hole	Gold	Blue	White	Red	Par	Red Par	HCP	Red HCP
1	406	373	293	282	4	4	11	13
2	529	504	482	437	5	5	3	3
3	151	136	107	85	3	3	17	17
4	360	353	331	309	4	4	13	9
5	419	402	373	324	4	4	5	5
6	442	426	388	351	4	4	1	1
7	355	349	318	250	4	4	15	15
8	538	516	469	414	5	5	9	7
9	207	191	168	152	3	3	7	11
Out	3,409	3,250	2,929	2,604	36	36		
10	310	293	260	221	4	4	16	18
11	195	178	126	108	3	3	6	14
12	332	325	286	243	4	4	14	12
13	512	478	433	402	5	5	8	6
14	377	348	339	294	4	4	12	10
15	169	154	140	129	3	3	18	16
16	392	385	357	322	4	4	10	8
17	431	412	380	338	4	4	2	2
18	577	552	530	470	5	5	4	4
In	3,295	3,125	2,851	2,527	36	36		
Total	**6,702**	**6,375**	**5,780**	**5,131**	**72**	**72**		

The bottom line is that this is a very decent, no-frills golf course that is best-suited to the midlevel player.

At 6,702 yards and par 72 from the back tees, it is plenty long and plays to a 127 slope. It can play as short as 5,131 yards (122 slope) from the forward tees. But more important, the fairways are generous, the rough is forgiving, there are few treacherous shots into greens, and you can go for holes and holes without feeling squeezed by OB stakes.

"The place suits my game perfectly," said a 22-handicapper with whom I played last week.

For my money, the back nine at Turtle Creek is more interesting than the front. But the front, which is mostly flat and straight, is home to one of the best holes on the course — the par-5 eighth — a double dogleg with a green that juts out into a pond.

The back nine, although shorter by about 100 yards, simply struck me as more challenging. Tougher holes, more trees, more water to negotiate. It also has the best one-two punch, the 17th and 18th.

The 17th is a 412-yard dogleg (No. 2 handicap), and the 18th is a 552-yard par-5 dogleg (No. 4 handicap) that's a true 3-shot hole, thanks to the ponds guarding the front of the green.

Is Turtle Creek going to get a low-handicapper breathing hard? No. Will the midlevel player have his or her hands full? Yes.

— July 26, 1998

If You Go

Address: 303 W. Ridge Pike, Limerick.

Phone 610-489-5133.

Greens fees: Weekends, $50 to ride, $50 to walk. Weekdays, $39 to ride (Mon.-Thur.) $25 to walk.

Carts: Walking is permitted anytime; cart fees included on weekends.

Amenities: Minimally stocked pro shop; snack bar, putting green, outdoor outing facility; driving range is next door.

Rating: Good course for mid-level player who likes to walk. Mid-price, good condition.

38. Twin Ponds Golf Club

Gilbertsville course short but sweet

For the last year or so, one of my regular golf buddies has been trying to get me out to the course he played growing up, a little family-run, no-frills operation called Twin Ponds Golf Club.

"I'm telling you, you'll like it," he'd promise.

"I'll get around to it," I'd tell him. The no-frills part didn't bother me. Out beyond the suburbs, there is a whole world of small-town, no-frills courses that are terrific. What gave me pause about Twin Ponds was that it's only 5,588 yards, which to me is woefully short. Why bother?

Last week, my buddy finally persuaded me to give the course in Gilbertsville, Montgomery County, a try, and I'm glad he did. I'm definitely going back.

If Twin Ponds comes up short in yardage, it's long on personality and panache. There are wide-open holes and there are tight holes with tree-lined fairways. A few holes are flat, but most are gently rolling doglegs that play into small, bunkered greens. Six ponds are scattered around the course, but they are not especially imposing. It's not a difficult course. Even from the back tees, the rating is 65.5 and the slope 111. Still, there is enough charm and challenge to make you happy.

As for the length, yes, Twin Ponds is short. But there are four par 5s — the 14th tops out at 573 yards, uphill and usually into the wind — and you will reach for the driver on most every hole. The course's lack of length comes more from its six par 3s and its healthy assortment of short par 4s. Granted, big hitters might not need more than a short iron into several of the par 4s, but you'd better be accurate.

If there is a bottom line, it's that Twin Ponds is ideal for golfers who want a good course, a challenge, but who can't handle those tracks full of 440-yard par 4s over water and wasteland.

"We like to say it's a fun course — you can miss a shot and par the hole," owner Ron Hoffman, 70, said last week.

It was back in 1963 that Hoffman, whose father and grandfather had operated a dairy farm on the property, decided that the farming life held no future for him and his wife.

"I'd never played a game of golf in my life, but my brother-in-law had started to play over at Arrowhead," Hoffman said. "He said, 'Why don't you build a golf course?'"

Hoffman decided he had heard dumber ideas in his life, even if golf wasn't as hot as it is today. He called in Leon Sell, not exactly a career architect but a man who had recently expanded Spring Ford Country Club in Royersford from nine to 18 holes. Sell now lives in a house off the sixth hole.

Hoffman, who is recovering from a yearlong bout with cancer, can still be found at the corner table in the casual clubhouse that was once a barn.

Scorecard

Hole	Blue	White	Red	Par	HCP	Red HCP
1	490	442	429	5	4	4
2	160	140	130	3	14	16
3	298	277	268	4	16	8
4	354	301	290	4	12	6
5	152	135	130	3	10	12
6	506	430	407	5	2	2
7	296	282	280	4	18	10
8	306	284	180	4	8	14
9	170	130	125	3	6	18
Out	2,732	2,421	2,239	35		
10	326	311	306	4	9	5
11	150	140	130	3	15	17
12	325	305	290	4	11	9
13	175	168	130	3	3	11
14	573	560	480	5	1	1
15	298	274	252	4	17	13
16	372	350	339	4	7	7
17	479	454	445	5	5	3
18	158	140	136	3	13	15
In	2,856	2,702	2,508	35		
Total	**5,588**	**5,123**	**4,747**	**70**		

"Used to have 70 head of cattle right here in this building," Hoffman said. "When I got mad at the cattle, I could kick them. I can't kick the customers."

Son-in-law Ron Boyles is the superintendent. Hoffman's daughters, Marcia and Sheila, who will one day inherit Twin Ponds, run the small pro shop and cook in the snack bar. Oh, the snack bar. Domestic beer runs toward $1.75; hot dogs are $1.50, hamburgers $1.80, cheeseburgers $2. A game of pool is 25 cents.

Those who get too full of themselves around Twin Ponds run the risk of finding their names on the plaque by the snack bar. "Twin Ponds Dummy of the Week," it says.

A round of golf is also easy on the wallet. The price on weekends with a cart is $38. You can walk anytime, and it's a very walkable course. Weekdays to walk costs you $20; after 4:30 p.m. it drops to $12.

Not surprisingly, Twin Ponds has its share of regulars, most of whom come from the surrounding area, as well as from Allentown and Bethlehem. Weekend mornings can get crowded, although Hoffman said it thins out after about 1 p.m. Weekday afternoons, the leagues swoop down.

"Tell people to call before they come," Hoffman said.

It's not a bad call to make.

— April 29, 2001

If You Go

Address: 700 Gilbertsville Rd., Gilbertsville.

Phone: 610-369-1901.

Greens fees: Weekends and holidays: $38 with cart, $28 to walk. Weekdays: $30 with cart, $20 to walk

Carts: Walking permitted anytime.

Amenities: Small, sparsely furnished pro shop; casual, inexpensive snack bar; practice range (must supply your own balls); picnic area for 200.

Rating: A short course, but charming and challenging. Excellent for short hitters. Easy to walk; a good course for family golf. Very affordable with a no-frills, friendly atmosphere. Worth a try.

39. Twining Valley Golf Club

Beginners are in luck

Once you've decided to take up the game, spent some time at the driving range, maybe done the pitch-and-putt or par-3 course scene, then what?

Where do you hone your game on a golf course that's not too long, not too tough and not too expensive?

You go to a place like Twining Valley Golf Club in Dresher in Montgomery County.

"We're a recreational course, not a country club," said Twining Valley director Hugh Reilly. "If you want to learn the game, come here. We try to keep it fun and keep it moving."

Keeping things moving sometimes can be a challenge. It's not unusual, Reilly said, to see golfers on the first tee whiff the ball, setting off groans among the group set to play behind them.

If you're just starting out, that's the kind of attitude and facility you're looking for — a course that knows it's not Augusta National and you aren't Tiger Woods.

That's not to say that Twining Valley is a complete pushover. With a slope of 114, it hovers right at the national average of 113 in degree of difficulty, although it is shorter than the national average of 6,300 yards by a couple hundred.

If that sounds a little vague, it's by necessity. Fact is Twining Valley has 19, not 18, holes, because there's always one hole closed for renovation. Golfers get rerouted as necessary to complete the full round of 18. Of course, that means the length of the course changes from time to time, depending on which hole is closed for repairs.

None of this should concern you too much. The important issue is that Twining Valley is a decent course for beginners and high- to mid-handicappers, as well as seniors and juniors who may be on a budget.

The track itself is mostly flat, although it does have a few hill holes, and it's not overly punishing with bunkers and water. The par 4s and 5s tend to be short and forgiving and, more importantly, so is the rough.

"We keep everything [rough] trimmed pretty short to keep play moving," Reilly said.

Reilly and his family have run Twining Valley for 16 years, ever since he signed a long-term lease with Upper Dublin Township. Since then, it has become a family affair.

Son Will is the head pro, son Hugh Jr. is the teaching pro and controller, mom Sue and daughter Trisha run the banquet facility. (Another son, Michael, is an assistant pro at Whitemarsh Valley Country Club in nearby Lafayette Hill.)

Nine holes at Twining Valley were designed and built in 1931 by a Scot, Jacques Mellville, who first leased, then bought the property off Susquehanna Road in Upper Dublin

Scorecard

Hole	Pro.	Men's	Seniors	Ladies'	Par	HCP
1	464	436	421	389	5	1
2	365	349	337	294	4	9
3	459	441	420	389	5	13
4	376	353	345	280	4	3
5	368	324	314	282	4	11
6	137	127	122	121	3	17
7	354	337	323	325	4	5
8	235	135	127	116	3	7
9	269	254	251	233	4	15
Out	3,027	2,756	2,660	2,429	36	
10	255	245	239	221	4	8
11	185	169	155	115	3	16
12	529	524	514	429	5	10
13	315	287	282	280	4	14
14	439	375	360	340	4	4
15	199	187	172	159	3	18
16	337	321	314	305	4	6
17	226	214	206	185	3	2
18	367	363	358	298	4	12
19	172	149	141	91	3	19
In	3,024	2,834	2,741	2,423	37	
Total	6,051	5,590	5,401	4,852	73	

Township. A second nine was added two years later.

In recent years, the Reilly family has been slowly renovating the course, most noticeably replacing the tiny, round, flat greens with larger, more receptive greens. So far, eight greens have been recast.

In two years, when the greens project is complete, the Reillys plan to remake another section of the course, closing the fourth and fifth holes to build a driving range and launch a golf academy.

Until the total makeover is complete, however, Twining Valley will likely have the look and feel of a course under construction.

As for the course in its current state, it won't challenge better golfers, but it's plenty to manage for lots of people.

The course starts you off with a short, uphill par 5 (436 yards), then a short par 4 (349 yards), then another short par 5 (441 yards). Even a relative newcomer to the game has a chance of reaching those greens in regulation.

The seventh, a par 3, and 9, a par 4, are very short — we're talking driver or wedge, at most, although you can get into trouble on the seventh because of the ravine fronting the green.

The backside is more interesting and slightly more difficult, perhaps because of the hillier terrain.

The favorite hole among Twining Valley regulars is the 15th, a 321-yard par 4 that requires a tee shot from an elevated tee down to a plateau, then a second shot over a pond into a small green nestled into a hillside.

"Lots of balls go into the water there," Reilly said.

The next three holes aren't so bad either — a 214-yard downhill par 3, a short dogleg par 4 into a tricky green, then an uphill par 3 that won't accept just any old shot.

If there is a criticism to be leveled at Twining Valley, it's that too many fairways and tees suffer from bare spots, perhaps a cost of the volume of play.

If You Go

Address: 1400 Twining Rd., Dresher.

Phone: 215-659-9917.

Greens fees: Weekends, $40 to ride, $26 to walk. Weekdays, $36 to ride, $22 to walk.

Carts: Walking permitted anytime.

Amenities: Moderately stocked pro shop, snack bar, club repair and custom clubmaking, putting green, no driving range, banquet facilities, outings welcome.

Rating: Nice course for beginners, high- and mid-handicappers, seniors and juniors.

40. Upper Perk Golf Course

Not a four-star course, but a nice place to try out

When I pulled into the parking lot of Upper Perk Golf Course recently, I was more curious than usual about the round I was about to play.

The Pennsburg course had always been one of those courses I kept pushing onto the back burner, mainly because friends who knew it assured me it was a fun, serviceable daily-fee loop, but one that wouldn't stand out if it were closer to Philadelphia.

But a few months ago, when the newest edition of *Golf Digest's 4,200 Best Places to Play* bumped Upper Perk from a three-star rating ("very good") to one of the area's select four-star courses ("outstanding"), it was time to find out for myself.

Put me in the three-star camp.

Family-owned and family-run, Upper Perk offers a casual, unpretentious atmosphere from the moment you walk into the modest pro shop until you tap in on the 18th. I also came away liking the golf course more than I thought I would, thanks to the back nine's strong mix of rolling doglegs and water holes.

With a slope of 117 from the back tees (6,381 yards), the course provides a test for mid- and high-handicappers without being the least bit penal. Fairways are forgiving, and there are no long forced carries on the course, meaning you can stone-cold top a tee shot without losing another ball in a waste area or water.

Still, for me, Upper Perk is not a four-star golf course. Blue Heron Pines, Sand Barrens and Scotland Run are four-star courses. Four stars, to me, suggests a country-club-for-a-day with a course that tests even a single-digit handicapper.

Upper Perk, pleasant as it is, is neither, which could cause some newcomers to have unreasonable expectations.

Linda Harbonis, who owns Upper Perk with her brother and sister, Rick and Wendy Eschbach, readily acknowledges that a championship course was not what her father set out to build 25 years ago when he transformed the family dairy farm.

"He had in mind to make it challenging, but not so the average golfer would get frustrated," Harbonis said.

In that respect, Upper Perk is a success.

Were Harbonis and her siblings surprised by the four-star rating? No, not surprised, she said, but they get around, and they know what else is out there.

"I would like to think it is due to the fact that we try to make it a pleasurable day for everyone who plays here," she said. "That's the way we get a lot of repeat play and quite a few outings and tournaments. And I think we have a nice

Scorecard

Hole	Blue	White	Red	Par	HCP	Ladies' HCP
1	369	349	332	4	11	7
2	541	523	405	5	5	1
3	362	352	343	4	13	3
4	162	152	142	3	17	17
5	366	336	309	4	7	9
6	350	340	328	4	9	5
7	481	463	355	5	15	15
8	447	430	319	4	1	11
9	230	219	165	3	3	13
Out	3,308	3,164	2,698	36		
10	358	352	346	4	12	8
11	400	381	318	4	8	12
12	395	387	300	4	2	6
13	396	382	320	4	4	2
14	347	330	320	4	4	2
15	158	144	133	3	18	16
16	335	323	302	4	16	10
17	504	492	385	5	6	4
18	180	162	127	3	10	14
In	3,073	2,953	2,551	35		
Total	**6,381**	**6,117**	**5,249**	**71**		

course."

The front nine at Upper Perk consists mostly of short, flat par 4s and a couple of lazy doglegs that had me wondering early on whether a three-star rating was generous.

But Upper Perk picks up considerably after the turn. Suddenly, you have gentle hills that add a little spice, a blind tee shot, a couple of sloping fairways, and doglegs that wrap around water hazards, plus a monster par 4 over water and a strong par 5 that pitches and rolls.

The monster par 4 in question is the 396-yard 13th, which is both testy and picturesque. After a blind tee shot over a crest, you soon find yourself considering a rather intimidating second shot from a downhill lie into a big but distant green that's tucked menacingly behind a small lake and flanked by bunkers.

— Oct. 15, 2000

If You Go

Address: Route 663 and Ott Road, Pennsburg.

Phone: 215-679-5594.

Greens fees: Weekends, $40 to ride, $30 to walk   (after noon). Weekdays, $30 to ride, $20 to walk.

Carts: Walking permitted anytime, although cart fees are included before noon on weekends and holidays.

Amenities: Moderately stocked pro shop, snack bar, putting green, short-iron practice range. Outings welcome.

Rating: Pleasant, casual, affordable daily-fee course with a strong back nine. Good course for mid- and high-handicappers and seniors. Good walking course.

41. Valley Forge Golf Club

No frills and few thrills

For every golfer who is looking for the newest, plushest, most difficult course in the area, there's another on the look-out for a track that offers decent, basic golf — inexpensive, convenient, and not so tough that six balls will be lost by the fourth hole.

That pretty much describes Valley Forge Golf Club, just about a solid 3-wood from King of Prussia Mall.

At Valley Forge, a staple for area golfers since 1928, don't expect to find a fancy clubhouse, a comfortable bar and grill, a well-stocked pro shop or a driving range. There's none of the above, except for a pro shop, which is spare at best. As for food, a halfway house serves sodas, hot dogs and crackers.

You have to work hard to lose a ball at Valley Forge. There are few bunkers, no marshes, no dense woods, no deep rough, and not a drop of water on the course, except for the drinking fountains. The fairways on this short, wide-open course tend to be generous and forgiving. The greens are also small and, except on a few holes, flat.

None of which bothered one chatty newcomer to the game, a Valley Forge semi-regular who was looking to get paired up on the first tee Friday.

"I know a lot of guys that wouldn't play this course," he said. "But I played Merion the other day, and I like this course. I say, if you like golf, you play anywhere and every-where."

Valley Forge is not to be confused with Merion — not by the longest of shots. *Golf Digest's 4,200 Best Places to Play* gives Valley Forge a one-star rating, meaning "basic golf," and lists such player comments as "good beginner's course," "nothing special," "acceptable," "old style" and "being so close to Philly, it's always crowded."

That may be, but assistant professional Frank Wright believes the course is just the ticket for more than a few players.

"It's enjoyable to the average golfer because there's not a lot of trouble, and a challenge to all golfers because of the small greens," he said.

Small as they are, the greens may be Valley Forge's strongest feature. Last week, they were in excellent condition — thick, true and freshly cut.

The back nine of the layout — the architect's name is long forgotten — turns hilly and is more interesting than the up-and-back front side.

The 12th hole, a 476-yard par-5, is over hill and dale to an elevated green that kicks anything to the left down an embankment. Regulars regard the par-4, 412-yard 14th hole as the toughest on the course. The fairway, which runs along a

Scorecard

Hole	Blue	White	Red	Par	Ladies' Par	HCP	Ladies' HCP
1	408	379	355	4	5	6	10
2	345	326	294	4	4	16	12
3	351	367	338	4	4	8	8
4	138	132	122	3	3	18	18
5	357	364	350	4	4	4	2
6	193	184	152	3	3	10	16
7	514	500	420	5	5	2	6
8	348	258	258	4	4	14	18
9	344	331	323	4	4	12	4
Out	3,008	2,841	2,612	35	36		
10	388	377	356	4	4	9	3
11	330	322	307	4	4	13	13
12	484	476	447	5	5	5	1
13	185	172	160	3	3	15	15
14	454	412	395	4	5	1	9
15	184	161	131	3	3	17	17
16	378	373	318	4	4	11	11
17	483	458	431	5	5	3	7
18	3,258	3,119	2,880	36	37		
Total	**6,266**	**5,960**	**5,492**	**71**	**73**		

busy street, slopes right to left, flanked by a few trees that can make things interesting.

The 15th, 161 yards with its elevated tee and green, is the most interesting par 3 on the course. That's quickly followed by the most scenic hole on the course, the par-5, 458-yard No. 17, with an elevated tee and a lazy, dogleg-right fairway.

Little surprise, as Wright confirms, that golfers who slip out of nearby office buildings for a quick nine definitely favor the back side.

Valley Forge is not the course to challenge low-handicappers. It measures only 5,960 from the white tees, with a course rating of 68.9 and a slope of 107, less than the national average of 113. (Despite what the scorecard says, there are no blue tees, only white and red).

But for mid- and high-handicappers, or for golfers on a budget, Valley Forge may be worth a try. It's convenient, it's forgiving, and it's in quite decent condition.

— October 6, 1996

If You Go

Address: 401 N. Gulph Rd., King of Prussia.

Phone: 610-337-1776.

Green fees: Weekends, $40 to ride; $27 to walk. Weekdays, $33 to ride, $20 to walk.

Carts: Walking permitted anytime

.Amenities: Minimally-stocked pro shop. Snacks in half-way house.

Rating: Price is right, golf is basic.

42. Westover Country Club

Relatively simple, one of Fazio's early designs

Writers have early works. So do painters, plumbers, cosmetic surgeons, architects, and virtually everyone in a creative craft or profession, including, of course, golf course designers.

Westover Country Club, a semiprivate course in his hometown of Norristown, is one of George Fazio's early works.

Whether he still lists it on his resume, well, you'd have to ask him — if you can reach him. Fazio is perhaps the most celebrated golf course designer in the world these days and one busy man. But his 1968 design of Westover — relatively flat, relatively simple, relatively unspectacular — stands as a signpost along what has become the superhighway of his superstar career.

"This was one of his launching pads," said superintendent Andrew Drevyanko Jr.

Now, said Drevyanko and Westover owner Vincent Piazza Sr., father of Los Angeles Dodgers all-star catcher Mike Piazza, the goal is to turn the course and club into "one of the best public facilities in the area."

Westover is something of a Piazza family affair. Vince Sr. has been an investor in the club for the last 10 years. About two years ago, he bought out his partners. Mike is an investor and another son, Vince Jr., is the general manager.

Since taking over, the Piazzas have sunk $1 million into refurbishing the clubhouse and significantly recasting four holes on the back nine to carve out room for a retirement village under construction on what used to be the 13th and 14th fairways.

"We didn't think the 13th and 14th were any great loss,"

Drevyanko said.

Perhaps not. Even as a young Fazio designed them, the 13th was a short and undistinguished flip wedge of a par 3 and the 14th was a short and undistinguished straightaway par 4. But whether the new holes are better is open to question.

In its current state, Westover is 6,263 yards from the back tees and plays to a 116 slope, both near the national average for length and difficulty. Other than two short and downhill par 3s — the fourth and the 12th — Westover remains a mildly rolling track with abundant, forgiving fairways, user-friendly rough, and midsize, flat greens.

The course has never taxed a low handicapper, but more than a few mid-handicappers, seniors, and young golfers find Westover plenty to handle.

The course starts off leisurely with a short, flat and

Scorecard

Hole	Blue	White	Red	Par	Ladies' Par	HCP	Ladies' HCP
1	330	315	295	4	4	17	10
2	481	471	461	5	5	9	2
3	412	388	370	4	4	5	6
4	173	132	106	3	3	15	18
5	418	368	299	4	4	3	8
6	347	294	267	4	4	13	14
7	455	434	384	4	4	1	4
8	190	153	131	3	3	11	16
9	374	348	271	4	4	7	12
Out	3,180	2,903	2,584	35	35		
10	364	344	293	4	4	14	15
11	464	454	444	4	5	2	3
12	395	361	327	4	4	6	5
13	206	146	106	3	3	18	17
14	403	311	294	4	4	8	9
15	349	291	268	4	4	12	11
16	371	361	325	4	4	10	7
17	333	320	280	4	4	16	13
18	372	320	280	4	4	4	1
In	3,257	2,908	2,625	35	36		
Total	**6,437**	**5,811**	**5,209**	**70**	**71**		

straight par 4. The second is a gentle 495-yard, par-5 dogleg right with trees up the right side; the third is an even milder dogleg left (though the green can be wicked).

The fourth is a steep, downhill par 3 into a sizable green that plays considerably shorter than its 177 yards from the blue tees.

The fifth and sixth are both straight, fairly narrow, tree-lined par 4s (430 and 357 yards) that offer opportunities to get into trouble if you're wrestling a wayward driver.

That brings you to the No. 1 handicap hole at Westover, the seventh, a 468-yard tree-lined par-4 dogleg that has definite double-bogey potential if you hang your tee shot out to the right.

It's not until the 11th, a nondescript 490-yard straight-away par 5 that the alterations to Fazio's design begin.

To make room for the retirement village's clubhouse, Piazza and Drevyanko have moved the tee to the left about 40 yards. (To create even more space, they're mulling shortening the hole into a par 4; if they do, they would lengthen either the fifth or seventh into a par 5.)

The significant and noticeable changes begin at the 12th, which had been the most unusual hole on the course. It is a mid-length but severe dogleg-right par 4 that started from an elevated tee and played down and around to a creek slashing across the fairway, leaving a short iron into the green.

Piazza and Drevyanko have basically cut the 12th into two holes: a short par 3 that plays from the original tee to the bottom of the hollow, over a small pond into a green protected by water and a rear bunker, and a straight, 305-yard downhill par 4 over a creek into an elevated green. Neither hole is as interesting as the original 12th.

The 14th, a 185-yard par 3 over a small ravine, is an altogether new hole that is longer and more difficult than the par 3 it replaces.

At the 15th, to make room for the retirement village, Piazza and Drevyanko have taken another of Fazio's doglegs and extended the fairway back into the woods and elevated the tees to create another straight, uphill par 4. It's a toss-up as to whether this is an improvement.

The 16th through 18th are untouched. The 16th is a nondescript, 387-yard par 4, and the 17th is a slightly shorter par 4 with a bit of a sloping fairway.

The 18th, depending on your perspective, is either one of the best holes on the course or the most ill-conceived. The No. 2 handicap hole, the 18th is a 410-yard par 4 that requires a mid- to long-iron off the tee to lay up short of a pond; from there it's about 150 yards to an elevated, bunkered green that can be hard to hit and hard to hold.

The bottom line on Westover? It's a basic two-star track.

In years past, brown fairways and splotchy greens detracted from the course's appeal. But Piazza has installed a sprinkler system for the greens, and a fairway irrigation system is in the plans for next year. That should help.

— June 22, 1997

If You Go

Address: 401 S. Schuylkill Ave., Norristown.

Phone: 610-539-4500

Greens fees: Weekends, $50 to ride, $30 to walk. Weekdays, $37 to ride, $25 to walk.

Carts: Mandatory before noon and weekends.

Amenities: Moderately stocked pro shop, driving range, banquet facilities; outings welcome.

Rating: Mid-level track, conditions improving.

43. Wood's Golf Center

It's no place for snobs,
but it can be some fun

Several years ago, when my children were little and sneaking away for a round of golf was a rare, guilty pleasure, a buddy told me to meet him on the first tee that Saturday morning at Woody's.

Woody's?

"It's short," he said. "We'll get around it quick."

To say I was disappointed, even dismayed, when it turned out that Woody's was an overcrowded par-3 course, with a chip-and-putt, a driving range, and a miniature golf course as part of a sprawling complex, would be an understatement. I couldn't believe that this was how I was using up one of my precious few rounds that summer.

My attitude has changed considerably since those days. I no longer look down on the Woody's courses of the world. I regard them as integral and valuable parts of the golfing land-scape. While on the road, covering golf tournaments, I have been known to pull off the road in Mississippi at 11 p.m., at the first sign of the magnificent glow of the lights, to pound a large bucket of balls at a driving range.

In addition to the sheer fun of them, Woody's and the like take a burden off of regular golf courses, welcoming novices, seniors, women, minorities, and people just messing around.

"We get a lot of people just starting the game," said Jena Wood, who works behind the counter at Woody's and is the granddaughter of founder John "Woody" Wood and the daughter of Pen Wood, the current owner. "We see them for a year or two on the range, then on the course. Then we don't see them much."

Places like Woody's — technically Wood's Golf Center at 559 W. Germantown Pike in Norristown — are the door to golf for a lot of people. Woody's is also a place where I can learn to hit a new club or drop off my son and his buddy for a Saturday-afternoon loop of their own. For the guys in my group at the par-3 course last week — I met three retirees on the first tee — it's also plenty of golf course as age takes a little off their tee shots.

Woody Wood himself laid out the course and, even as par-3 courses go, it is not a towering achievement. Greens tend to be small, round and flat. Bunkers are few. There is one pond, but it's not very threatening as ponds go.

What teeth Woody's has comes in the form of distance. Five of the 18 holes measure more than 200 yards, with one stretching to 246 and another to 228. For a lot of golfers, anything more than 200 yards is a short par 4.

They do 40,000 rounds a year at Woody's, so good luck finding a blade of grass on the tees in the summer. And at the end of the day, the greens can look as if they took a shelling.

During any round at Woody's, you never know what you're going to encounter — teenagers goofing around, old men just glad to be alive, upright and outdoors, or beginners so raw that the rangers have to explain the most basic rules and etiquette. There are, however, always the regulars.

Scorecard

Hole	Blue	Par
1	211	3
2	168	3
3	173	3
4	138	3
5	203	3
6	113	3
7	122	3
8	175	3
9	193	3
Out	1,496	27
10	134	3
11	180	3
12	246	3
13	119	3
14	248	3
15	105	3
16	228	3
17	176	3
18	144	3
In	1,580	27
Total	**3,076**	**54**

"We have always had a consistent senior-citizen crowd because of the reasonable rates and the length of the course," Jena Wood said. "On weekends, we get a lot more women now. And a lot of Koreans and more minorities."

Woody's doesn't take tee times, so weekend mornings at the height of the season can see a 90-minute logjam that looks like a committee meeting at the United Nations.

"It can be awkward because, a lot of times, you're pairing people who don't speak English," said Jena Wood, who spends many of her weekend mornings mixing and matching singles and twosomes to create foursomes. "But a lot of people meet and end up playing together more or keeping in touch."

More and more, Wood sees better golfers turning up at Woody's because they don't have time to devote the better part of a day to a round at a full-blown course.

"It's kind of a trend in the industry," she said.

From her perspective, Woody's is on the downside of Tigermania.

"The year he came out was really big for us and everybody," she said. "It has kind of leveled off."

Oh, well. Saturday night will still be crowded.

— Nov. 12, 2000

If You Go

Address: 559 W. Germantown Pike, Norristown.

Phone: 610-279-0678.

Greens fees: Weekends and holidays, $13 to walk. Weekdays, $10 to walk. Weekdays for seniors, $8 to walk. Carts are $13.

Carts: Walking permitted anytime.

Amenities: No pro shop. Par-3 course. Driving range with 35 outdoor mats, eight heated outdoor stalls, room for 40 on grass. Putting course. Snack bar.

Rating: A Montgomery County institution. No frills. Big, popular complex.

Other Montgomery County Courses

Butter Valley Golf Port
S. Seventh Street, Bally.
610-845-2491
Weekdays, $18 to walk, $29 to ride; weekends, $38 to ride.

General Washington Golf Club
2750 Egypt Rd., Audubon.
610-666-7602
Weekdays, $17; weekends, $29. Carts are $11.

Gilbertsville Golf Club
2944 Lutheran Rd., Gilbertsville.
610- 323-3222
Weekdays, $20 to walk, $28 to ride; weekends and holidays,
$29 to walk, $38 to ride.

Limerick Golf Club
765 North Lewis Rd., Limerick.
610-495-6945
Weekdays, $22 to walk, $33 to ride;
weekends, $32 to walk, $43 to ride.

Rolling Turf Club
Smith Road, Schwenksville.
610-287-7297
Weekdays, $9.50; Weekends, $10. Carts are $8.

Twin Woods Golf Club
2924 East Orville Road, Hatfield.
215-822-9263
$12 weekdays; $14 weekends

Northampton
C O U N T Y

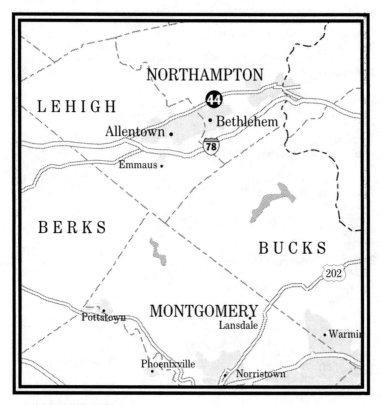

44. Whitetail Golf Club

44. Whitetail Golf Club

Pleasant course offers few severe challenges

With a name like Whitetail Golf Club, you half expect to encounter the occasional deer grazing at the edge of the rough or the woods just beyond. I never did.

But that doesn't mean that Whitetail, a six-year-old daily-fee layout in Bath, just north of Bethlehem, was a disappointment. Truth is, I had no idea what to expect. All I knew was that Golf Digest awarded Whitetail a very respectable 3½ stars in its latest edition of *4,200 Best Places to Play,* so it deserved checking out.

What I found was a casual, comfortable small-town place with a welcoming feel and plenty of course for most levels of golfers.

Designed by Jim Blaukovitch, a Lehigh Valley architect who is making a name for himself, Whitetail is well-conceived and well-maintained. At 6,432 yards from the back tees, it's certainly not the longest track around, nor is it the most difficult. Although it plays to a 128 slope from the back, Blaukovitch has made sure that you have to take some nasty hacks to get yourself into deep trouble. Fairways are forgiving, bunkers are less than plentiful, the rough is manageable, and there is little water and almost no forced carries.

Of course, Whitetail was never intended to be the severest of tests.

"We didn't want to build a new course and make it super, super punishing," Whitetail general manager Chad Kulp said. "It was designed to be a course most everybody could play and enjoy."

That said, Whitetail is no pushover. It hosted the Eastern Pennsylvania Amateur a couple of years ago, as well as a Nike Tour qualifier. The assistant pros in the Philadelphia Section of the PGA thought enough of the course to hold their championship there in 1997.

Still, after a very pleasant loop last week, I came away feeling that 3½ stars were fair for the facility overall, but it struck me as about a half-star too generous — at least in terms of the challenge. For 3½ stars, you ought to suffer more for a misplayed shot.

By way of general description, Whitetail's strength is its mix of short to mid-length par 4s, most confronting the player with twists, turns, hills or combinations thereof.

Scorecard

Hole	Blue	White	Red	Par	HCP
1	326	312	276	4	18
2	322	306	254	4	16
3	106	96	80	3	12
4	514	502	434	5	6
5	352	340	320	4	14
6	378	360	312	4	4
7	382	358	270	4	8
8	602	546	482	5	2
9	132	125	114	3	10
Out	3,114	2,944	2,542	36	
10	510	492	406	5	17
11	176	152	118	3	13
12	398	352	318	4	7
13	354	342	268	4	11
14	508	490	390	5	5
15	458	440	382	4	1
16	136	122	104	3	15
17	356	338	304	4	9
18	422	400	320	4	2
In	3,318	3,128	2,610	36	
Total	**6,432**	**6,072**	**5,152**	**72**	

The fifth hole comes immediately to mind. At 352 yards, it's hardly intimidating. But it's downhill from the tee, and a lake comes into play on the right side in the driving area, just at the point where the hole doglegs left. Although the second shot is only about 100 yards, another lake looms to the right of the green. Only two par 4s on the course exceed 400 yards, making for a lot of short- and mid-iron approach shots.

Unquestionably, the two best holes on the course are par 5s. The eighth — Kulp calls it the signature hole — is quite a sight from the highly elevated tee that provides one of the panoramic views of the surrounding farmland. From there, the hole tumbles ever downward before curling right and upward again, then down again. At 602 yards, even big hitters will be playing their third shots into this green.

The other toughest test is the 14th, a 508-yard par 5, with a blind chasm on the left that chokes the tee shot landing area to about 10 yards. Hit it long here off the tee and even a dead-center tee shot bounds down and out of bounds. The second shot is another beast — over the chasm — into a green that's 250 yards away because of the layup shot off the tee.

The 18th is also a fine finishing hole: It's straight, but 422 yards uphill. You'll work for a par there.

A couple of other interesting footnotes about Whitetail. There's the free bag of range balls with greens fees. Kulp's theory is that it helps get you loosened up and ready to play, which leads us to Whitetail's slow-play policy.

Hold up the course and initially you'll get a polite warning; a second infraction and you'll be asked to pick up your ball and move to the next tee. Three strikes and you're out. You'll be asked to leave the course, although you'll be given a prorated gift certificate to return at a future date.

Bravo.

— May 9, 1999

If You Go

Address:2679 Klein Rd., Bath.

Phone: 610-837-9626

Greens Fees: Weekends, $50 to ride, $50 to walk. Weekdays, $35 to ride, $23 to walk.

Carts: Walking permitted anytime; cart fees included Friday, Saturday, Sunday and holidays until twilight.

Philadelphia

C O U N T Y

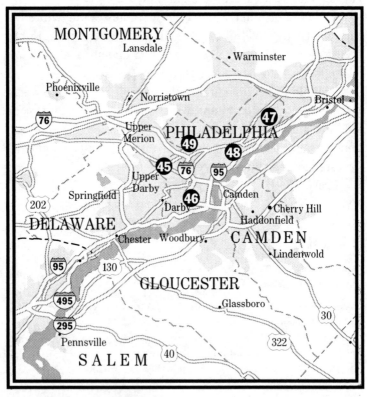

45. Cobbs Creek Golf Club
46. Franklin D. Roosevelt Golf Club
47. John F. Byrne Golf Club
48. Juniata Golf Club
49. Walnut Lane Golf Club

45. Cobbs Creek Golf Club

Despite flaws, still a gem of a course

It's probably fair to say that more golfers have played enjoyable rounds at Cobbs Creek Golf Club over its 81-year history than at any other course in the Philadelphia area.

It's also fair to say that at one time or another over the years, many of those same golfers have found themselves fuming, seething and wondering why they went to Cobbs in the first place.

This is because the crown jewel of the six city-owned municipal courses can get more crowded than a Tokyo subway car. Because some golfers can't fathom having to hammer a tee into bare ground or fix crater-size ball marks left by previous groups.

Because of fairways burning out in hot weather for lack of a sprinkler system, and the choking waves of dust left by carts with no cart paths to follow.

Because of neighborhood kids who wander the course with impunity, sometimes acting as if the paying customers are the intruders.

We could go on.

It's all part of the catch-22 and, yes, even the charm, of Cobbs Creek.

The thing is, what makes the course such a valuable asset to the city — its affordability, convenient location, classic layout, open arms to any and all golfers — also is precisely what can make a round there so maddening.

At Cobbs Creek, it's not uncommon to be transfixed by the grandeur of the 12th, the awesome 638-yard par-5 hole designed by Hugh Wilson, who also laid out world-famous Merion East.

Yet it's also not unusual to find yourself searching for a blade of grass on the tee, all the while wondering if that guy in the middle of the fairway teaching his girlfriend how to play will ever notice you. Will he ever think to let you play through? Does he even know to let you play through?

"It's all part of Tigermania," assistant pro Michael Kummer said last week.

"People see Tiger, and they just want to get out on the course. It's great for us, but at the same time, people come out without knowing the rules or etiquette of the game. When somebody walks up to the counter, there's just no way to know whether they know to fix ball marks."

Tigermania? Certainly, Tiger Woods' phenomenal rise may have contributed to, even exacerbated, the situation at Cobbs Creek. But anyone who has played there over the years can testify that it has been this way at least since Tiger was in diapers.

And that's a shame. Cobbs Creek is like a grand old mansion gone to seed. Underneath it all, it's a wonderful layout. And, truth be told, the course is probably in as good a condition as it has been in years — during a round last week, only the first green and several tees were in bad shape.

But it could be so much more. With a healthy dose of tender loving care — or, more accurately, cash — Cobbs Creek could be a showpiece.

Scorecard

Hole	Blue	White	Red	Par	HCP
1	484	423	412	5/4	7
2	361	343	307	4	11
3	304	277	263	4	5
4	168	136	110	3	15
5	413	349	336	4	1
6	122	117	109	3	17
7	470	416	391	5/4	13
8	194	178	162	3	13
9	264	259	253	4	9
Out	2,780	2,498	2,343	35/33	
10	297	288	277	4	10
11	431	399	374	4	6
12	440	431	422	4	2
13	377	368	356	4	12
14	614	589	574	5	8
15	447	392	378	4	4
16	275	266	225	4	18
17	193	166	154	3	16
18	348	339	330	4	14
In	3,422	3,238	3,090	36	
Total	**6,202**	**5,736**	**5,433**	**71/69**	

None of this is necessarily blaming the people who run the place — Golf Corp. of Dallas, which has a long-term management contract with the city. Golf Corp. is caught between a need for cash to improve the place and a city that wants to keep greens fees as affordable as possible.

The result, of course, is that Cobbs Creek, like that grand old mansion, gets the occasional metaphorical coat of paint but none of the badly needed structural improvements.

Will things ever change? Probably not.

Golf Corp. wants out of its contract in order to focus on upscale resort courses. The company that wants to take over, Meadowbrook Golf Group Inc. of Chicago, may make an initial infusion of cash but would eventually face the same problems.

Fact is, unless they reduce the number of rounds played and increase the greens fees, there are no simple ways to transform Cobbs Creek into the course it could be. And so it remains what it is: a crown jewel without most of its luster.

As aggravating as that can be, if you play the course when it's not too crowded, Cobbs can provide a pleasant round of golf. There are, after all, several terrific holes.

Is there, for instance, a better par 4 in the area than the third, with its 493 yards of treachery in the form of a creek that runs right up the middle of the fairway? From the tee, do you play it safe and take it left of the creek, or do you chance it to the right for the short iron into the green?

The eigth, though only 311 yards, is another terrific par 4 — uphill, fairway mounds, and a hungry bunker guarding a small, flat green. Or how about the 447-yard 10th, with its sloping fairway and tricky second shot into a green with bunkers left and back?

The 12th, at 638 yards, is perhaps the longest par 5 in the area. Even from the elevated tee, nobody, with the possible exception of Tiger, is going to reach this green in two.

Still, perhaps the most fiendish hole on the course is the 486-yard 13th, an uphill beast with a sloping fairway that kicks most any tee shot far to the right. Problem is, for a decent shot at the green, you're advised to drive up the left side. Even then, the green is hard to hit. It's a wonderful golf hole.

As it lies, Cobbs is a treasure. Maybe, just maybe, it will someday become even grander.

— Aug. 24, 1997

If You Go

Address: 72d Street and Lansdowne Avenue.

Phone: 215-877-8707.

Greens fees: Weekend, $35.25 to walk, 49.91 to ride. Weekday, $29 to walk, $43.66 to ride.

Carts: Walking permitted anytime.

Amenities: Well-stocked pro shop, snack bar, driving range, putting green. Outings welcome.

Rating: Crown jewel of city courses, needs tender loving care.

46. Franklin D. Roosevelt Golf Club

Course is sorely lacking, but has its fans

It was somewhere in the middle of the front nine during a round at Franklin D. Roosevelt Golf Club that I began thinking what a sad sack of a golf course it is. That's when my playing partner piped up with some interesting information.

"Oh, it's much better since that new company took over," said Will, a Peco employee and regular at FDR, one of the six city-owned courses. "The greens are better, the fairways are better, everything is just better."

Hmmm, everything in life is relative, I suppose.

If you were to ask me, I'd have to say that except for one par 3 on the front nine and a refreshing three-hole stretch on the back, FDR is an utterly forgettable golf course. It gets a single star in Golf Digest's Places to Play, as in "basic golf," and only a golfer who doesn't get around much would quibble with that assessment.

What FDR lacks in length (5,894 yards, par 69) it frankly doesn't make up for in layout, design or challenge. Far too many holes at FDR, which is tucked away in FDR Park across Broad Street from Veterans Stadium, are short, flat and straight. Driver, short iron; driver, short wedge; on and on it goes. Yawn.

In some ways, FDR seems a sad golfing legacy for one of the most popular presidents in history, not to mention a man known for extending a helping hand to those most in need. If only he were alive today to extend a hand to this golf course.

But, hey, like Will, my partner that day last week, said, things are better — and getting better still.

While Meadowbrook Golf Group Inc., which took over

management of the city courses early this summer, is promising no miracles, the company is promising improvements.

The most immediate bit of work has been to give golfers better conditions at the course. While FDR is hardly manicured, head pro Jack O'Neil is encouraged.

"Tremendous difference," O'Neil said. "We have equipment now we only dreamed of and more people to get the job done. We used to have three people [on the maintenance crew], and now, some days, we have seven. It's great to be able to look out the window and see people working."

Sometime in the fall, Meadowbrook also plans to give FDR's clubhouse the same kind of face-lift that Cobbs Creek has already gotten — renovations that include new carpet, wall coverings and ceiling tiles, an expanded and improved food-service area, and a small pro shop.

The idea, said Joe Zaleski, Meadowbrook's vice president

Scorecard

Hole	Blue	White	Red	Par	Ladies' Par	HCP	Ladies' HCP
1	398	354	340	4	4	8	8
2	277	268	260	4	4	18	18
3	406	397	388	4	4	6	6
2	418	401	381	4	4	2	2
5	182	172	165	3	3	4	4
6	284	273	271	4	4	14	14
7	371	355	305	4	4	10	10
8	158	150	142	3	3	16	16
9	485	456	425	5	5	12	12
Out				35	35		
10	420	410	401	4	4	1	1
11	322	317	276	4	4	13	13
12	386	377	276	4	4	3	3
13	159	151	143	3	3	15	15
14	382	376	370	4	4	5	5
15	379	370	361	4	4	11	11
16	376	369	362	4	4	9	9
17	201	190	179	3	3	7	7
18	290	283	276	4	4	17	17
In				34	34		
Total				**69**	**69**		

for operations for the city courses, is to make the clubhouse "more inviting."

That's a start, to be sure. Those loyal regulars at FDR, of whom there are many, deserve at least as much.

Next on Meadowbrook's agenda, perhaps as early as the spring, is to begin improving the course itself. Zaleski is a little more vague on those specifics for a couple of reasons. First, the architect who has been hired is still mulling over the possibilities for FDR and the five other courses. Second, given the available space and the cost of such course changes, Zaleski doesn't want to promise wholesale changes Meadowbrook can't deliver.

A good place to start, as Zaleski readily acknowledges, is FDR's drainage system. Much to its detriment, FDR sits on a floodplain, especially the front nine. Most any rain creates problems; heavy rain, such as the seven inches from Hurricane Floyd, causes an outright nightmare.

When I played there early last week, walking on several fairways was like slogging through the Dismal Swamp. As it turned out, the course had been closed for several days the previous week.

"This time last week, the whole front nine was a lake," Will said.

Information about the course's history is not easy to come by. What everybody seems to agree on, however, is that FDR opened about 1933, evidently having been built during the Depression as a Works Progress Administration project.

Suffice it to say, the result was not golf course exotica. The first few holes are about as flat, straight and unimaginative as golf holes can get. Greens tend to be small and flat; bunkers are minimal and not very ominous.

The fourth, a 418-yard par 4 with a long second shot over a creek, offers a glimmer of hope and challenge. And the fifth, a 182-yard par 3 with a bunker crowding the green from the right side and a big tree on the left, is a breath of fresh air. But then it's back to ho-hum.

The back nine, with a three-hole stretch of doglegs (14, 15, 16) and mild elevation changes, is better but hardly inspired. There is only one par 5, the 485-yard ninth, and it barely qualifies as such. It all adds up to a 113 slope, which makes it exactly average for golf courses in the United States.

All this criticism aside, FDR, like all the city-owned courses, has its legion of devoted regulars, who get as much pleasure from a day at FDR as many members get from the spoils of Merion.

Actually, what I found unchallenging about FDR is precisely what attracts many of the regulars.

"We have a large group of seniors who favor it because it is flatter and easier to walk," O'Neil said.

I also saw a foursome of teens on the course enjoying themselves.

— October 10, 1999

If You Go

Address: 20th Street and Pattison Avenue, in FDR Park.

Phone: 215-462-8997.

Greens fees: Weekends, $25 to walk, 38.70 to ride. Weekdays, $21.25 to walk, $34.95 to ride.

Carts: Walking permitted anytime.

Amenities: Driving range, putting green, practice bunkers, clubhouse with snack bar in need of renovation. Outings welcome.

Rating: Basic, affordable, no-frills golf. Good course for mid- to high-handicappers, seniors, juniors and beginners.

47. John F. Byrne Golf Club

Forgotten course worth getting to know

I'll be honest. Driving to John F. Byrne Golf Club last week, I wasn't exactly excited, and I wasn't expecting much.

It's not that I'd heard bad things about Byrne. Truth is, I hadn't heard much of anything about it. I'd never set foot on the golf course before, and all I really knew was that it was one of the city's six municipal courses, it was across the street from Torresdale-Frankford Country Club, and frankly, it didn't look all that inviting from the street the times I'd passed it.

Shows you how wrong you can be.

I'm not going to get carried away here and say Byrne is some classic layout in pristine condition. It is neither. But I will say it is a heck of a lot better golf course — with more potential — than I ever imagined. It was enough to make me wonder if the reason you don't hear much talk about Byrne is because all those golfers in the Northeast want to keep outsiders away.

While it's not to be confused with Torresdale-Frankford, the rolling, tree-lined Donald Ross layout a stone's throw away on the other side of Grant Avenue, Byrne does benefit from the same hilly terrain that practically begs to be turned into a golf course.

Fortunately, Alex Findlay, who also designed Walnut Lane in Roxborough, did just that in the 1930s. The result is a short course — Byrne is just 5,234 yards from the back tees — but with plenty of twists and turns, elevated tees and greens, fairways that roll, and mildly devilish par 3s, making for a course that plays tougher than its 107 slope. If Meadowbrook Golf Group Inc., the company that took over management of the city courses in the summer of '99, will make a few improvements to the conditions, Byrne could be a delightful track.

"It's a shot-maker's course, and I think it has character," said pro Dan Hoban, who grew up on Henry Avenue and was the golf equivalent of a gym rat at Walnut Lane.

"It gives you different looks. It gives you some risk and reward shots, and on a few holes you run the risk of knocking in the water or out of bounds. There are four greens out there about the size of a Volkswagen. All the greens are challenging, which I think makes up for the lack of length."

Scorecard

Hole	Blue	White	Red	Par	HCP
1	340	310	280	4	8
2	205	197	160	3	10
3	300	288	253	4	14
4	310	290	245	4	4
5	330	310	270	4	16
6	176	160	134	3	12
7	283	275	260	4	18
8	190	180	170	3	6
9	385	379	373	4	2
Out	2,519	2,389	2,144	33	
10	338	333	287	4	7
11	149	143	137	3	15
12	522	515	508	5	3
13	119	114	104	3	17
14	240	225	186	3	5
15	166	161	156	3	13
16	470	462	454	5	11
17	375	370	365	4	1
18	341	336	321	4	9
In	2,715	2,664	2,518	34	
Total	**5,234**	**5,053**	**4,662**	**67**	

All true.

Byrne's strongest feature is the wonderful kind of rolling ground that even today a fleet of earthmovers couldn't produce if you gave the developers a $5 million cost overrun. Add plenty of trees and a couple of decent creeks meandering through the property, and it's hard not to come up with a decent golf course.

I got no farther than the first tee before I realized Byrne was going to be better than I expected. Unlike Walnut Lane and Franklin D. Roosevelt, which start with straight, flat, boring holes, Byrne gets you thinking and sweating right out of the blocks. The first, a 340-yard par 4, plays from an elevated tee, over a creek and back up hill. The 10th is a very similar hole.

The weakest hole on the front is the third, a short, flat, ho-hum par 4, which I feared was a bad omen for what lay ahead. Not to worry. While there are no par 5s on the front nine to test your driver, your long irons and possibly your fairway woods will get a workout on the three par 3s, which measure 205, 176 and 190 yards. The ninth, the No. 2 handicap hole, is the beast of the front nine — 385 yards, elevated tee, uphill fairway onto a blind green that is protected by large bunkers that squeeze it from the left and right.

The back nine is where you'll find both of Byrne's par 5s: the 12th (522 yards) and the 16th (470). Neither is a particularly dramatic hole, but neither is easily reachable, either. The back nine, however, is also where the only bum hole on the course is to be found: the forgettable little flip-wedge 13th, which is more like something you'd find on a par-3 course.

While the 18th is a toned-down version of the ninth, the best hole on the back nine is the 17th, a 375-yard par-4 dogleg right with trees up the left side, out of bounds up the right, and a waste area short of the green.

If Byrne has problems, it's in the conditioning, not the layout. Like the other city courses, years of neglect have left Meadowbrook scrambling to improve life for city-course golfers. Hoban is encouraged.

"Budgets are increasing, things are getting mowed on time, and every week they want to know what piece of maintenance equipment is broken," he said of Meadowbrook.

As for other improvements, Hoban said Meadowbrook's first move was to fill the bunkers with sand — a good sign — and company officials have plans on the drawing board to build badly needed cart paths.

— Oct. 31, 1999

If You Go

Address: 9500 Leon St.

Phone: 215-632-8666.

Greens fees: Weekends, 38.40 to ride, 23.75 to walk. Weekdays, 34.40 to ride, $20 to walk.

Carts: Walking is permitted anytime.

Amenities: Moderately stocked pro shop, snack bar, practice putting green. No driving range. Outings welcome.

Rating: Hilly, fun layout with a variety of holes. A working stiff's golf course in look and feel. Good walking course. A challenge for all but single-digit handicappers.

48. Juniata Golf Club

City course's many problems giving way to much promise

As golf courses go, Juniata Golf Club, the city-owned course in the Northeast neighborhood of the same name, would not be at the top of the list. Any list.

What it lacks in length (5,275 yards), regrettably, it doesn't make up for in variety or challenge (it has a 106 slope). And what it lacks in variety and challenge, well, don't get me started on conditioning. Not the condition of the fairways and greens — I have no serious complaint in that regard — but the walkways and cart paths have more mud holes, bumps and ruts than my career. I rented a cart there, but after two holes, I was tempted to go back to the pro shop and ask if they had something in an all-terrain vehicle.

Did I mention the graffiti? True, Juniata is fighting a losing battle against punks with spray paint. They have even hit the signs on the course. You also ought to know that when I played there last week, three of the holes had no flags — there were pins, all right, just no flags. (I suppose you could say two holes, because on one of the three, the flag was technically there — it was lying on the green next to the pin.)

And then there was the hike from the 12th green to the 13th tee. We're talking about a quarter-mile trek that takes you under a bridge for Wyoming Avenue and is so spooky and dark and dank and nasty and graffiti-ridden that not even a self-respecting troll would live under there.

"We call that the safari," head pro Bob Ewing said later, chuckling — at least he sounded as if he was chuckling; he might have been crying.

My purpose here is not to poke fun at Juniata. There are too many good people there who work too hard to make it as good as it is. Also, I recognize that a lot of avid golfers play the course regularly and almost religiously.

Rather, my reason for laying out the problems at Juniata is to establish a baseline from which to measure improvement. When the folks at Meadowbrook Golf Group Inc. assumed management of the six city-owned courses in the summer, they vowed to make things better. Well, at Juniata, they have their work cut out for them. From what I've seen of the other city courses, this will be the ultimate test of their abilities, their commitment and, in the end, their word.

Truth is, Ewing said, things already are getting better under Meadowbrook. Despite last summer's drought, the fairways and greens are in passable shape.

"Without a doubt, the aesthetics are better," he said. "We've seen a dramatic difference since they took over."

Other improvements are also on the way. Come spring,

Scorecard

Hole	Blue	White	Red	Par	HCP	Ladies' HCP
1	180	150	140	3	17	17
2	290	260	250	4	13	13
3	420	390	370	4	3	3
4	400	380	300	4	9	9
5	415	360	350	4	5	5
6	360	350	290	4	1	1
7	280	275	270	4	15	15
8	200	190	180	3	11	11
9	400	380	370	4	7	7
Out	2,945	2,735	2,520	34		
10	190	150	140	3	12	12
11	380	360	300	4	2	2
12	320	300	290	4	18	18
13	180	160	140	3	8	8
14	290	240	210	4	4	4
15	140	130	130	3	6	6
16	310	275	210	4	16	16
17	350	320	290	4	14	14
18	170	135	130	3	10	10
In	2,330	2,070	1,840	32		
Total	**5,275**	**4,805**	**4,360**	**66**		

Juniata expects to get a new fleet of carts — and not a moment too soon, if my clunker was typical. Of course, how long can new carts be expected to hold up at Juniata? So Meadowbrook is promising new paths by spring. That's a believable claim, because construction workers already are building a new cart barn. (The old barn has burned down twice in the last five years.)

During the coming months, Meadowbrook also has promised to expand the smallish tee boxes, which take a brutal beating at the height of the season, and improve the bunkering and irrigation on the course.

No matter how bad the situation has gotten at Juniata, the little oasis of green grass in the middle of a tough neighborhood has always been a popular meeting place for nearby residents and regulars.

"It's a middle-class golf course set tight in a blue-collar neighborhood, a classic 'muni' course," Ewing said. On any given morning, the combination pro shop/snack bar, which is clean and functional but rather barren, takes on the air of a corner store.

"The old guys come in here and [have] their coffee and play golf, and then argue over nickels and dimes," Ewing said.

The golf course itself, designed in the 1960s by architect Edmund Ault, is cramped and rarely more than passable. Squeezed as it is onto a tight chunk of land, Juniata has six par 3s, no par 5s, no truly long par 4s, and plays to a par of 66. But despite it all, thanks to the hilly terrain, Ault was able to make sure the course does have its moments.

Most notably is the sixth hole, a 360-yard dogleg par 4 with an uphill and sloping fairway that plays into an elevated, bunkered green that's tough to hold. It's the toughest and most interesting hole out there. There's also the 11th, a 380-yarder that plays from an elevated tee over a creek down to a tight, tree-lined fairway. The best par 3 on the course is the 200-yard eighth, which does not easily yield pars.

But too often, as Ewing acknowledged, Juniata suffers

from the "up and back" syndrome — short, uninspired par 4s that offer little challenge to better players. Still, on the day I was there, the course was full of working stiffs who couldn't have cared less — it was an uncharacteristically balmy fall afternoon, and they were sneaking in a round of golf.

Even if Meadowbrook wanted to enhance Juniata, there is no real room to squeeze much more length out of the course. Given the cost, it's probably not realistic to expect a dramatic renovation or makeover anyway.

But if Meadowbrook's people can dress up what is already there, they can markedly raise the pleasure quotient of a round at Juniata. Grass, they can grow. Flags, they can replace. Cart paths, they can pave.

The tough question is, what can they do to make sure all of their work is not undone by hoodlums every night when the sun goes down? Build a taller fence around the course? Hire security guards? Should that kind of responsibility even fall to Meadowbrook?

What Juniata becomes in the next few years will say a lot about Meadowbrook. But, no question, it will say just as much about the neighborhood.

— November 28, 1999

If You Go

Address: L & Cayuga Streets.

Phone: 215-743-4060

Greens fees: Weekends, $22.50 to walk, $36.50 to ride. Weekdays, $18.50 to walk, $32.50 to ride.

Carts: Walking permitted anytime.

Amenities: Snack bar, putting green, and minimally stocked pro shop. Outings welcome.

Rating: A course that takes a beating but keeps on ticking. A true "muni" course. Short and hilly, best suited for beginners to mid-level players, juniors and seniors.

49. Walnut Lane Golf Club

A jewel in much need of polishing

Pointing out the shortcomings of Walnut Lane Golf Club is like shooting fish in a barrel.

Aside from the fact that it's woefully short — 4,509 yards from the back tees — it's too often packed cheek to jowl with golfers. Then there's the conditioning, even at the height of spring — no sense in beating a dead horse when it comes to the course's lack of care and feeding of the grass on the tees, fairways and greens; the weeds in the bunkers; or the trees badly in need of care.

Yet, in spite of it all, you would be hard-pressed to find a golf course in the area that has provided more enjoyable rounds of golf to more people than the city-owned Walnut Lane.

Inexpensive and conveniently located in Roxborough, Walnut Lane is a neighborhood course to thousands of golfers, a place for others to sneak in a quick round after work. For countless golfers, a round at Walnut Lane is their introduction to the game.

Best of all, even as short as it is, even in its sad state, there is no denying that Walnut Lane boasts more than a few fun and creative holes.

For now, the biggest hope for Walnut Lane is Meadowbrook Golf Group Inc., which last week took over management of the city's six municipal courses. If Meadowbrook lives up to its promises, Walnut Lane could be transformed into a small golfing oasis in the city. If Meadowbrook fails — well, let's hope it doesn't.

"We've got plans and proposals for it," Joe Zaleski, vice president for Meadowbrook, said last week.

Chief among the plans is to improve the abysmal condition of the grass, from tee to green. That alone could vastly improve the environment at Walnut Lane. Meadowbrook will do what it can for now, Zaleski said, but the best time for major overseeding is in the fall.

For now, the company will get to work on what it can: repairing a leaky clubhouse roof, repairing a bridge on the course, clearing fallen trees, and installing benches around the course and signs on each hole. An overall cleanup is also in the works.

Scorecard

Hole	Blue	White	Red	Par	HCP
1	325	305	290	4	6
2	196	186	176	3	12
3	320	307	292	4	7
4	228	218	208	3	1
5	200	184	175	3	8
6	177	157	145	3	17
7	370	357	343	4	5
8	360	344	334	4	2
9	237	227	217	3	9
Out	2,413	2,285	2,180	31	
10	153	143	133	3	16
11	336	316	306	4	3
12	341	331	320	4	10
13	140	134	130	3	11
14	337	317	287	4	13
15	135	125	120	3	14
16	162	152	132	3	15
17	340	326	316	4	4
18	152	142	132	3	18
In	2,096	1,986	1,889	31	
Total	**4,509**	**4,271**	**4,069**	**62**	

Other long-range improvements and enhancements will be hammered out in meetings with Fairmount Park officials.

"I think within 30 to 60 days, people will be able to see a difference," Zaleski said.

Once a semi-regular at Walnut Lane, I hadn't played there in more than a year until a week ago. Its condition contributed to driving me away, as did the challenge. At only 4,509 yards, it has no par 5s and 10 par 3s; the longest hole on the course is 370 yards.

But last week, with a chance for another evaluation, I came to understand the charm and appeal the course holds for so many regulars. True, better golfers can easily leave their drivers in the trunks of their cars, but the course is rich with tough par 3s and short but testy par 4s.

The first hole is about as ho-hum as golf gets: a short, straight, flat par 4. But the fourth and fifth holes — 228 and 200 yards, respectively — can hold their own with most any par 3s in the area. The fifth, with its elevated tee over a ravine into an elevated, bunkered green, is especially dicey. The eighth, a 360-yarder with major tree intrusion from the right, is a classy little par 4. The ninth, at 237 yards, is certainly no pushover par 3.

The real fun doesn't begin until the back nine, home to several short, tight, tree-lined dogleg par 4s that pitch and roll. Here, you have to work to make pars.

The best of the bunch is a toss-up. The 11th, a 336-yard par 4 over another ravine, requires an accurate drive to have any chance to go for the well-protected green. The 13th is the only truly lousy hole on a coarse, 140-yard par 3 that plays drastically uphill into a blind green. Bad idea for a golf hole.

All is quickly forgiven, however, at the 14th, a 337-yard par 4 that swings left and up a hill like a banked turn on the NASCAR circuit. Short but nice — and difficult.

None of the par 3s on the back nine compares with the fourth and fifth holes, but other than No. 13, they are fun and fair.

Along with the eigth and 14th, the other serious candidate for best hole is the 17th, a 340-yard dogleg par 4 that begins from an elevated tee and swoops down and around to the right. It's a little short but still a terrific golf hole.

Walnut Lane is not a championship course by any means. But it can be a fun and challenging track, especially for mid-handicappers on up. No matter who you are, you had better be accurate off the tee and with your short irons.

Now, if they would only spruce it up so it can reach its potential.

— April 25, 1999

If You Go

Address: 800 Walnut Lane. Philadelphia.

Phone: 215-482-3370

Greens fees: Weekends, $35.66 to ride, $21.00 to walk. Weekdays, $31.91 to ride, $17.25 to walk.

Carts: Walk ing permitted anytime.

Amenities: Moderately stocked pro shop, snack bar, putting green.

Rating: Short but sweet. Excellent course for beginners, juniors, seniors, and anyone who likes to walk. Also good for a family outing or a quick round. Crowding is a problem, especially on weekends. Conditions need to be improved.

York

C O U N T Y

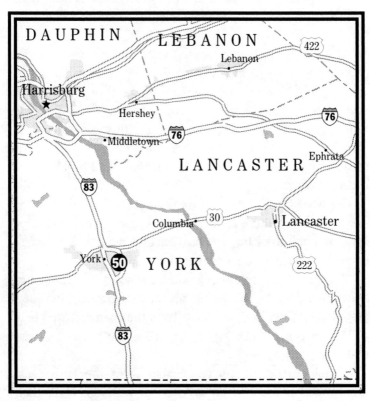

50. Springwood Golf Club

50. Springwood Golf Club

It's affordable, it's terrific

If you like your golf courses short, flat and easy, stop reading right now. If you like them long, hilly and demanding, call Springwood Golf Club.

If it were a little closer to Philadelphia and a little better known, Springwood would be competing for business with the area's two top daily-fee courses: Wyncote Golf Club and Hartefeld National.

If Springwood hasn't crossed your radar screen yet, it's probably because it has kept a relatively low profile since opening last May. First, there were financial problems, with cost overruns forcing the local owners to file for bankruptcy. When a new management team, Billy Casper Golf Management, came on board several months ago, the company quickly realized what it had on its hands and began a promotional campaign.

So, what's to like about Springwood?

For starters, there is the clubhouse, a sprawling, country-club-for-a-day affair that sits on a hill and commands a majestic view of the rolling course beyond.

But for Philadelphia-area golfers starved for top-quality daily-fee tracks, the course itself is the real draw. Springwood plays longer than its 6,826 yards from the championship tees and tougher than its 131 slope — it's a thinking player's course that rarely lets up.

Consider this: If you're playing from the back tees, Springwood starts you off with a 587-yard downhill, then uphill par 5 (forget going for the green in two) that falls off to an abyss on the left side.

Then, just when you're recovering from that rude awakening, you're staring down the barrel of the second hole, a testy 400-yard par 4 that begins from an elevated tee and proceeds over a creek, then swerves almost 90 degrees left. Try to bite off too much of the dogleg from the tee and you'll never find the ball in the woods.

I started bogey and double-bogey, then stood on the third tee scratching my head as Tony Cianci, Springwood's general manager and director of golf, told me how tough Springwood got on the back nine.

He was right: Springwood did get tougher — and better. Prime example: the fourth, a short (297 yards) downhill par 4 with the green tucked on the other side of that same creek from the second. You can hit an iron off the tee and a wedge into the green and still walk away wondering how this hole beat you up so badly.

All across Springwood, the holes pitch and roll. You better know how to hit from a sidehill lie, and because there are vast, open areas on this slab of former farmland, you better

Scorecard

Hole	Black	Blue	White	Green	Red	Par	HCP
1	587	560	535	515	440	5	4
2	400	370	355	330	315	4	6
3	185	175	155	140	115	3	18
4	297	272	260	245	245	4	10
5	425	410	395	375	300	4	2
6	307	283	275	260	240	4	16
7	550	535	517	480	430	5	8
8	200	187	170	150	125	3	14
9	357	335	320	300	250	4	12
Out	3,308	3,127	2,982	2,795	2,460	36	
10	429	406	385	365	355	4	3
11	465	415	400	380	345	4	1
12	204	182	130	115	90	3	15
13	454	425	410	390	320	4	5
14	216	210	185	160	140	3	11
15	352	340	315	300	260	4	17
16	558	525	490	475	420	5	7
17	325	310	290	265	230	4	13
18	515	496	475	455	455	5	9
In	3,518	3,309	3,080	2,905	2,615	36	
Total	**6,826**	**6,436**	**6,062**	**5,700**	**5,075**	**72**	

know how to play in the wind.

Springwood's designers — Ault, Clark and Associates from Washington, D.C., which also was responsible for TPC at Avenel in Potomac, Md. — played to the strength of the topography to ensure that most every hole offered some kind of elevation change.

Some are dramatic (see Nos. 1, 2, 4, 7, 8, 12 and 18), others less so. Nothing out there could remotely be considered a lousy hole.

The best holes are in the stretch from the 10th to the 14the, two par 3s and three par 4s.

The 10th, a 429-yard downhill par 4 with out of bounds right and mounds left, will get your juices flowing. But the 11th is probably the crown jewel of Springwood.

If you are bold (foolhardy?) enough to play from the back tees, the 11th confronts you with a 235-yard carry off the tee over a lake that slashes diagonally across the fairway and presents trouble all up the left side. Even better players are looking at least at a mid-iron — usually into a prevailing wind — into a deep, narrow green.

The 12th, a long par 3, is one of the toughest and most confounding holes on the course. If you play from the back tees, it's 204 yards uphill into a blind green. Not user-friendly. If you move up to the shorter tees, the 12th suddenly plays downhill. From there, the green is at least visible, but the hole is only slightly less forgiving.

By the way, if the par 3s are dicey, which they are, the par 5s are brutish. None is shorter than 500 yards, and each one is up hill and dale. You work for pars, let alone birdies.

If all this seems a bit foreboding for high handicappers, well, Springwood can be. With five sets of tees, you can bite off as much of the course as you wish. Still, bring your best game or you will be frustrated.

For better players, Springwood offers the kind of challenge that will get you to think, work and, I'm betting, come back.

— May 30, 1999

If You Go

Address: 601 Chestnut Hill Rd., York.

Phone: 717-747-9663.

Greens fees: Weekends, $55 to ride, $55 to walk. Weekdays, $40 to ride, $40 to walk.

Carts: Walking is permitted anytime, although cart fees are included.

Atlantic

C O U N T Y

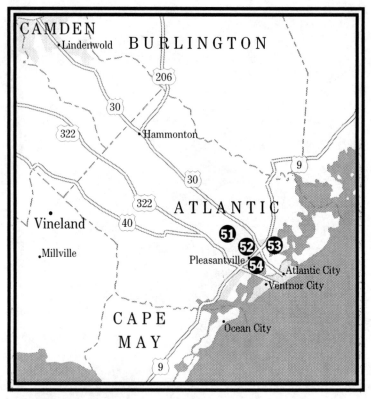

51. Blue Heron Pines, East
52. Harbor Pines Country Club
53. Marriott Seaview –
    Pines Course
54. Twisted Dunes Golf Club

51. Blue Heron Pines East

New layout isn't a letdown

Of all the new golf courses opening in the region this season, the most anticipated had to be Blue Heron Pines East. Would the new East course be as good as its sister course across the street, the popular and respected Blue Heron Pines West?

In a word, yes.

The East course, which has been open for about a month, is different from the West, to be sure. The East, on a sprawling 170-acre tract just across Tilton Road from the West, is more of a links-style layout where the wind can become a significant factor on several wide-open stretches of holes.

The East is also longer: 7,221 yards versus 6,810. It has less water to worry about, fewer forced carries, and a little less sand, although the sand that's there is strategically placed and can be troublesome.

I'm inclined to agree with the consensus of the assistant pros, who, like the slope and course rating (73/136 West; 74.8/135 East), indicate that the East is a little tougher.

The bottom line is that Blue Heron Pines East is a winner, a surefire four-star course and another welcome, albeit pricey, option for Shore golf.

A few years ago, when developer Roger Hansen decided it was time to add a second course at Blue Heron, he wasn't sure what he wanted. He just knew he wanted something different from the West course, which was designed by Stephen Kay in 1993.

Early in his research, Hansen bumped into Bradley Klein, the well-traveled course critic for Golfweek, who suggested that he consider Steve Smyers, a top amateur player and busy designer who is best known for his work in his home state of Florida. Hansen sampled some of Smyers' handiwork and set up a meeting.

Smyers, comfortable working with South Jersey's sandy soil and low-lying terrain, slashed a swath through the heavily wooded area, opened up clusters of holes, and swayed back and forth through the Pine Barrens. There wasn't much water to work with, and he didn't try to dress it up with fake-looking, man-made ponds. Instead, he took what the land gave him and created sweeping, rolling holes that play into well-bunked, crowned greens that often feature the kind of swales and collection areas found at Pinehurst No. 2.

Being an accomplished player himself — he was on the 1973 Florida team that won the NCAA championship — Smyers also made sure he built some oomph into the course. You will hit some long approach shots, and if you get too far off the fairway, you will be in knee-high undergrowth that is not pleasant.

East Course

Hole	Gold	Blue	White	Green	Red	Par	HCP
1	406	396	315	300	266	4	12
2	438	416	400	358	318	4	10
3	471	433	393	379	326	4	8
4	565	545	510	492	446	5	2
5	225	197	178	155	149	3	14
6	462	442	402	370	322	4	6
7	169	159	153	110	103	3	18
8	367	353	330	291	280	4	16
9	448	427	396	354	319	4	4
Out	3,551	3,368	3,077	2,809	2,529	35	
10	433	409	379	325	315	4	11
11	473	435	387	370	360	4	1
12	537	519	494	450	393	5	9
13	187	173	149	134	130	3	17
14	465	420	395	357	310	4	3
15	522	499	470	421	415	5	7
16	341	333	310	290	268	4	15
17	237	213	184	165	145	3	13
18	475	438	410	383	300	4	5
In	3,670	3,439	3,178	2,895	2,636	36	
Total	7,221	6,807	6,255	5,704	5,165	71	

Playing from the tips, the East opens with par 4s that go 406, 438 and 471 yards, respectively. If that doesn't wake you up, Smyers then comes at you with the only par 5 on the front, a split-fairway affair. The tee shot is white-knuckle, no matter how you play it.

The fifth isn't the most exotic par 3 around, but it plays 225 from the back tees. I've played it twice now, and I'm still trying to figure out the best way to handle it, especially in the wind.

The far more interesting par 3, however, is the seventh, shorter at 169 from the back, but tricky because it plays into a two-tiered green with a brutal slope.

There are a couple of short but sweet par 4s on the back, but the stars of the inward nine are the two par 5s, both mid-length but hard-to-reach doglegs, both heavily bunkered, both with those Pinehurst-style crowned greens that can turn a

West Course

Hole	Gold	Blue	White	Green	Red	Par	HCP	Ladies' HCP
1	315	307	290	278	221	4	14	15
2	180	165	150	129	119	3	10	11
3	5333	517	485	473	369	5	2	13
4	183	173	160	151	138	3	18	17
5	413	405	390	373	348	4	4	1
6	412	400	366	351	284	4	12	7
7	323	305	283	258	225	4	6	9
8	575	555	520	449	443	5	8	5
9	420	370	347	329	308	4	16	3
Out	3,354	3,197	2,991	2,791	2,455	36		
10	395	382	367	327	315	4	5	2
11	135	124	114	101	90	3	14	17
12	415	405	386	375	330	4	9	12
13	374	365	342	330	305	4	9	12
14	518	498	483	471	358	5	1	10
15	421	408	383	331	321	4	3	4
16	218	196	176	150	132	3	11	18
17	451	438	401	387	342	4	7	8
18	529	511	471	457	405	5	13	16
In	3,456	3,327	3,123	2,929	2,598	36		
Total	**6,810**	**6,524**	**6,114**	**5,720**	**5,053**	**72**		

sure par into a frustrating double bogey.

If the wind whips up, as it is wont to do at the Shore, you have even more problems on your hands. On those wide-open holes, nothing shields the wind, and a hole that played driver/8-iron yesterday can suddenly become driver/3-wood.

The only water on the course comes late in the round, with a lake that separates the 16th, a short par 4, and the 17th, a long par 3. It shouldn't be a problem, though, for the mid-level player on up.

Unless you play from tees beyond your ability, there aren't any problematic forced carries on the course.

In general, the East has a big, substantial feel to it. It's easy to imagine the course hosting qualifiers and tournaments down the road. Blue Heron Pines now delivers a very strong one-two punch.

— July 2, 2000

If You Go

Address: 550 W. Country Club Drive, Cologne.

Phone: 888-4STAR-GOLF

Web: www.blueheronpines.com

Greens fees: East Course. Weekends, $130 to ride, $130 to walk. Weekdays, $105 to ride, $105 to walk. West Course. Greens Fees: Weekends, $125 to ride, $125 to walk. Weekdays, $100 to ride, $100 to walk.

Carts: Walking is permitted anytime, although cart fees are included.

52. Harbor Pines Country Club

Shore course is worth the trip

If you've been waiting for another upscale championship resort course to play while vacationing at the Shore, it has arrived in Harbor Pines Country Club.

Open only six weeks, Harbor Pines is the latest addition to daily-fee golf at the Shore, and, though not the second coming of Galloway National, it's a welcome addition.

Weaving through mature pines and hardwoods, as well as around a nature preserve, Harbor Pines is a midlength course (6,478 yards from the blue tees) that challenges better golfers, yet it won't overwhelm mid- and even high-handicappers.

From the championship tees, Harbor Pines measures 6,827 yards and sports a 72 par and 127 slope. From the blues, Harbor Pines plays to a very manageable 123 slope; from the whites, 120.

In many respects, Harbor Pines calls to mind three-year-old Blue Heron Pines in nearby Galloway, no doubt because the course is carved from similar topography by the same golf architect, Steven Kay. That said, Blue Heron, with its long carries over wetlands on several holes, has a little more diversity in its layout and is probably a bit more intimidating than Harbor Pines for high-handicappers and seniors. Blue Heron's slope ratings — 136 from the back, 128 from the middle — are significantly higher than Harbor Pines'.

Unlike so many modern courses dominated by unruly fescue grass and marshland, Harbor Pines is characterized more by generous, often forgiving fairways. A topped tee shot needn't spell utter disaster.

And, even though there is water on eight holes at Harbor Pines, in most cases only the truly errant or awful shot gets wet. Only two holes — the par-3 eigth and the par-4 12th — require a significant carry over water, and even there danger can be minimized by carefully choosing from the five sets of tees.

Because of its proximity to the Shore, Harbor Pines is flat — no hilly lies and very little of the fairway perimeter mounding overdone on so many new courses. But there are plenty of vast, sprawling collection bunkers and grisly greenside bunkers to present problems.

The greens, like those on most new courses these days, are huge and undulating; the pin placement can radically change the difficulty of a hole.

Harbor Pines has the look and feel of a young course — in places, its otherwise natural setting also has the look and feel of a construction site. Owned and developed by Max Gurwitz & Son Inc. of Northfield, N.J., Harbor Pines is the centerpiece

Scorecard

Hole	Black	Blue	White	Green	Red	Par	HCP
1	505	480	465	430	412	5	15
2	380	360	340	282	271	4	13
3	170	153	143	125	123	3	17
4	400	370	347	313	296	4	5
5	452	422	402	378	360	4	3
6	394	364	345	279	263	4	7
7	526	502	474	435	418	5	9
8	215	190	170	159	137	3	11
9	460	435	419	367	346	4	1
Out	3,502	3,276	3,105	2,768	2,626	36	
10	540	530	511	440	419	5	8
11	182	172	162	142	130	3	12
12	339	333	291	266	233	4	18
13	400	383	351	318	296	4	6
14	335	325	315	279	252	4	14
15	179	158	150	117	108	3	16
16	402	385	367	321	298	4	4
17	461	437	409	364	335	4	2
18	487	479	458	423	402	5	10
In	3,325	3,202	3,014	2,670	2,473	36	
Total	**6,827**	**6,478**	**6,119**	**5,438**	**5,099**	**72**	

of a pricey residential community.

Harbor Pines opens with a fairly forgiving, short par-5 — 480 yards from the blues, 465 from the whites — that should cough up more than its fair share of birdies.

In fact, the course doesn't take a turn for the tough until the fourth, a 370-yard par-4, the sharpest dogleg in the layout and the No. 5 handicap hole. That's followed by the third and seventh handicap holes, both par 4s with water ready and willing to become home to sprayed tee shots. The most scenic hole on the course may well be the eigth, a 190-yard par 3, with water as a threat from the back tees and a green encircled by sand, sand, sand.

Designer Kay reserves the toughest challenge on the backside for the 16th and 17th, both long par 4s, and the fourth and second handicap holes, respectively. The 17th, at 437 yards, has trees left and right and a half-acre collection bunker plopped down right in the middle of the fairway that comes into play on the second shot. Steer clear unless you packed sandals and a camel.

For now, facilities are minimal. A two-trailer combination serves as the pro shop and snack bar; there are rest rooms, but no locker rooms. An 18,000-square—foot clubhouse overlooking the first and ninth holes is scheduled for completion next spring.

The bottom line on Harbor Pines: It's a fun golf course, not great, not awe-inspiring. But in an area with few quality daily-fee courses, Harbor Pines immediately vaults into the top two or three.

— Sept. 8, 1996

If You Go

Address: The Harbor Pines development entrance is at 3071 Ocean Heights Ave., Egg Harbor Township.

Phone: 609-927-0006 or 1-800-GOLF-222.

Greens fees: Weekends, $120 to ride, $120 to walk. Weekdays, $95 to ride, $95 to walk.

Carts: Mandatory at all times.

Web site: www.harborpines.com

Amenities: Minimal for now. Small pro shop and snack bar in trailers until the clubhouse is completed next spring. Driving range.

Rating: Welcome. One of the two or three best daily-fee courses at the shore. Note: Harbor Pines is a nonmetal-spike course. If you don't have nonmetal spikes, the staff will change them.

53. Marriott Seaview – Pines Course

Tucked within the Shore's pines, a most understated challenge

At the mention of Seaview Marriott Resort, most golfers probably think of the dignified and storied Bay Course. As its name suggests, the charming Donald Ross design unfailingly serves up seagulls and gentle sea breezes, along with eye-catching views, as it wends its way along the wetlands and waters of Absecon Bay.

Indeed, back in 1914, the Bay Course was the centerpiece of the old Seaview Country Club, which utilities baron Clarence Geist built as his personal playground when he grew tired of waiting for preferred tee times at other courses at the Shore. The Bay Course later would become the setting for Sam Snead's dramatic win in the 1942 PGA Championship, and in recent years has become home to the ShopRite LPGA Classic.

Yet, for all that pedigree, any golfer who has spent any time around Seaview knows that the far better course sits across the street, tucked quietly and unobtrusively behind the resort's hotel. Also aptly named, that layout is called the Pines Course.

Granted, the Pines doesn't quite share the Bay's legacy. The Pine's original nine holes were built in 1929 by Howard Toomey and William Flynn, the team behind so many fine courses in the region, and a duo only now beginning to get its due. The second nine at the Pines was completed in 1957, thanks to William Gordon, a Toomey and Flynn disciple and colleague who left behind an impressive body of work of his own (Saucon Valley, Sunnybrook).

Truth is, here's a case where Donald Ross got outdone.

The Pines Course, at par 71 and 6,731 yards from the championship tees, is as engaging, endearing and demanding as many of the best private courses around Philadelphia.

It lies only a few hundred yards from the bay, yet the Pines might as well be somewhere 80 miles inland on the Main Line. Before you are nothing but towering pines and oaks enveloping each hole, and gently undulating fairways and greens. It tends to be quiet back there, as if you were a 1,000 miles from the hustle and bustle of Shore activity.

Scorecard

Hole	Blue	White	Red/Gold	Par	HCP
1	357	345	293	4	9
2	434	421	341	4	1
3	484	464	394	5	7
4	360	347	290	4	11
5	301	291	255	4	15
6	393	380	319	4	5
7	190	180	110	3	17
8	319	392	288	4	13
9	415	401	325	4	3
Out	3,253	3,131	2,615	36	
10	419	403	321	4	2
11	204	193	150	3	16
12	377	366	294	4	8
13	115	104	92	3	18
14	230	221	179	3	14
15	320	311	275	4	12
16	476	463	411	5	6
17	352	337	272	4	10
18	501	482	408	5	4
In	2,994	2,880	2,402	35	
Total	**6,247**	**6,011**	**5,017**	**71**	

It's hard to point to one or two holes as breathtaking or even impressive. Because Gordon integrated his work into that of Toomey and Flynn's, creating a rather seamless whole, I dare all but the most sophisticated students of design to even identify who laid out what. I sure couldn't.

Holes on the Pines are not dramatic — no eye-popping views, no massive carries required, nothing to make you stand back and marvel. That's a function of the terrain, certainly, but it is also perhaps a testament to the understated design techniques of Flynn and Gordon.

Instead, what you have at the Pines is hole after hole that is tightly framed by trees, with flat or mildly contoured fairways, most complicated by gentle twists and turns and masterfully placed bunkers. As with their courses around Philadelphia, Flynn and Gordon's greens run toward midsize with significant but not severe undulations.

From the tips — my tees of choice — the Pines measures a respectable 6,731 yards and plays every bit (and then some) of its 71.7 rating and 128 slope. More than a few of the tee shots play out of tree-lined chutes into tight fairways just waiting to cause you misery. Approach shots are rarely simple. Greenside bunkers loom, tree limbs intrude, and your hands sweat.

I later learned that almost nobody plays the Pines from all the way back. Most regulars gravitate to the more manageable white tees, from which the course plays 6,211 yards to a 126 slope.

If the Pines has a problem, it has nothing to do with the course itself. It's the greens fees. In season, from April 29 through Oct. 8, a round goes for $110 during the week and $139 on weekends and holidays. True, that includes the cart and a forecaddie, but it's still steep.

Because of competition in recent years from the spate of new, quality daily-fee courses at the Shore, there are ongoing discussions about reducing the rates. Maybe it will happen, maybe it won't. Until then, the best bet is waiting for twilight (after 3 p.m., it's $59 on weekdays and $69 on weekends) or waiting until Oct. 9, when the price drops to $99 on weekends and $79 on weekdays. Better still, come November, when the weather is still generally pleasant at the Shore, the price drops to $49 on weekdays and $59 on weekends.

— Aug. 13, 2000

If You Go

Address: 401 S. New York Rd., Absecon.

Phone: 609-652-1800.

Web site: www.gacga.com (Greater Atlantic City Golf Association).

Greens fees: April 29 through Oct. 8, $110 weekdays, and $139 weekends and holidays.

Carts: Mandatory until Oct. 30. Greens fees include carts and forecaddie.

Amenities: The Pines is part of the Seaview Marriott Resort, a posh facility that includes an upscale hotel, a top-100 pro shop, practice facilities, an Elizabeth Arden spa, and a Faldo Golf Institute. Seaview is first-rate from top to bottom.

Rating: The Pines is pricey, but it has a terrific and classic layout, challenging for all levels of players.

54. Twisted Dunes Golf Club

A twisted, yet fascinating, new course

By the time I walk off the 18th green of most every golf course I play, I know whether I like the course, and I like to think I have a sense of whether others golfers will, too.

I can't say that about Twisted Dune.

The new and unusual — and much-awaited — high-end daily-fee layout, which opens Friday, remains an enigma after one round there the other day.

You know you're in for something different at Twisted Dune as you approach Ocean Heights Avenue. You don't see fairways and greens or trees and people. You see dunes so big and tall and deliberate that they seem to be obscuring something ominous (like a secret military installation?). It certainly gets your attention.

The facility is still taking shape — the clubhouse isn't built yet — but it's easy to see that the owners are trying to do something special here. We'll be able to tell better in a year how successful they are.

By the time you reach the first tee, it becomes obvious that if nothing else, Twisted Dune is big. The course sprawls, it rolls, it stretches in every direction with dune-lined fairways so wide that even Ian Baker-Finch couldn't have missed them in the throes of his worst driving slump.

Twisted Dune never disappoints from there on out — or at least it never ceases to fascinate. I liked it. I swear I liked it a lot. I'm pretty sure I did.

I'm not nearly so ambivalent about the golf holes themselves. Them, I like. There is not a bad hole out there. Long, devilish par 4s that are unreachable in the wind. Great 1-shot par 3s. Deceptive risk/reward par 5s. And — my personal favorite — a healthy sampling of treacherous short par 4s.

You and your game will be tested. You'll never be bored.

And all the while I was playing Twisted Dune, I was trying to figure out what the place reminded me of.

Sand Barrens? Maybe a little, given all the sand.

Galloway National? Yeah, in places, it has the same kind of look and feel, which is a very good thing.

A couple of treeless, seaside courses I've played in Scotland? Hmmm, yeah, that too. Twisted Dune is some kind of amalgam of all that.

"I wanted to replicate a kind of Irish look," said Archie Struthers, the designer. "I tried to build a modern course that looks like it occurred rather than being built."

Struthers is quite a character, a former caddie and assistant pro at Pine Valley, who has gone on to become the managing partner of the company that owns Greate Bay and now, with Twisted Dune, a developer.

Scorecard

Hole	Tourn.	Daily	Forward	Par	HCP
1	400	334	399	4	11
2	432	402	363	4	7
3	235	199	145	3	13
4	584	556	477	5	1
5	357	333	284	4	15
6	425	384	331	4	9
7	438	417	357	4	5
8	162	128	104	3	17
9	529	496	411	5	3
Out	3,562	3,249	2,772	36	
10	565	542	432	5	6
11	435	402	334	4	10
12	565	515	449	5	2
13	198	178	146	3	18
14	414	377	292	4	4
15	425	386	325	4	12
16	217	176	130	3	16
17	416	384	326	4	14
18	486	472	411	4	8
In	3,721	3,432	2,845	36	
Total	**7,283**	**6,681**	**5,617**	**72**	

Until Twisted Dune, Struthers never had designed a course, and he didn't intend to design this one. Originally, with substantial financial backing, he hired Rees Jones, one of the top architects working today. Jones' company produced an initial routing plan. But Jones, who never visited the property, and Twisted Dunes soon parted company, and the resulting course is emphatically not a Jones design.

"We weren't on the same page," said Struthers, preferring not to discuss the matter further. "This is not a Rees Jones course."

Struthers stepped into the design breach. Lacking formal training, Struthers relied largely on his own instincts and some of the design philosophy tips he overheard during those seven years as a caddie at Pine Valley while toting the bags of some of the greats, among them Tom Fazio, Arnold Palmer, Jack Nicklaus and Ben Crenshaw.

On most every hole, Struthers began by designing the green complex — mid-size, with Pinehurst-style swales — then working backward up the fairway toward the tee. Like George Crump once did at Pine Valley, Struthers would hit shots into the green until he decided how the fairway and the hole ought to go. If he had doubts, he would ask some of his buddies — all strong players — what they thought.

"It's not rocket science," Struthers said.

He also moved a lot of dirt.

The result is a course with fairways lined by dunes. But the dunes aren't so much stacked as the fairways and green complexes are dug out. "Thirty and 40 feet deep, in some cases," Struthers said. At times, you feel like you're playing sunken holes carved out of canyons of dunes.

"We tried to build the best course we could, given our abilities and our money," Struthers said.

Twisted Dune is still so new, still so much in the birthing process, that it's hard to tell what it will be like in a year or two, once all the native grasses have grown in. But it is going to turn heads, and it's definitely going to be a course everyone will want to play to decide whether they love it or hate it.

"Hate it?" said Struthers, taken aback. "What's there to hate? I think it's going to look more intimidating to the average golfer than it plays."

He's probably right. Twisted Dune is more bark than bite. The tournament tees (7,336 yards) play to a rating of 74.7 and a slope of 132 — respectable but not overly difficult; and the regular "daily" tees play to 71.8/124 — manageable even for mid-handicappers.

One final point. Struthers and his partners are all golfing purists, and for that reason, they have established a greens fee schedule that literally invites golfers to walk. Talk a cart and you'll pay $125 ($105 until mid-June), but take a caddie and you'll pay just $85.

"It's not a penalty for riding; it's a bonus if you walk," Struthers said. "It promotes our caddie program, and it takes a little wear and tear off the golf course. . . . You appreciate the golf course better when you walk."

— April 20, 2001

If You Go

Address: 2102 Ocean Heights Ave., Egg Harbor Township

Phone: 609-653-8019.

Greens fees: All days, $125 to ride (introductory rate of $105 until mid-June); $85 to walk, with a caddie.

Carts: Walk anytime. Trained caddies available.

Amenities: Clubhouse due to be completed in the fall.

Rating: A striking new addition to the daily-fee scene at the Shore. Golfers will love it or hate it. Very different from other Shore courses. Solid test without being too tough for mid-handicappers. Must-try for any curious golfer in the area.

Other Atlantic County Courses

Atlantic County John F. Gaffney Green Tree Golf Course
1030 Mays Landing-Somers Point Rd., Egg Harbor Township.
609-625-9131
Weekdays, $30; $36 weekends (non-residents)

Brigantine Golf Links
Roosevelt Blvd. & The Bay, Brigantine.
609-266-1388
Weekdays, $50; Saturdays, $70; Sundays, $65.

Buena Vista Country Club
Country Club Lane, Buena.
609-697-3733
Weekdays, $35; Friday-Sunday, $49.

Greate Bay Resort and Country Club
901 Mays Landing Rd., Somers Point.
609 927-0066
Weekdays, $78 (in season); weekends, $88 (in season).

Hamilton Trails Country Club
Ocean Heights & Harbor Ave, McKee City.
609-641-6824
Weekdays, $21, weekends, $24. Carts are $6 per person.

Latona Country Club
Oak & Cumberland Roads, Buena Vista.
609-692-8149
Weekdays, $15; weekends, $18. Carts are $8 per person.

Mays Landing Golf Club
1855 Cates Road, McKee City.
609-641-4411
Weekdays, $58, Friday-Sunday, $70

Pomona Golf and Country Club
400 West Moss Mill Rd., Pomona.
(609) 965-3232
Weekdays, $13; weekends, $15.

Burlington

C O U N T Y

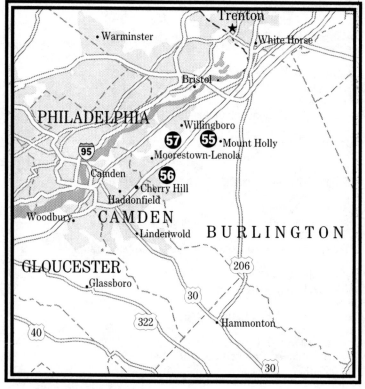

55. Deerwood Country Club
56. Ramblewood Country Club
57. Rancocas Golf Club

55. Deerwood Country Club

Overlooked course is pleasant surprise

There was certainly no reason to expect much from Deerwood Country Club, the three-year-old semiprivate course just outside Mount Holly, in South Jersey.

There had been no clamor about it, to my knowledge, not even a mild buzz, really. And judging from the length (6,231 yards from the back tees) and the difficulty (126 slope from the back), it wasn't going to be the most severe test of golf around.

Sure enough, Deerwood wasn't a backbreaker.

But as I made my way around the wetlands-filled "Carolina-style" layout, as the owner bills it, one question kept coming to mind: Why hasn't there been more talk about this place?

Deerwood is a pleasant, challenging, if overlooked little gem.

For starters, it has a fairly upscale, club-for-a-day feel to it. It is rarely crowded, doing only about 20,000 rounds this year, which is below the figure for even most top-dollar country clubs.

As for the course, Deerwood boasts several delicious holes, particular the closing five. Thanks to several considerable forced carries, it plays longer than 6,231 yards. And credit superintendent Joel Collura, because it is a safe bet you are not going to find many daily-fee golf courses in better condition.

So, why haven't you heard of Deerwood?

"We've done absolutely no marketing," head pro Greg Farrow said.

The reason is simple and somewhat ominous. Next year, construction begins on 400 single-family homes and townhouses around the perimeter of the 507-acre site, and

Deerwood owner Dick Alaimo doesn't want to fill the membership roster of the semiprivate club before that happens.

Time will tell whether the construction and the housing intrude too much on the course. But for now, anyway, Deerwood, designed by Alaimo and area architect Jim Blaukovitch, is an engaging, fun track more like what you might expect to find around Myrtle Beach, S.C.

It is a curious blend of flat wetlands, wooded area and bordering farmland, which makes for a mix of wide-open and tight golf holes.

Because almost half of the property is protected wetlands, better than half of the holes at Deerwood require some kind of forced carry off the tee or into the green on the approach shot. Others simply run alongside trouble. Yet other holes — the 12th and 13th, the back-to-back par 3s on the back side, for example — are enshrouded by trees from tee to green, offering a more traditional, parkland style of golf.

Scorecard

Hole	Blue	White	Green	Red	Par	HCP
1	380	371	354	316	4	9
2	383	369	353	273	4	11
3	365	349	347	294	4	5
4	136	130	123	114	3	17
5	465	436	419	367	4	1
6	350	325	315	294	4	13
7	513	481	471	405	5	7
8	209	197	185	131	3	3
9	334	323	314	267	4	15
Out	3,135	2,981	2,881	2,461	35	
10	375	364	354	300	4	10
11	368	330	318	303	4	12
12	176	164	151	137	3	16
13	139	130	127	118	3	18
14	398	380	325	221	4	4
15	310	287	265	224	4	14
16	398	383	366	311	4	8
17	556	546	534	441	5	2
18	376	363	349	291	4	6
In	3,096	2,947	2,789	2,346	35	
Total	**6,231**	**5,928**	**5,670**	**4,807**	**70**	

If the fifth, a 465-yard par 4 over marsh off the tee, is the best and toughest single hole on the course, it only is preparing you for the closing five holes.

The fun, or misery, starts at the 14th, 398 yards from the tips, over a yawning chasm of weeds and water that looks almost impossible from the tee. The fairway is barely visible.

The 15th, a short par 4 (310 yards) dogleg over more mess off the tee, is another challenge entirely. Here, a well-placed iron off the tee is the prudent shot, before heading upward to a small, heavily bunkered green. Then there is the 398-yard 16th, which is forgiving on the tee shot but deadly on the long approach shot over still more wetlands.

"Sometimes, high handicappers play up the 17th fairway, around the marsh," Farrow said of the 16th.

The 17th, one of only two par 5s on the par-70 layout, is the longest hole at Deerwood at 556 yards, not to mention the No. 2 handicap. The closer is a sweeping, sloped 376-yard dogleg right around marsh that forces you to decide how much to bite off. Slice here and you are sunk.

As pleasant as Deerwood is, it's not for everyone. Even with four sets of tees, some high-handicappers, seniors, women and juniors are going to struggle against the marshy areas.

Others may not like that carts are mandatory — but it is for good reason. Matters of revenue aside, there are some l-o-n-g hauls between several greens and the next tee.

Still, for more than a few golfers, Deerwood will be a welcome change from many of the daily-fee options in the area.

— Aug. 9, 1998

If You Go

Address: 18 Deerwood Dr., Westhampton.

Phone: 609-265-1800.

Greens Fees: Weekends, $84 to ride, $84 to walk. Weekdays, $72 to ride, $72 to walk.

Carts: Mandatory.

Amenties: Comfortable, country-club-style clubhouse, locker rooms, banquet facilities, driving range, putting green. Outings welcome.

Rating: A bit pricey, but an innovative, fun, manicured course with a coastal feel.

56. Ramblewood Country Club

Keeps small-town country club appeal

I remember almost 20 years ago, when I moved to Philadelphia, trying to find a golf course to call my own. I lived in Center City at the time and didn't know the town, so I played Cobbs Creek a number of times. I tried Walnut Lane, FDR, and a couple of other places long forgotten. I'd grown up playing at a small-town country club, and none of them had quite the feel I wanted.

Then one day at work, somebody suggested a place over in Jersey called Ramblewood.

It wasn't perfect, but it was close enough. For the next year, until I moved, most every weekend found a couple of buddies and me making the trek to Mount Laurel and Ramblewood. Granted, it was often too crowded, but Ramblewood had a better than decent course and something of a small-town country club feel to it. And, not least important, I could afford it.

Last week, I discovered not much had changed. Ramblewood Country Club is pretty much as I left it — 27 holes of basic but solid golf, nothing fancy, but well-run, comfortable, and accommodating to golfers of all levels, ages and genders.

"We like to call it user-friendly," said general manager John Goodwin, whose grandfather and father developed the course and semiprivate club in the early 1960s. "You can go to tougher courses and beat your brains out, or you can come here and have a fair shot at shooting a good score."

Not a bad assessment.

Not many holes at Ramblewood give you reason to stand on the tee and admire the handiwork of the designer, the late Edmund Ault. But there aren't any that give you reason to cuss his name, either.

Red Course

Hole	Blue	White	Red	Par	Par	HCP	HCP
1	380	375	352	4	4	4	8
2	367	354	345	4	4	8	7
3	549	526	439	5	5	3	1
4	485	457	439	4	5	1	3
5	250	176	122	3	3	5	9
6	490	464	415	5	5	7	2
7	391	382	369	4	4	6	4
8	418	409	354	4	4	2	5
9	161	144	131	3	3	9	8
Total	**3,491**	**3,287**	**2,966**	**36**	**37**		

White Course

Hole	Blue	White	Red	Par	Par	HCP	HCP
1	390	384	279	4	4	3	3
2	384	353	323	3	3	9	6
3	200	168	132	3	3	7	8
4	513	503	457	5	5	2	1
5	400	385	374	4	5	1	4
6	210	196	152	3	3	8	9
7	537	502	423	5	5	6	2
8	386	365	292	4	4	5	7
9	372	355	343	4	4	4	5
Total	**3,392**	**3,211**	**2,775**	**36**	**37**		

Blue Course

Hole	Blue	White	Red	Par	Par	HCP	HCP
1	221	187	165	3	3	6	9
2	325	303	242	4	4	8	6
3	540	520	418	5	5	1	1
4	203	181	165	3	3	7	8
5	385	359	283	4	4	5	7
6	381	352	307	4	4	3	3
7	357	333	315	4	4	4	4
8	483	460	381	5	5	2	2
9	337	307	257	4	4	9	5
Total	**3,232**	**3,002**	**2,533**	**36**	**36**		

Ramblewood offers straightforward golf. True, a few holes stand out — a couple of par 3s, a couple of par 4s, and a couple of par 5s come to mind — but for the most part, you find mid-length, tree-lined par 4s with greens flanked by bunkers and just enough teeth to satisfy good golfers without demoralizing high handicappers.

With three nines, you can mix and match the courses at Ramblewood, although oftentimes the choice is not yours but the starter's. That's too bad, because the three nines are not created equal. I happen to prefer the Blue course, which is a little tighter and less forgiving. But if keeping tee shots in the fairway is not your strength, you're definitely better off on the Red and White courses.

"The White and the Red are very wide," Goodwin said. "You have room for error, and you can still recover." A couple of holes on the Blue are wooded corridors.

Ault, a designer from Washington, D.C., who left a legacy of courses from Maryland to Pennsylvania, tackled the Red and White courses first, a few years after the Goodwins bought an old dairy farm from another South Jersey family, the Joneses. Ault added the Blue course, which is built on more wooded adjacent property, in 1971.

Although a few holes play from slightly elevated tees, the topography of Ramblewood is basically flat. That, of course, makes it a welcoming layout for juniors, seniors and women. Except for weekend mornings, you can walk, which is also appealing to many players.

Depending on the tees and the courses you play, a round at Ramblewood can range from a slope of 123 to 130, which are respectable numbers. Unless you play the back tees, Ault rarely confronts you with a long forced carry, nor does he tuck his greens behind nasty bunkers. Almost always, he gives you space to roll the ball onto the green. The greens tend to be medium-sized, rarely with tiers, and almost always pitched from back to front.

None of this is to say that Ramblewood can't jump up and

bite you. I happened to play my round last week with a certain nameless editor. Wide as the fairways were, he visited the rough. He also rinsed a few balls at two of the watery par 3s.

Discretion, and the prospect of some horrid assignment, prevents me from divulging his score. But it was a beautiful day, and he had a heck of a time. Reports from the office had him working on his take-away next to his desk for days afterward.

— Nov. 14, 1999

If You Go

Address: 200 Country Club Parkway, Mount Laurel.

Phone: 856-235-2118.

Greens fees: Mon.-Thurs., $35 to walk, $50 to ride. Fri., $58 to ride. Sat.- Sun., $63 to ride.

Carts: Carts are mandatory, Fri.-Sun.

Amenities: Minimally stocked pro shop; putting and chipping green; restaurant, snack bar and banquet facilities. No driving range. Outings welcome.

Rating: Busy but well-run course that should appeal to most every level of golfer. Comfortable, unpretentious feel.

57. Rancocas Golf Club

A popular challenge

Ask anybody in South Jersey to name the daily-fee courses they play and it's a pretty sure bet they'll mention Rancocas Golf Club.

Rancocas, a Robert Trent Jones Sr. design in Willingboro, gets about 52,000 rounds a year, which makes it one of the most popular public courses in the area.

The facility is well-managed, the price is reasonable ($38 to ride, weekends after 1 p.m.), and the course itself — in quite decent shape considering the volume of play — is a respectable challenge.

Rancocas plays as long as 6,629 yards and a 130 slope from the championship tees, or as short as 5,284 yards and a 122 slope from the forward tees. It gets three stars from *Golf Digest's 4,200 Best Places to Play.*

What's most noticeable about the course is the difference in the two nines. The front side is flat and wide open, and the back is tight, tree-lined and loaded with doglegs. Prudence suggests sheathing your driver at the turn.

The greens at Rancocas can also bite you. They are generous enough — most are midsize and mildly undulating — but they are almost all at least slightly elevated and well-bunkered.

"You had better bring your short game when you come, because if you miss the greens here, it's almost impossible to get up and down," head pro Joe Casey said.

Rancocas was built in 1966 as the now-defunct, semiprivate Willingboro Country Club. There have been no significant changes to the original layout by the prolific and successful Jones, who helped launch the design careers of his sons, Robert Trent Jones Jr. and Rees Jones.

About 1990, with Willingboro Country Club on hard times,

National Golf Properties, the giant of the golf-course industry, bought the course and turned it over to its management subsidiary, American Golf Corp. The name came from Rancocas Creek, which runs along the dicey, par-3 11th hole.

Rancocas starts you off with a straightaway, narrow par 5 that should be no problem unless you hook your tee shot OB.

From there through the seventh hole, the course is a string of mid-length, relatively wide-open holes that are adequate but nothing special.

The first truly nice hole is the eighth, a short (316 yards), severe dogleg left, with woods and three well-placed fairway bunkers that make you think twice about trying to cut the corner. Assuming you play it safe, the second shot is a short iron onto a elevated green guarded by bunkers on the left and right.

The 485-yard ninth is the more interesting of the par 5s

Scorecard

Hole	Champ.	Middle	Forward	Par	Ladies' Par	HCP	Ladies' HCP
1	585	549	499	5	5	1	1
2	192	156	133	3	3	17	17
3	355	320	298	4	4	13	13
4	420	396	383	4	5	3	3
5	380	346	319	4	4	7	7
6	390	350	311	4	4	11	11
7	202	167	141	3	3	15	15
8	348	316	292	4	4	11	11
9	523	485	393	5	5	5	5
Out	3,395	3,085	2,796	36	37		
10	406	365	334	4	4	12	12
11	165	126	57	3	3	18	18
12	568	522	409	5	5	2	2
13	568	522	409	5	5	2	2
14	402	368	284	4	4	6	10
15	396	381	368	4	4	10	8
16	400	374	344	4	4	4	4
17	165	145	120	3	3	16	16
18	402	373	345	4	4	8	6
In	3,234	2,955	2,515	35	35		
Total	**6,629**	**6,040**	**5,284**	**71**	**72**		

on the front, thanks to a dogleg, a pond fronting the green, and a very shallow green. Even if you can reach it in 2, the hard-to-hold green, with OB if you're long, makes the ninth a 3-shot par 5 for most golfers.

The 11th is the best par 3 on the course. It plays only 126 yards from the middle tees, but it's almost all carry over wetlands into a long, narrow green with a fence on the right and Rancocas Creek on the left.

In fact, the 11th is really the beginning of the best stretch of holes here. The 12th is a short, 301-yard, par-4 dogleg guarded on the right by trees and fairway bunkers.

The 13th, a 522-yard par 5, is the signature hole. It's a downhill, then uphill, double-dogleg, with fairway bunkers on the left, and once you've negotiated the first leg, a narrow, tree-lined approach.

Then comes the 368-yard dogleg 14th, with yet another tight fairway and another pond fronting the well-bunkered green.

And you haven't seen the last of the doglegs on the back side. At 373 yards, the 18th is also tight and also turns, once again ending with a bunkered green.

— July 13, 1997

If You Go

Address: Clubhouse Drive, Willingboro.

Phone: 609-877-5344.

Greens fees: Monday through Thursday, $38 to ride, $32 to walk. Friday through Sunday and holidays, $48 to ride before 1 p.m; after 1 p.m., $38 to ride, $32 to walk.

Amenities: Moderately stocked pro shop, snackbar, driving range.

Rating: Respectable, well-run course. A bit difficult for high handicappers, good test for mid and low handicappers.

Other Burlington County Courses

Golden Pheasant Golf Course
141 Country Club Dr. & Eayrestown Rd., Medford.
609-267-4276
Weekdays, $40 to ride, $28 to walk; weekends, $49 to ride.

Hanover Country Club
133 Larrison Rd., Jacobstown.
609-758-8301
Weekdays, $31 to walk, $41 to ride; weekends, $43 to walk, $55 to ride.

Indian Spring Golf Course
115 S. Elmwood Rd., Marlton.
856-983-0222
Weekdays, $28; weekends, $32. Carts are $14.

Willow Brook Country Club
4310 Bridgeboro Rd., Moorestown.
856-461-0131
Weekdays, $18 to walk, $33 to ride; weekends, $21.50 to walk, $36.50 to ride.

Camden

C O U N T Y

58. Pine Hill Golf Club
59. Pennsauken Country Club

58. Pine Hill Golf Club

Has country-club feel

Awesome, flat-out awesome. I don't know how else to describe the brand new Pine Hill Golf Club in South Jersey.

I'll admit, when they announced plans a couple of years ago to build a "public Pine Valley," I was skeptical, even if the property was a stone's throw from the real Pine Valley and even if none other than Tom Fazio had signed on as the architect.

But I have now played a preview round at Pine Hill, and I am here to tell you that you can count me among the officially optimistic, the excited, the totally converted believers. Pine Hill, which is scheduled to open in the spring (limited public play is available now through Dec. 10), is nothing short of breathtaking, beautiful and brutal.

Let's be honest, though. Pine Hill is not Pine Valley. There is only one Pine Valley, the world-famous enclave discreetly tucked away in the piney woods near Clementon, Camden County, and universally ranked by the golf magazines as the No. 1 golf course anywhere. Beyond the exquisite golf course itself, there are also the history and mystique of the ultra-private Pine Valley.

For us nonmembers, Pine Hill will have to do — and that is not such a bad thing.

As far as I am concerned, as of the day it opens, Pine Hill will become the undisputed No. 1 daily-fee course in the area.

Think half-again better than Fazio's other recognized work in the area, Hartefeld National. Think Bulle Rock without the 90-minute drive south in Maryland. Think of a golf course where most every hole is a treat for your eyes and a test of your game, a golf course where fairways are engulfed by trees, isolating most holes from the others.

Naturally, Pine Hill is also a strain on your finances —

greens fees will be in the $125 range — but worth every penny of it.

"We are going after people who want something superb," said developer Eric Bergstol, who eventually will sink $20 million, including $6 million for the clubhouse, into Pine Hill. "We think there is a market for it."

With stratospheric greens fees and posh country-club-for-a-day treatment, Bergstol realizes Pine Hill will attract a few corporate memberships and a ton of expense-account and special-occasion golf. That means few golfers ever will get a chance to learn every nook and cranny of the course.

So, the solution was to have Fazio, who is masterful with a bulldozer, design a course with a Pine Valley look and feel, but not make it so difficult and penal. He has done just that. Though Pine Hill, at 6,969 yards, pitches and pitches, twists and turns, it has nothing like the teeth of Pine Valley.

Scorecard

Hole	Black	Blue	White	Gold	Red	Par	HCP	Ladies' HCP
1	520	504	480	455	389	5	16	8
2	174	165	150	132	107	3	18	12
3	467	442	416	369	331	4	4	6
4	437	420	395	353	326	4	8	10
5	210	185	171	154	105	3	14	16
6	410	397	370	340	315	4	10	14
7	577	566	546	450	387	5	2	2
8	205	190	170	150	95	3	12	18
9	448	423	397	375	292	4	6	4
Out	3,448	3,292	3,095	2,778	2,347	35		
10	447	449	430	411	360	4	5	7
11	408	387	369	353	332	4	11	5
12	399	390	375	360	289	4	13	13
13	170	163	145	115	93	3	17	15
14	534	517	477	457	390	5	7	3
15	471	444	409	381	341	4	1	1
16	203	180	155	145	122	3	15	17
17	453	435	422	404	338	4	3	9
18	406	385	371	341	310	4	9	11
In	3,521	3,350	3,153	2,967	2,575	35		
Total	**6,969**	**6,642**	**6,248**	**5,745**	**4,922**	**70**		

"It is an accepting golf course," said Bergstol, a single-digit handicapper. "The carries are shorter, and the greens are bigger and gentler. The whole course is more subtle."

I couldn't have said it better myself.

As with most every other Fazio course I've played, the real test of your game comes on the second shot. He perches greens above the fairways, he tucks them behind high-faced bunkers, he somehow makes even the most routine approach shot seem intimidating.

At Pine Hill, he also had a wonderful piece of land on which to work his magic. Fazio gives you sandy waste areas, but not on the scale of Pine Valley, and not so hair-raising. Rare is the hole that is flat. Equally rare is the hole that doesn't have you standing on the tee, shaking your head at the view, the whole scene. On three holes, when you step to the tee, looming in the distance is the Center City skyline.

"Do you realize this is about the eighth hole you've described as gorgeous or beautiful?" a buddy informed me as I made notes to myself into a tape recorder during our round.

Even if Pine Hill isn't as difficult or penal as Pine Valley — who would want it to be? — it is more than enough of a challenge, even for the best of players. The course hasn't been rated yet, but I suspect it will likely come in with a slope of 130-plus.

It's impossible to pick a signature hole at Pine Hill because at least half a dozen qualify for a picture postcard, but the 10th had to be one of my favorites. From the back tee, it's a monster par 4, 477 yards, that requires two monster shots.

It starts high up on a hill with a commanding view. No matter how hard you hammer your tee shot, you're looking at 200 yards to a green that's guarded by an imposing-looking, ball-eating crevasse and a couple of sizable, nasty bunkers.

"Do you believe this hole?" my buddy asked me.

No, I didn't. Except, yes, I did.

If there is a disappointment about Pine Hill, it is that it's not a course you'd want to walk. Because of wetlands and environmentally protected areas on the 360-acre property that were off-limits to Fazio, the trek from one green to the next is considerable on several holes.

That complaint aside, however, Pine Hill is out of this world.

— Oct. 22, 2000

If You Go

Address: 500 W. Branch Ave., Pine Hill.

Phone: 856-435-3100, or toll free, 1-877-450-8866.

Web site: www.golfpinehill.com

Greens fees: Fees for next season have not been finalized, but expect $125 to $140.

Carts: Walking permitted anytime, but expect some long hikes between holes.

Rating: Excellent, potential 4 1/2-star to five-star course. Best daily-fee course in the area, like Bulle Rock without the drive. Upscale country-club-for-a-day facility. Still a work in progress; clubhouse will be completed in the spring.

59. Pennsauken Country Club

A success – but not a challenge

Pennsauken Country Club, the municipal course in its namesake township, is never going to wow anybody with its length (5,749 yards from the white tees) or difficulty (117 slope).

But thanks to lush fairways, user-friendly greens and several fine, fun holes — none of them especially penal — Pennsauken never lacks for golfers.

For the low-handicapper, Pennsauken is a place to score well. For the mid- and high-handicapper, Pennsauken is a course to make your way around without hunting all day for lost balls or hacking your way back onto the fairway.

"I'd say people like it the most because it's always in good condition," said Bob Prickett, the golf superintendent and general manager. "If I had to point out a weakness, it's that we don't have enough tee times. We did 7,600 rounds in July."

For most of its 67 years, Pennsauken was known to area residents as Iron Rock, which Prickett, a municipal employee, thinks was a private club. He doesn't know who designed the course. But in 1982, with Iron Rock closed, the township stepped in to maintain the land as "open acres," Prickett said, rather than see the site become yet another apartment complex.

"The city fathers thought it was in the best interest of everyone," Prickett said. "Golf courses produce more oxygen than 800 apartments, plus it's not a burden on the school system or the police and fire departments. It has been a tremendous success."

As for the layout itself, the back nine has a little more spice than the front, which suffers from too many open, up-and-back holes.

Pennsauken starts you off with a short (309 yards), flat,

mild dogleg left. Even stumbling out of the car cold (there's no driving range), you'd have to work to make double bogey here. The second hole is only slightly longer (344) and dead straight, although there are out of bounds and a railroad track up the left side.

The seventh is the favorite hole among many Pennsauken regulars; at 216 yards from the whites, it's easily the longest par 3 on the course and a test for even better players.

The 10th — long (461 yards), narrow and tree-lined on both sides — is another favorite of regulars, as well as the No. 1 handicap hole. It's the one hole at Pennsauken where even low-handicappers will likely find themselves hitting at least a mid-iron into the green.

Come to think of it, the 10th is the beginning of the best stretch of holes on the course. The par-3 11th is a picturesque 117-yard shot over a pond, with trees right and left.

Scorecard

Hole	Blue	White	Red	Par	Ladies' Par	HCP	Ladies' HCP
1	325	309	304	4	4	15	13
2	353	344	306	4	4	10	8
3	156	142	111	3	3	13	14
4	397	387	317	4	4	2	1
5	319	301	290	4	4	14	15
6	341	323	302	4	4	12	10
7	240	216	189	3	3	4	3
8	526	510	433	5	5	8	9
9	388	386	278	4	4	6	5
Out	3,045	2,918	2,530	35	35		
10	471	461	320	4	4	1	6
11	127	117	88	3	3	16	16
12	336	326	300	4	4	11	11
13	339	313	294	4	4	9	4
14	485	469	401	5	5	7	2
15	113	98	85	3	3	18	18
16	392	379	288	4	4	5	12
17	283	271	254	4	4	17	17
18	415	397	300	4	4	3	7
In	2,961	2,831	2,330	35	35		
Total	6,006	5,749	4,860	70	70		

The 13th, despite being only 313 yards, is a delightful little easygoing dogleg over a crest and a pond into a sloping yet receptive green.

The weakest hole is easily the 17th, barely a par 4 at only 271 yards and nearly defenseless with only two feeble fairway bunkers and a flat, unguarded green.

"The whole back nine is better, except for the 17th," said Prickett, who is considering moving the green back into the woods to give the hole more muscle.

The 18th is another short, leisurely dogleg par 4 that should allow even high-handicappers to walk off the course with a par, bogey at most.

— Aug. 10, 1997

If You Go

Address: 3800 Haddonfield Rd., Pennsauken.

Phone: 856-662-4961.

Greens Fees: Weekends, $47.50 to ride, $ 47.50 to walk. Weekdays, $47.50 to ride, $32 to walk (Mon.-Thurs.).

Carts: Mandatory until 3 p.m. on Fridays, weekends, and holidays..

Other Camden County Courses

Freeway Golf Course
1858 Sicklerville Road, Sicklerville.
856- 227-1115
Weekdays, $20 to walk, $28 to ride; weekends, $45 to ride.

Kresson Golf Course
298 Kresson & Gibbsboro Roads, Voorhees.
856-435-3355
Weekdays, $22 ; weekends, $26.

Pinelands Golf Course
887 South Mays Landing Rd., Winslow.
609-561-8900
Weekdays, $25 to ride, $20 to walk; weekends, $35 to ride.

Ron Jaworski's Valley Brook Golf Course
200 Golfview Drive, Blackwood.
856-227-3171
Weekdays, $28 to walk, $42 to ride; weekends, $49 (cart included).

Cape May

C   O   U   N   T   Y

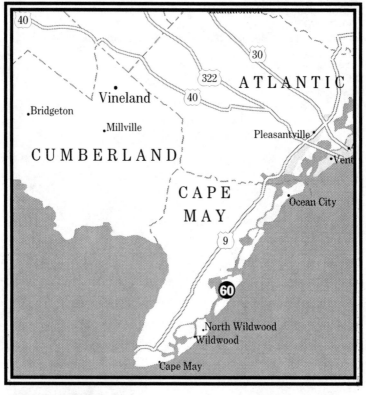

60. Sand Barrens Golf Club

60. Sand Barrens Golf Club

Designer found key underfoot

In the beginning, the plans were to call Sand Barrens Golf Club, the new upscale resort track just north of Cape May, Royal Oakes. It made sense, given the evergreen- and oak-lined fairways.

But that was before the backhoe experiment.

It was during the winter of '96, after work had begun on clearing trees for what would become fairways, that lead designer Dana Fry came for one of his frequent visits.

"We were standing on the eighth hole, and there was snow everywhere," Mike Gaffney, the project manager then and Sand Barrens' general manager now, recalled last week. "Dana said, 'What kind of soil do you have under here?' I said, 'Pure sand once you get down three or four feet.'

"Dana said, 'Go back and get a backhoe, will you?' We dug a test hole, and when he saw all that sand, his eyes lit up."

That's when Fry, who was simultaneously designing a desert course out West, looked at Gaffney and said, "I've got some other ideas."

Within days, Fry's plans for a leisurely loop through the tall pines and oaks of tiny Swainton got tossed into the trash.

Starting tomorrow, when Sand Barrens officially opens, 12 miles north of Cape May, you can decide for yourself whether Fry made the right decision. It's a unique, first-class resort track that's the closest thing you'll find to a desert course in this neck of the woods. And Fry managed to pull it off without creating a course that feels too gimmicky.

Virtually every hole features sand — long stretches that run alongside fairways like gutters on a bowling lane; ribbons that zigzag across the fairway, that strategically bloat to add treachery to a tee or approach shot, that wrap around greens like a deadly anaconda. On a couple of holes, Fry became

South Course

Hole	Pro	Champion	Regulation	Rookie	Forward	Par	HCP
1	365	353	329	305	254	4	8
2	188	179	163	145	105	3	6
3	399	372	354	328	308	4	4
4	429/439	406/416	381/391	353/363	329/339	4	1
5	439	428	415	358	328	4	2
6	546	523	491	459	443	5	3
7	204	186	157	129	109	3	5
8	295	285	276	255	210	4	9
9	511	500	485	461	387	5	7
Total	3,376/ 3,386	3,232/ 3,242	3,051/ 3,061	2,793/ 2,803	2,473/ 2,483	36	

West Course

Hole	Pro	Champion	Regulation	Rookie	Forward	Par	HCP
1	386	375	362	319	250	4	6
2	561	548	530	510	448	5	3
3	175	165	141	130	113	3	9
4	398	379	356	335	279	4	8
5	514	499	478	422	400	5	2
6	203	182	177	140	97	3	7
7	204	186	157	289	242	4	5
8	448	432	413	373	351	4	1
9	440	425	409	374	308	4	4
Total	3,509	3,366	3,209	2,892	2,488	36	

South Course

Hole	Pro	Champion	Regulation	Rookie	Forward	Par	HCP
1	401	385	355	325	266	4	4
2	411	395	377	347	282	4	6
3	401	389	365	335	273	4	5
4	391	355	345	325	255	4	7
5	161	150	140	125	90	3	9
6	580	557	539	513	425	5	2
7	442	430	416	395	308	4	3
8	595	562	545	518	479	5	1
9	201	183	171	140	85	3	8
Total	3,583	3,406	3,253	3,023	2,463	36	

especially fiendish, fashioning one bunker so deep that it has been dubbed "Halfway to Hell" and another with steps that is "The Coffin."

No matter the level of your game, no matter how accurate your shots, figure on spending part of your round honing your sand game. There's so much sand — 25 acres — that it isn't treated as a hazard. Rather, the sand at Sand Barrens is played as "waste area," meaning golfers will be able to ground their clubs in the sand, even take divots on practice swings.

Rakes will be provided, but there will be no real effort to maintain the waste areas in the manner of a sand trap. If a shot comes to rest in a footprint or a rut, local rules allow golfers to lift the ball, smooth the lie with a foot or rake, and replace the ball — a "smoothie" is what Gaffney called it.

On several holes the only way to get from the green to the next tee is to walk directly through the sand. "But that's the way Fry designed it," Gaffney said.

All this might seem intimidating, but don't be scared away. On a number of holes, the sand is as much psychological as it is strategic. It may run along the far side of a fairway, or directly in front of the tee, but it often will catch only the truly errant shot. In addition, if you choose correctly from the five sets of tees, you can generally avoid those jaw-dropping forced carries.

There is also the matter of the sand itself. It wasn't trucked in; it was unearthed from the course site. So, unlike the fluffy, fine-grained sand found in the bunkers on your course back home, the sand at the Sand Barrens is coarse and pebble-laden, reducing the number of buried lies and making approach shots much more manageable.

Fry, a young designer who is increasingly making a name for himself, has provided a healthy sampling of short and long holes, straightaways and doglegs, even a couple of par 3s over water. The greens, for the most part, are huge and undulating. On most holes, Fry has given higher handicappers a choice of rolling the ball onto the green.

As you wind your way around the course, no matter what else a hole features, you always come back to the sand. But on some holes, the sand is more predominant than others.

Take the eighth hole, a par 5, the No. 1 handicap hole. Standing on the tee, you half expect to see Lawrence of Arabia riding up on a camel. Sand runs up the right side of the fairway about halfway to the green, then meanders across the fairway, then continues up the left side the rest of the hole. On top of that, it's long — 562 yards. After a great 3-wood off the tee, and another from the fairway, I still had 100 yards in to the green.

My favorite holes include two of the shorter holes: the 285-yard, par-4 14th, which big hitters will be tempted to go for on their drive; and the 17th, a downhill, 179-yard par 3 over sand and water, into a sloped, tiered green roughly the size of Grandma's Christmas tree farm.

From the pro tees, Sand Barrens measures 6,902 yards, well beyond the 6,300-yard national average. As you move forward on the tees, you can choose to play the course from 6,615 yards, 6,304, 5,857 or even 4,817.

Sand Barrens hasn't yet been evaluated by the U.S. Golf Association for slope or course rating, but based on a round last week from the champion tees — normally the blue tees, but here they're yellow — my guess is it'll come in somewhere in the low- to mid-130s for slope. That's a serious test.

Will you like Sand Barrens? You'll either love it or vow never to come back until Castro turns capitalist.

— May 18, 1997

If You Go

Address: 1765 Route 9 North, Swainton, N.J

Phone: 609-465-3555.

Web: www.sandbarrens.com

Greens fees: Weekends, $79 to ride, $79 to walk; weekdays, $69 to ride, $69 to walk.

Carts: Walking permitted anytime, but cart fees are included.

Amenities: Moderately stocked pro shop, snack bar, driving range.

Rating: Unique, first-class resort course well worth a try.

Gloucester

C O U N T Y

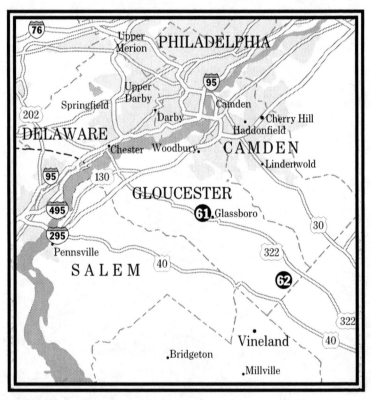

61. Scotland Run
62. White Oaks Country Club

61. Scotland Run

It may well be worth the price

Like many people, I suppose, I had already heard good things about South Jersey's newest upscale daily-fee course, Scotland Run, in Williamstown.

The word was that it was built on and around an old quarry, making for some beautiful holes and difficult carries over mess you didn't want to get into. It had bent grass from tee to green, which is a must these days. And it was the latest work from Jersey's own Stephen Kay, whose previous courses include the respected, high-end resort tracks Blue Heron Pines and Harbor Pines at the Shore.

But as I stood in pro shop and plunked down my credit card only to hear, "$95, please," all I could think was: $95? On a Wednesday? This had better be good.

Well, Scotland Run was good. Very good. I wouldn't say it was so good I would pay $95 in the middle of the week too many times, but then maybe owner Chip Ottinger Sr. knows the market for quality daily-fee courses in South Jersey better than I do. And it is true that Scotland Run, open only since June 21, is still a work in progress.

"Salem, Gloucester and Cumberland Counties don't have any upscale facilities," Ottinger said last week. "I don't think we'll have a problem. It might be until the clubhouse is built. Then we'll be able to provide the total golf experience."

For now, Scotland Run's pro shop is in a renovated old house. But in the next few months, construction is slated to begin on a posh 28,000-square-foot clubhouse with a pro shop, locker rooms, grill room, and banquet facilities for 250 to 300.

As for the course, it's a test — with a 131 slope from the tips — and it has the familiar look and feel of Stephen Kay's other work, which is to say plenty of sand, plenty of picturesque views, and plenty of demanding golf holes.

All three — the sand, the views and the difficulty — come largely thanks to the old sand-and-gravel quarry that Ottinger's other business, a road construction company, excavated for 25 years. When the construction company had extracted all the sand and gravel it could, Ottinger opted to develop the quarry and some adjoining farmland into Scotland Run, a tough, first-rate 6,810-yard layout that draws its name from a creek that borders the property.

The back nine, where the old quarry mostly comes into play, is vastly superior to the front, not to mention much more scenic. In fact, if you're like me, through about five holes you'll be wondering how Scotland Run can expect to get away with $95 during the week, $105 on weekends.

Not that the front nine is bad; it isn't. It's just unremarkable as it wends its way through relatively wide-open flat-

Scorecard

Hole	Black	Blue	White	Green	Red	Par	HCP
1	520	510	493	470	420	5	10
2	454/414	435/395	418/378	392/352	371/331	4	4
3	370	365	332	271	241	4	8
4	165	153	143	112	90	3	18
5	457	451	431	394	367	4	2
6	315	312	303	265	230	4	12
7	372	357	340	302	285	4	14
8	406	385	353	304	281	4	6
9	223	212	191	167	135	3	16
Out	3,282	3,180	3,004	2,677	2,420	35	
10	545	510	492	468	438	5	11
11	404	374	338	318	302	4	13
12	465	445	434	380	290	4	1
13	217	200	172	155	130	3	9
14	315	304	275	252	238	4	15
15	164	153	140	135	118	3	17
16	402	375	360	332	272	4	7
17	486	461	421	372	363	4	3
18	530	514	502	465	439	5	5
In	3,528	3,336	3,134	2,877	2,590	36	
Total	**6,810**	**6,516**	**6,138**	**5,554**	**5,010**	**71**	

lands, much like several of the newer links-style courses in the region.

The first hole is a simple, straightforward par 5 that starts you off easy. The difficulty of the second, a 454-yard dogleg left bordered by woods, depends almost entirely on which of the hole's two greens are in play that day — that's right, Kay has designed a hole with two greens that can completely change the character of the hole.

The seventh, a short, dogleg par 4, is the first hole to bring the quarry into play, although nothing like what you'll encounter in later holes. But it is about then that you sense Scotland Run is going to get better.

By the time you make the turn, Scotland Run is starting to earn that $95.

The par-5 10th might be reachable by Tiger Woods and John Daly, but not by the likes of you and me. Not because it's overly long — it's 545 yards from the tips — but because the elevated green is well-protected behind a moat-like fairway bunker and an imposing wall of railroad ties. It's a 3-shot hole, for sure.

By the 12th, a long, rolling par 4 with the green hidden in a bowl, Scotland Run is truly picking up steam. Kay follows that with a beastly 217-yard par 3, over water, into an elevated green also guarded by a nasty-looking front bunker that creates narrow entryways on either side. It's a lot of golf shot to fly that green, then stop it.

The three closing holes — especially the 16th and 18th — are the memories most golfers will take away from Scotland Run. The par-4 dogleg 16th is truly a sight — and a monster shot over a yawning chasm of sand quarry into a fairly narrow landing area. Bite off as much as you want, fully aware of the risk and reward.

The day I was there, some poor hack in the group in front of ours was down in there, flailing away. When he finally got the ball up and out, he raised his arms in exultation.

The par-5 dogleg 18th, however, is the true signature hole.

The tee shot is downhill, with a lake on the right coming into play for long hitters. But for any hope of reaching the distant, uphill green in two strokes, you've got to get it down there, right? Right.

Even with a good drive, the sensible second shot is to forget about attempting the 200-yard-plus carry over the awesome expanse of sand and water. But if you're a single-digit player, you'll itch to go for the green. What the heck, give it a shot.

In a couple of places, Scotland Run's yardage book makes reference to holes with a Pine Valley look and feel. Make no mistake, while the course does offer a taste of the kind of waste areas you will find at the famous neighboring course, the similarity ends there.

At Pine Valley, every hole is enshrouded by trees. Not so at Scotland Run, where Ottinger's construction company in the distance detracts from the overall viewing experience.

There is one other, um, situation you should know about. Although it's nearly invisible behind the trees near the 18th green, there is a township sewage treatment plant lurking nearby. The day I was there, it, too, came into play, just as surely as the quarry, if you get my drift.

Ottinger says this is not usually a problem — only once before did the plant rear its stinky head, and the township quickly took care of it. For the sake of anyone spending time at Scotland Run, let's hope they come up with a permanent solution.

Overall, though, Scotland Run is a winner.

— Aug. 1, 1999

If You Go

Address: Route 322 and Fries Mill Road, Williamstown.

Phone: 856-863-3737.

Web site: www.scotlandrun.com

Greens fees: Weekdays, $95 with cart. Friday through Sunday, $105 with cart.

Carts: Walking permitted anytime, although cart fees are included.

Amenities: Small, sparely stocked temporary pro shop. Driving range and putting green. Posh clubhouse planned to open next fall.

Rating: Pricey, but a badly needed addition to the upscale daily-fee scene in South Jersey. A fine course, with fine amenities to follow. A work in progress that has definite promise.

62. White Oaks Country Club

One of S. Jersey's rare jewels

White Oaks Country Club, a mid-priced, top-quality, semi-private facility near Vineland, deserves to turn heads on the daily-fee golf scene.

I had a good feeling about this place as soon as I turned into the parking lot. For one thing, even though the club staged its grand opening only a month ago, the comfortable clubhouse was up and running. Thank goodness, not another construction trailer. But best of all, the golf course did not disappoint.

At 6,510 yards, par 71, and with a slope of slightly above-average 118, White Oaks is plenty of course for most golfers. It has wide-open holes and also tight, tree-lined fairways. It has waste areas, and it has a little water to negotiate. It makes you think and it makes you work, but it won't beat you to death.

Do I see White Oaks supplanting Blue Heron Pines and Harbor Pines as the main attractions in South Jersey? No. Do I think we're looking at another solid 3½-star, perhaps even 4-star course in golf travel books? Yes.

White Oaks also has an interesting story. It's owned by a couple of young brothers, Arret Dobson, 29, and Emory Dobson, 26, who inherited the family business, Dobson Construction Inc., a few years ago when their parents were killed in a plane crash.

Rather than try to run the company, the brothers, both passionate golfers, decided to sell it and build a golf course they could run together. Once they found a suitable tract amid the Pine Barrens, the Dobsons brought in Billy Casper Golf as a consultant. Steve Phillipone, a staff designer from Casper, routed the course, but most of the shaping and detail work were done by Michael Gaffney, the onetime general manager of Sand Barrens now working in golf-course construction.

What I liked most about White Oaks was that it's just a good, solid golf course. It has enough muscle and enough risk-and-reward to interest a single-digit handicapper, yet it shouldn't overwhelm beginners or discourage high-handicappers.

For instance, take the par-5 seventh, a 621-yard dogleg right. From the back tees, it takes a 210-yard tee shot to clear trouble and safely reach the fairway. Then you have a decision to make: Bite off a big chunk of the dogleg by blowing a fairway wood over the yawning waste area and between two towering trees already dubbed the "goal posts," or, for the faint of heart, tiptoe your way around the sandy death via the wraparound fairway provided.

There's not a lousy par 3 on the course. The first (No. 4) goes 197 yards, the second (No. 8) 190, and the third (No. 12) 168, although it may be the most deceiving. But the star of the

Scorecard

Hole	Blue	White	Gold	Red	Par	Pace of Play
1	368	349	325	320	4	:14
2	342	312	292	270	4	:14
3	487	455	415	400	5	:16
4	197	176	134	124	3	:13
5	343	328	306	302	4	:14
6	410	382	366	363	4	:15
7	621	562	530	446	5	:16
8	190	179	150	143	3	:13
9	375	350	320	310	4	:15
Out	3,333	3,093	2,838	2,678	36	2:10
10	570	552	530	518	5	:16
11	438	419	392	308	4	:14
12	168	140	130	114	3	:13
13	401	388	364	360	4	:14
14	338	325	283	274	4	:13
15	344	322	290	254	4	:14
16	312	296	254	235	4	:14
17	240	220	202	170	4	:13
18	366	358	320	284	4	:14
In	3,177	3,020	2,765	2,517	35	2:05
Total	**6,510**	**6,113**	**5,603**	**5,195**	**71**	**4:15**

par 3s is definitely the last one, the 17th, a 240-yard behemoth that plays downhill and into a slippery green.

White Oaks also has a good mix of par 4s, ranging from relatively short and testy doglegs that demand deft approach shots to a couple of long, straight holes that can give you fits. Most every green can be attacked by land or air.

In the end, you come away from White Oaks with a sense that it probably won't be the star of South Jersey, but it will be a course that earns a loyal and sizable following.

— June 25, 2000

If You Go

Address: 2951 Dutch Mill Rd., Newfield.

Phone: 856-697- 8900.

Greens fees: Weekends, $69 to ride, $69 to walk. Weekdays, $54 to ride, $54 to walk.

Carts: Walking permitted anytime, but cart fees are included.

Web site: www.whiteoaksgolf.com

Amenities: New, comfortable clubhouse and restaurant; well-stocked pro shop; banquet facilities. No driving range yet.

Rating: A good challenge for low handicappers, but not overwhelming for higher handicappers. A good mix of holes. A hint of Sand Barrens and Pine Barrens in it, but not nearly as extreme. Definitely worth a try.

Other Gloucester County Courses

Beckett Golf Club
Kings Highway, Swedesboro.
856-467-4702
Weekdays, $20 to walk, $28 to ride; weekends, $24 to walk, $37 to ride.

Maple Ridge Golf Club
1705 Glassboro Rd., Sewell.
856-468-3542
Weekdays, $23 to walk, $28 to ride; weekends, $45.

Pitman Golf Course
501 Pitman Rd., Mantua.
856-589-6688
Weekdays, $18 (residents), $27 (non-residents) to walk, $32 (residents), $33 (non-residents) to ride; weekends, $23 (residents), $37 (non-residents) to walk, $41 (residents), $47 (non-residents) to ride.

Washington Township Municipal Golf Course
197 Fries Mill, Turnersville.
856-227-1435
$11 weekdays; $13 weekends

Westwood Golf Club
850 Kings Highway, Woodbury.
856-845-2000
Weekdays, $22 to walk, $36 to ride; weekends $49 to ride.

Mercer

C O U N T Y

63. Miry Run Country Club
64. Mountain View Golf Club
65. Mercer Oaks Golf Course

63. Miry Run Country Club

Nothing special, nothing gained at this course

I almost always take the bait when I see an ad for some course that's "formerly private, now public." For some reason, I feel as if I'm intruding where I don't belong. So, off I went to Miry Run Country Club in Robbinsville, just on the other side of Trenton.

In no time at all, I was eagerly striding across the lawn toward the pro shop and the first tee.

Four hours later, I was headed back to my car, reminded that "private" doesn't necessarily mean "exclusive" or "excellent."

Not that Miry Run is a lousy golf course. It is not. Of course, I also wouldn't call it especially interesting, inspired or inviting, either. Was it a wasted round, a misspent afternoon? No. Would I drive the better part of an hour to play there again? No.

Despite a few bright spots and even a couple of intriguing holes, overall, Miry Run struck me as a rather tired and ordinary golf course. And that's before you even factor in the small airport next door that cannot be ignored.

"Wait till we get to the 16th and 17th," said Bob, a semi-regular at Miry Run, who saw me looking at the airport as we stood on the first tee.

At the 16th hole, a long par 4 and one of the two or three best holes on the course, the runway runs parallel to the fairway. At the 17th, a brutish 231-yard par 3, the green sits at the end of the runway.

Not good.

Open since 1963, Miry Run operated as Sharon Country Club until the early '80s, when it was aptly renamed Skyview Country Club. It became Miry Run, so named for a creek that slashes across the course, when a Pennsylvania family bought the facility in 1995 and took it semiprivate. It has been welcoming daily-fee customers ever since, but began advertising in earnest only recently.

Miry Run draws regulars from the Trenton area, of course, but lately more and more folks are fleeing the golf congestion of New York and North Jersey for a comparatively cheap ($40 with cart on weekends) and tranquil round down around Trenton.

"It's a good, affordable course, and the bar-restaurant has a nice atmosphere," head pro Jeff Bonicky said. "The course looks easy, but when it was private and they played some of the country club events here, it played tougher than many of the surrounding country clubs."

From the tips, Miry Run can play as long as 6,849 yards, which is significant, but the rather average 116 slope is proof

Scorecard

Hole	Blue	White	Red	Par	Red Par	HCP	Red HCP
1	543	528	463	5	5	15	6
2	166	151	1222	3	3	13	12
3	386	371	330	4	4	1	2
4	382	367	300	4	4	9	14
5	520	505	460	5	5	17	8
6	385	370	305	4	4	7	16
7	394	379	341	4	4	5	10
8	197	182	167	3	3	11	18
9	405	389	354	4	4	3	4
Out	3,378	3,242	2,842	36	36		
10	221	206	141	3	3	10	17
11	405	390	355	4	4	4	5
12	403	388	375	4	4	6	1
13	345	330	315	4	4	18	15
14	377	362	347	4	4	12	9
15	552	537	422	5	5	8	11
16	434	419	400	4	5	2	3
17	231	216	170	3	3	14	13
18	503	488	435	5	5	16	7
In	3,471	3,336	2,960	36	37		
Total	**6,849**	**6,578**	**5,802**	**72**	**73**		

that the course will not have most single-digit handicappers groping for their "A" games.

In some ways, Miry Run leaves me scratching my head. Granted, the airport is an annoyance, and the course is generally flat and forgiving, with midsized, push-up greens. But on the plus side, it's plenty long (the par 5s all exceed 500 yards), it's got a few doglegs and fairway bunkers that demand well-placed tee shots, and water comes into play on a few holes. The par 3s may be the strongest feature of the course. It's also priced quite reasonably.

Still, if you ask me, when you add it all up, Miry Run is merely adequate, nothing more.

— April 30, 2000

If You Go

Address: 106B Sharon Rd., Robbinsville.

Phone: 609-259-1010.

Greens fees: Weekdays, $40 to walk, $55 to ride; weekends, $50 to ride.

Carts: Mandatory before 1 pm. on weekends.

Amenities: Moderately stocked pro shop, driving range, putting green, restaurant-bar, snack bar on the course. Outings welcome.

Rating: Uninspired but adequate mid-priced daily-fee track. The airport is a factor.

64. Mountain View Golf Club

The earlier the better

If you want to get an idea of what it must be like to play golf in Japan, head over to Mountain View Golf Club in West Trenton, some warm Saturday about 3 a.m.

What you will see are carloads and vanloads of golfers who have been there an hour or so, drinking coffee, playing cards, and waiting for the starter to arrive at 4 a.m.

Why? At Mountain View, a quite decent track owned by the Mercer County Parks Department, the price is right for county residents ($13 on weekends) and there are no starting times — first-come, first-served.

And what do the early birds do after they sign up? They go back to drinking coffee and playing cards — or napping, if they can.

"Once they sign up, they can't leave the grounds," county park manager Lenny Dewrocki said. "You leave, you go to the back of the line."

Is Mountain View worth that kind of wait?

Hey, Augusta National isn't worth that. But Mountain View is not a bad layout at all. It's in decent shape, and on a weekday you may not have to wait at all.

Opened in 1958, Mountain View is the oldest of three courses owned by Mercer County. (The others are Princeton Golf Club and Mercer Oaks in Trenton.) Designed by a committee of forgotten architects and the parks commissioner, it was so named because it is the highest point in the county.

On certain holes, especially on the front nine, it is easy to believe that Mountain View was designed by a committee. The first three holes, in particular, are rather uninspired, short par 4s, all under 400 yards.

The front side gets better toward the end, but not enough to leave you wondering how the course earned a 2½ star rating from Golf Digest's Places to Play.

The back nine, however, is considerably better, beginning with back-to-back par 5s at the 10th and 11th.

The 11th, at only 440 yards from the white tees, is short for a par 5, but it is a genuinely attractive hole. Standing on the tee, gazing at the creek on the left, the trees on the right, fairway bunkers in the distance, and a decidedly sloping fairway, it's enough to make you think this course might get better.

It does. The 12th, 405 yards from the whites, is another terrific hole — over a crest, a heavy tree line up the right side, another sloping fairway, and a small pond on the other side of the crest. Even if you crush your tee shot, you are facing a long iron into a small green protected by water and bunkers. Tough golf hole, even for better players.

That is followed by a nice downhill par 3 over a creek,

Scorecard

Hole	Blue	White	Red	Par	Ladies' Par	Strokes
1	390	365	330	4	4	13
2	375	350	300	4	4	15
3	350	335	290	4	4	16
4	235	190	165	3	3	11
5	545	450	410	5	5	5
6	410	380	340	4	4	8
7	145	135	125	3	3	18
8	420	395	300	4	4	1
9	425	405	330	4	4	3
Out	3,295	3,005	2,590	35	35	
10	530	490	460	5	5	9
11	470	440	375	5	5	7
12	440	405	350	4	4	2
13	165	140	110	3	3	17
14	375	340	320	4	4	10
15	345	330	310	4	4	10
16	430	390	380	4	5	4
17	210	190	155	3	3	6
18	515	490	450	5	5	14
In	3,480	3,215	2,910	37	38	
Total	**6,775**	**6,220**	**5,500**	**72**	**73**	

which is followed by a short (340 yards), steep, uphill par 4. The 15th is another short par 4, only 330 yards, but it is a classic, sweeping, tree-lined hole like you might find at a grand old country club.

In the end, whatever the front side lacks, the back side makes up for, both in beauty and in difficulty (the back side has three par 5s).

Mountain View, with its sort of working-man's feel, will never be confused with the fancy clubs in the area, nor with the great golf courses. Then again, you don't have to look far to find a lot less enjoyable courses.

— Nov. 10, 1996

If You Go

Address: Bear Tavern Rd., West Trenton.

Phone: 609-882-4093.

Greens fees: Weekends, $28 to ride plus $25 per cart, $28 to walk. Weekdays, $24 to ride plus $25 per cart, $24 to walk. (Mercer County resident-members pay reduced fees).

Carts: Walk permitted anytime.

Amenities: Moderately stocked pro shop, grass driving range, snack bar.

Rating: Great price, great back nine.

65. Mercer Oaks Golf Course

Not too long on frills, but it offers challenge

The small clubhouse/pro shop looks more like the double-wide office for a construction site. The halfway house is actually a halfway trailer.

But so what?

Five-year-old Mercer Oaks Golf Course in West Windsor Township, is a fine, fun course that is starting to turn heads.

The designers, Bill Love and Brian Ault of the Maryland design firm of Ault, Clark & Associates, created an enjoyable place to play for most golfers of any level.

Golf Digest's 4,200 Best Places to Play gives Mercer Oaks 2¹/₂ stars, which is somewhere between, "Good, not great, but not a rip-off, either," and "Very good. Tell a friend it's worth getting off the highway to play."

That's a fair assessment. Unless your current daily-fee course is a dog track, Mercer Oaks probably won't blow you away. But it's a solid, challenging course, and definitely better than several public tracks in the area.

From the tips, Mercer Oaks plays long — 7,017 yards — but it goes a much more manageable 6,305 from the whites, right at the national average. From the blue tees, the slope is a respectable 126 (and 120 from the whites).

The course is fair — no cheap or trick holes — and scenic in several spots.

What may be most appealing is that Mercer Oaks is quite playable, no matter what your level of golf. The fairways are for the most part generous and forgiving, many offering mounding to help keep errant tee shots from bounding into the woods.

Even better, especially for higher-handicappers, are the clear openings to virtually every green, allowing approach shots to roll onto the putting surface. On far too many modern courses today, greens are guarded in front by yawning bunkers or wetlands that gobble approach shots without mercy.

That's fine for the low-handicapper who doesn't flinch at such hazards. But for lesser golfers, you're talking disaster. So credit Love and Ault with knowing their clientele and providing an option.

"When you're building public courses, your market is the middle of the road," said Frank Ragazzo, executive director of the Mercer County Park Commission and the man who oversaw the building of Mercer Oaks.

"You can't make it so difficult they become frustrated and don't come out to play. You want a course that's pretty, not boring, yet good enough that it's challenging."

That's what they have in Mercer Oaks. It's one of three

Scorecard

Hole	Blue	Gold	White	Red	Par	Ladies' Par	HCP
1	395	375	360	320	4	4	15
2	365	350	335	310	4	4	13
3	445	400	375	340	4	4	5
4	535	520	505	445	5	5	7
5	213	170	160	110	3	3	9
6	454	435	400	360	4	4	1
7	600	550	535	460	5	5	3
8	165	160	155	110	3	3	17
9	380	365	350	275	4	4	11
Out	3,552	3,325	3,175	2,730	36	36	
10	390	380	360	325	4	4	14
11	450	400	380	340	4	4	2
12	425	400	380	340	4	4	6
13	160	150	130	115	3	3	18
14	355	340	325	300	4	4	16
15	505	490	465	415	5	5	12
16	240	200	185	155	3	3	10
17	405	385	365	300	4	4	4
18	535	525	510	335	5	5	8
In	3,465	3,305	3,130	2,625	36	36	
Total	**7,017**	**6,630**	**6,305**	**5,355**	**72**	**72**	

courses owned and operated by the Mercer County Park Commission — the others are Mountain View in West Trenton and Princeton Golf Club in Princeton. Mercer Oaks is newer and the only course the county built on its own.

Mercer Oaks first opened for a month in the fall of '91, but the first full season was '92. It could use a few more years of maturity, but its youthfulness isn't a real problem.

The most boring hole is probably the first, an ever-so-slight 375-yard plain-Jane dogleg that starts you off nice and easy.

Things pick up after that — there are doglegs, water holes and fairways with huge fairway bunkers.

Although the front side boasts a 600-yarder (the seventh) from the blue tees, the best hole going out is probably the ninth. It's a short 365-yard par 4, dogleg right, that will require most players to hit a long iron or fairway wood from the tee, then fly their second shot over a small lake into a green nestled against the water.

The best holes at Mercer Oaks, however, are probably the three finishing holes. The 16th is a long par-3, 240 yards from the blue tees, into an elevated green guarded by bunkers and mounding.

The 17th is perhaps the most picturesque. It's a 405-yard, par 4 with a lake all the way up the right side that squeezes the fairway at about the point a good tee shot would land. Again, like No. 9, the second shot is a testy shot over water, if your tee shot has hugged the right side of the fairway. The 18th, a long par 5, is another nice hole that wraps up a nice round.

If there's a gripe to be lodged against Mercer Oaks, as well as the two other county courses, it's that credit cards aren't accepted. But Ragazzo said that, too, will change with the installation of a new computer system.

Mercer Oaks is not to be confused with a ritzy country club. But if you take the plunge once, there's a good chance you'll go back.

— May 20, 1997

If You Go

Address: Village Road West, West Windsor Township.

Phone: 609-936-9603.

Greens fees: For Mercer County residents, weekdays, $17 to walk; weekends, $19 to walk. For nonresidents, weekdays, $34 to walk; weekends, $38 to walk.

Carts: Walking is permitted anytime. $25 per cart.

Amenities: Minimally stocked pro shop; snack trailer; grass driving range. Outings welcome on Mondays.

Other Mercer County Courses

Avalon Golf Club
1510 Rt. 9 North, Cape May Court House.
609-465-4653
Weekdays, $59; weekends, $72 . Carts are mandatory.

Cape May National Golf Club
Route 9 & Florence Ave. Cape May.
609-884-1563
Weekdays, $57, (Mon.-Thurs.); Fri.-Sun., $69.

Ocean City Golf Course
26th and Bay Ave., Ocean City.
609-399-1315
$9 everyday.

Ponderlodge
7 Shawmont Ave., Villas.
609-886-8065
$33 to walk, $45 to ride.

Ocean

C O U N T Y

66. Pine Barrens Golf Club

66. Pine Barrens Golf Club

Another Shore course offers up sandy challenges

There was a time when finding a top-notch daily-fee golf course at the Jersey Shore was about as likely as stumbling across a decent Chinese restaurant in rural Mississippi.

Things have changed. Blue Heron Pines, Harbor Pines, Cape May National and Sand Barrens — all relative newcomers — have helped improve the Shore's public golf landscape. Now comes still another quality, upscale public course "downashore," albeit a little farther north, near Toms River: Pine Barrens Golf Club.

Pine Barrens is on the pricey side — but, frankly, that puts it in the mid-price range in the growing market of "private club for a day" facilities.

How about the course itself? Think Sand Barrens, the three-year-old upscale layout near Cape May, only slightly milder and more forgiving.

Pine Barrens features the same vast expanses of natural sandy waste areas on many holes, the same towering pine trees bordering fairways, and the same generous landing areas and sizable greens. Pine Barrens, though, doesn't seem quite as intimidating for the mid- and high-handicapper as Sand Barrens.

"It is similar and does have the same look, except it's a little more peaceful because it's off the beaten path," Rudy Virga, Pine Barrens' head pro and general manager, said last week.

Just as at Sand Barrens, more than a few holes at Pine Barrens can be visually foreboding from the tee — the kind of waste areas first perfected at Pine Valley often run alongside the fairway from tee to green. Truth is, more than not, they cause trouble for only the truly sprayed shot.

At Pine Barrens, developer and designer Eric Bergstol has also made sure that only players venturing back to the championship tees face long carries over trouble. In most cases, fairways are plenty wide before funneling down as they wend their way closer to the green. Rare is the green that doesn't afford the weaker player or high-handicapper the chance to run the ball up onto the putting surface.

Even if you find your way into one of Pine Barrens' waste areas, recovery doesn't require a yeoman's work. As at Sand Barrens, local rules allow you to ground your club, remove loose pebbles, and even take a practice hack or two. Sand around the greens, where rakes are provided, will be treated as traditional sand hazards.

All in all, with five sets of tees, Pine Barrens can provide as little or as much of a challenge as you want to bite off.

"We're not all tour players," Virga said. "This course is

Scorecard

Hole	Black	Blue	White	Yellow	Red	Par	HCP
1	389	365	333	289	263	4	12
2	409	383	354	306	276	4	16
3	204	190	183	165	140	3	6
4	453	427	391	364	320	4	2
5	187	172	161	144	112	3	14
6	562	546	521	480	450	5	10
7	302	293	271	248	213	4	18
8	437	415	390	372	333	4	8
9	558	558	495	448	409	5	4
Out	3,501	3,313	3,099	2,816	2,516	36	
10	446	424	384	312	282	4	9
11	377	362	339	321	298	4	7
12	175	164	149	122	104	3	17
13	396	378	359	337	310	4	13
14	226	212	195	174	150	3	3
15	518	501	488	443	414	5	11
16	415	391	365	340	316	4	15
17	469	456	406	382	349	4	1
18	602	572	556	520	486	5	5
In	3,624	3,460	3,241	2,951	2,709	36	
Total	**7,125**	**6,773**	**6,340**	**5,767**	**5,225**	**72**	

designed to accept shots by average players."

From the black tees, the course measures a whopping 7,125 yards and plays to a 74.2 rating and a 131 slope. With that kind of length, we're talking plenty of doglegs, a couple of unreachable par 5s, long irons into several par 4s, and one super 226-yard par 3 over sand, sand, sand.

That said, even most mid-level players should be able to take on Pine Barrens from the proper set of forward tees. From the middle tees, it plays 6,340 yards to a 70.6 rating and 124 slope. That should be manageable. From the forward tees, the course can play as short as 5,225 yards.

Several holes stand out. The seventh is only 302 yards from the championship tees, but it's a bogey waiting to happen. A nasty ditch slashes diagonally across the fairway, forcing a layup with a mid-iron to long-iron. If the pin is tucked close to the front, more than a few suckers will dump it in the ditch trying to make birdie.

There are no bad par 3s at Pine Barrens, but the 14th — the beast over the desert — is the strongest and most visually striking. From the black tees, it's 226 yards — much of that over waste area — into a large green that is choked on the right by sand and bordered on the left by a slope.

The four closing holes are perhaps the most consistent stretch of holes on the course, especially the dogleg par-5 15th (518 yards), with trouble all up the right side, and the sweeping dogleg par-5 18th. Even with a big tee shot at the 18th, you're looking at 300 yards to get home.

Pine Barrens is still a work in progress. An impressive-looking clubhouse is under construction, but it won't be completed until mid to late summer. For now, there are virtually no club-like amenities; the pro shop operates out of a trailer.

In addition, the course will need a year or two of maturing before reaching its full potential. For now, there remain patches where turf has been recently laid down.

If you're eager to try a new, quality, challenging track,

however, none of this should discourage you from heading to Pine Barrens.

— April 11, 1999

If You Go

Address: 540 S. Hope Chapel Rd., Jackson.

Phone: 877-746-3227.

Greens fees: Weekends, $112, cart included.   Weekdays, $97, cart included.

Carts: Walking permitted anytime; however, cart fees are included.

Web site: www.pinebarrensgolf.com

Amenities: Posh clubhouse with pro shop, locker rooms, restaurant and veranda; excellent driving range.

Rating: First-rate upscale public.

Other Ocean County Courses

Bey Lea Golf Course
1536 North Bay Avenue, Toms River.
732-349-0566
Weekdays, $14 (residents) $16 (non-residents);
weekends, $28 (residents) $32 (non-residents). Carts are $26.

Cedar Creek Golf Course
Forest Hills Parkway, Bayville.
732-269-4460
Weekdays, $27; weekends, $31. Carts are $14 per person.

Forge Pond County Golf Course
301 Chambers Bridge Rd., Brick Township.
732-920-8899
Weekdays, $14 (residents), $24(non-residents);
weekends, $16 (res.), $28 (non-residents).

Lakewood Country Club
West County Line Road and Hope Rd., Lakewood.
732-364-8899
Weekdays, $27; weekends, $47. Carts are $30,
and are mandatory on weekends.

Ocean County Golf Course at Atlantis
Country Club Blvd., Tuckertown.
609-296-2444
Weekdays, $18 (residents), $35 (non-residents);
weekends, $24 (residents), $42 (non-residents).

Delaware

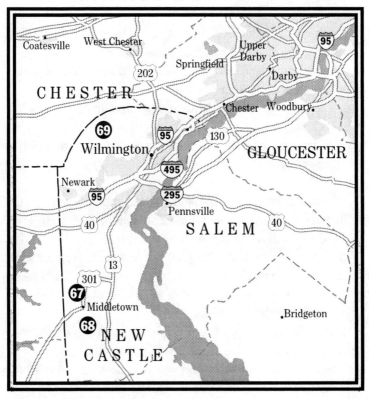

67. Back Creek Golf Club
68. Frog Hollow Golf Club
69. Three Little Bakers Country Club

67. Back Creek Golf Club

Challenge at right price

The last time somebody built a public golf course in Delaware, Richard Nixon was president. The wait is over.

Back Creek Golf Club. If you play daily-fee golf, write it down.

Given the spate of new private and public courses in the region — several are still under construction — it's hard to say exactly where Back Creek will stand when all the earth-movers finally grind to a halt. But it's absolutely fair and accurate to say that if you're a public-course player, Back Creek should go on your "must try it" list.

It's long, it's lush, it's challenging, and, although it wends its way through a housing development, never once do you feel hemmed in. Best of all, Back Creek is very reasonably priced at only $48 during the week and $62 on weekends — with a cart.

"People around here think that's too much," said Allen Liddicoat, the Back Creek managing partner who largely designed the rolling, mostly links-style layout.

Maybe it is expensive for golfers from rural New Castle County, about 20 minutes south of Wilmington. But trust me, at that price, for what Back Creek is, Liddicoat won't hear a peep out of Philadelphians.

How to describe Back Creek? Open only a few months, it's really still a work in progress. But so far, so good.

The clubhouse, though temporary, is nothing fancy — a perfectly adequate modular building. Not some trailer, but an actual building. (Note: Other than a soft-drink machine, there is no food service yet, so pack a snack; the snack bar is expected to open within the next couple of weeks.) Because of some quirk of state law, Liddicoat says the permanent club-house can't be built for another few years, when better streets are in place to accommodate the increased traffic.

The golf course is another story — a success story.

Built on farmland that was originally owned by the first governor of Delaware, Joshua Clayton, Back Creek is laid out across what is essentially a flat, ordinary piece of real estate. No problem — not even for a developer who had never designed a course.

It's not as if Liddicoat is an egomaniac. It's just that he did the research on what the market would bear in terms of greens fees and decided he was the biggest-name architect he could afford. An avid golfer himself, he embarked on his own education program.

"I read every book on course architecture I could find and attended every seminar I could get to," Liddicoat said. Next, he sat down with David Horne of Architerra PC in Allentown, and together they came up with what was both good and pos-

Scorecard

Hole	Back Creek	New Castle	Kent	Sussex	Par	Timer	HCP	Ladies' HCP
1	417	384	360	307	4	:14	16	10
2	210	182	168	126	3	:28	14	16
3	450	426	415	301	4	:43	2	4
4	355	341	325	274	4	:57	12	12
5	541	505	480	408	5	1:12	8	2
6	341	319	300	201	4	1:27	6	14
7	433	386	366	288	4	1:41	10	8
8	156	137	116	93	3	1:53	18	18
9	460	438	414	293	4	2:08	4	6
Out	3,354	3,118	2,944	2,291	35	2:08		
10	460	435	405	287	4	:15	3	13
11	530	496	470	409	5	:30	9	3
12	446	396	365	314	4	:44	11	11
13	462	440	407	339	4	:59	1	5
14	191	173	159	98	3	1:12	17	17
15	413	390	353	317	4	1:25	13	7
16	540	500	480	450	5	1:41	5	1
17	170	152	137	109	3	1:54	15	15
18	437	405	385	301	4	2:08	7	9
In	3,649	3,387	3,161	2,624	36	2:08		
Total	**7,003**	**6,505**	**6105**	**4,915**	**71**	**4:16**		

sible.

The result is a playable, pleasurable course that's open and devoid of trees in places, yet something of a more traditional park-land course in others.

Depending on how much you want to bite off, Back Creek can play as long as 7,003 yards from the back tees, or as short as 4,915 yards from up front. Front or back, it's no cake walk: 134 slope from the tips, 126 slope up close.

Where the land is utterly flat, Liddicoat and Horne have added contours and framed the holes with mounds and knolls. By diverting water, they have also created three man-made ponds that come into play on six holes. With the aid of dump trucks, they have added 81 bunkers for your golfing misery.

Granted, all that may make Back Creek seem somehow contrived, but it doesn't feel that way. For my money, Back Creek will eventually debut at a solid 3½ stars in *Golf Digest's 4,200 Best Places to Play.*

The front and back have nice stretches of holes. It begins with the fourth, a short, par 4 dogleg that forces you to decide whether to lay up in front of a marshy area off the tee or try to bomb one over. The second shot is into an elevated well-bunkered green.

The fifth is a very reachable (505 yards on the New Castle course) dogleg par 5 over a crest, followed by a another short but tricky uphill dogleg par 4.

On the inward nine, the 13th, a 440-yard straightaway par 4, requires two nice shots to get home and avoid the pond that wraps around the left side and bunkers flanking the front.

That's followed by a mid-length, slightly downhill par 3 with a saddleback green and a huge collection bunker in front. The par 5 dogleg 16th is also reachable, if you keep your tee shot far enough left. But too far left is wet, and too far right is in the woods.

One of the nicest aspects about Back Creek is it won't torture the mid- or high-handicapper. Liddicoat and Horne have made sure to provide avenues to run the ball up to most greens. But low-handicappers looking to go low will often find themselves firing at pins tucked behind bunkers and mounds. For a first-time designer, Liddicoat can slap himself on the back.

— April 24, 1998

If You Go

Address: Churchtown Road, Middletown.

Phone: 302-378-6499

Web site: www.backcreekgc.com

Greens Fees: Weekends, $62 to ride, $62 to walk. Friday's, $58 to ride, $58 to walk. Weekdays, $48 to ride, $48 to walk.

Carts: Walking permitted anytime, but cart fees are included

68. Frog Hollow Golf Club

New Delaware course boasts a fine back nine

When Allen Liddicoat unveiled Back Creek Golf Club in Middletown, four years ago, the obvious question was whether it was a fluke.

Even if Liddicoat was an avid golfer, how could a developer with no experience in golf-course architecture read a few books and attend a few seminars, then design a pleasurable, testy track that soon cracked Golfweek's list of the top 100 modern courses in America?

Who knows, but it turns out Back Creek wasn't a fluke.

With Frog Hollow Golf Club, which opened in August just five minutes up the road from Back Creek, Liddicoat has created another winner that is sure to attract carloads of golfers in search of a quality course for a reasonable price.

At 6,608 yards from the tips, Frog Hollow is respectable in length, but it doesn't necessarily require the long ball. With a course rating and slope that top out at 72.1/128, it's got plenty of bite without being too frustrating for the mid- and high-handicapper.

"What we tried to do was to build a slight upgrade from Back Creek but keep it at a modest cost," Liddicoat said last week. "A lot of people think it is tighter and tougher."

Liddicoat, who has continued his self-education in golf course design, brings new techniques to Frog Hollow that he hadn't yet learned when he undertook Back Creek. Specifically, with judicious use of 51 jagged, natural-looking bunkers, generous mounding, and midsized, undulating greens, he has created a course that has illusions, deceptions and nuances, and that demands thought and strategy.

He has also done it at a fair price. In a golf-course climate in which greens fees increasingly top $100, a round at Frog

Hollow can be had for $48 on weekdays, or $65 during the prime time of weekend mornings.

Frog Hollow is still a work in progress. The course is complete and in commendable condition, but the sizable clubhouse won't be finished until early summer. For many golfers, however, the bigger distraction in the coming months will be that Frog Hollow is the centerpiece of a golf course community that is still very much under construction.

Hammers pound, workers talk and laugh, curious potential home buyers cruise slowly by.

By the time Liddicoat was called in, the homesites had

East Course

Hole	Red	White	Green	Par	HCP	Green HCP
1	375	352	280	4	8	12
2	505	480	403	5	6	6
3	166	145	101	3	16	16
4	427	405	315	4	2	2
5	495	470	391	5	10	10
6	209	180	140	3	12	8
7	380	357	277	4	4	4
8	154	135	82	3	18	18
9	369	350	270	4	14	14
In	3,080	2,874	2,259	35		

West Course

Hole	Red	White	Green	Par	HCP	Green HCP
1	394	370	291	4	9	9
2	533	514	426	5	11	7
3	390	360	248	4	13	11
4	360	330	223	4	7	15
5	177	155	107	3	15	13
6	450	417	330	4	1	5
7	219	165	127	3	17	17
8	435	409	325	4	3	3
9	570	530	414	5	5	1
Out	3,528	3,250	2,491	36		
Total	6,608	6,124	4,750	71		

already been laid out for the flat, treeless slab property that would become the East Course, which is being played as the front nine.

Liddicoat did as much as he could to overcome the routing limitations on the East Course, moving tons of earth to create mounds to separate holes and letting native grasses grow to give it a linksy feel. Still, the result is an outward nine that's good but not great, and plagued by some awkward separations between green and tee on some holes that make walking the course out of the question for most golfers. It also makes for a front nine that isn't nearly as strong as the back nine, or West Course.

Ah, the back nine.

Here, where homesites are yet to come and Liddicoat had a much freer hand, Frog Hollow moves away from the construction and gets better with each successive hole.

My favorite stretch starts at the second hole on the West, or the 11th, an uphill 533-yard dogleg par 5 over a lake, where you can bite off as much of the water off the tee as you wish.

After a mid-length (390-yard) straightway par-4 follow-up, Liddicoat has you gulping over a short (360-yard) but dicey par 4.

"The island fairway," Liddicoat devilishly called it, referring to what isn't truly an island but has a pond to the left and to the right, pinching the landing area to perhaps 40 yards wide. Keep it in the short grass, however, and you're left with a little sand wedge into a green guarded by a hungry front bunker.

Next comes the first of two strong par 3s on the West Course — a 177-yard poke entirely over water onto an elevated green that juts out into the water. For the meek and mild, Liddicoat has provided a bailout area left and short of the green. Two holes later comes the 219-yard, par-3 seventh (or 16th), where wind, oceans of sand and a big, tiered green can give you fits.

The two closing holes are perhaps the best on the course.

The eighth on the West Course (17th) is a 435-yard, slightly uphill, lazy dogleg. Even for low handicappers, a big tee shot can leave almost 200 yards into a green that slopes away from you. Leak it to the right and you're into trees that run all the way up the right side; venture left and you're in a pond that protects the left front of the green.

The closing hole is a monster: 570 yards, with mounding left and right off the tee and a labyrinth of bunkers on the right awaiting an errant tee shot. Farther up the fairway, dead center, another yawning chasm of sand poses problems for the second shot. Can you clear it? Can you steer left or right? You won't know until you try.

— April 8, 2001

If You Go

Address: 1 E. Whittington Way, Middletown.

Phone: 302-376-6500.

Web site: www.froghollowgolf.com.

Greens fees: Monday through Thursday, $48; Friday, $58; Saturday, Sunday and holidays, $65. (All fees include cart.)

Carts: Walking permitted anytime, but cart fees are included. There are long stretches between some holes.

Amenities: The clubhouse and pro shop are to open in early summer.

Rating: A strong new addition as a challenging, mid-priced course. Links style. Housing on the East Course can be a distraction. Not a good walking course for most golfers.

69. Three Little Bakers Country Club

A sweet surprise

Ask golfers from Wilmington what they think about Three Little Bakers and don't be surprised if you get a blank stare and a "never heard of it."

They've heard of it all right — they just don't want you to hear about it.

Three Little Bakers Country Club — and yes, it has to be good with a name like that — is a hidden gem of a semiprivate golf course near Wilmington. It's hilly, it's tight, it's demanding, it's superbly conditioned. The greens are large and undulating. At least a half-dozen times during a round you'll stand on the tee and marvel at what a terrific golf hole you're about to play.

So, why have you probably not heard of it?

Because, basically, Three Little Bakers doesn't need to chase your business — there are so few public tracks in Delaware that people there already know about it.

"It is something of a secret," said head professional Dick Matthias. "It's a great little course that a lot of people don't know about. But we already get 40,000 rounds a year, and we can't handle much more."

Golf Digest's 4,200 Places to Play rates TLB three stars — and it's easily that. The course, which plays to a 130 slope and measures 6,609 yards from the back tees, has no bad holes, plenty of good holes, and at least six terrific holes.

Superintendent Steve Segui and his staff have the place groomed — manicured bent fairways and greens — as if it were a pricey country club instead of some public loop.

It's hard to pick a favorite hole. Would it be the fifth, a devilish, 410-yard par 4 that's way downhill, then doglegs around a lake on the left into a tight green?

Or the 17th, a 205-yard par 3 into a boomerang-shaped green with a nasty bunker guarding the front?

Or maybe the 18th, the 512-yard downhill, then sidehill, then uphill, dogleg left?

The drawbacks? There are several holes that wend their way through condo developments but, frankly, it's a small price to pay.

The course is part of a semiprivate country club and dinner-theater complex owned by three brothers who once were, literally, three little bakers. The Immediato brothers — Hugo, Nick and the late Al — were an acrobatic act during the big-band era. When one of them hurt his back, the brothers turned to baking, which they had learned from their immigrant parents.

The baking business became successful enough that they launched a dinner theater, Three Little Bakers, in Kennett

Scorecard

Hole	Back	Middle	Forward	Par	Ladies' Par	HCP	Forward HCP
1	167	148	129	3	3	18	16
2	392	363	317	4	4	4	2
3	369	343	265	4	4	10	14
4	363	342	324	4	4	14	4
5	410	373	310	4	4	2	6
6	399	377	315	4	4	6	8
7	504	478	402	5	5	12	10
8	186	165	112	3	3	16	18
9	524	484	379	5	5	8	12
Out	3,314	3,073	2,553	36	36		
10	381	356	331	4	4	11	5
11	383	364	347	4	4	5	3
12	206	183	164	3	3	17	15
13	423	402	302	4	4	7	17
14	163	153	142	3	3	13	7
15	439	415	401	4	5	3	9
16	583	554	443	5	5	1	1
17	205	185	152	3	3	15	11
18	512	480	374	5	5	9	13
In	3,295	3,092	2,656	35	36		
Total	**6,609**	**6,165**	**5,209**	**71**	**72**		

Square. By the early 1980s, they were looking for a larger facility, and they found it in what was then a private country club, Pike Creek Valley.

None of the brothers played golf, but the course, designed in the early '70s by Ed Ault (Toftrees, Waynesboro), was part of the deal, and they decided to continue operating it.

Three Little Bakers has 350 members, but the bulk of its play is daily-fee. You could do worse than join that bulk.

— June 15, 1997

If You Go

Address: 3542 Foxcroft Dr., Pike Creek Valley.

Phone: 302-737-1877.

Web site: www.tlbinc.com

Greens fees: Weekends, $52 to ride, $52 to walk. Weekdays, $47 to ride (Mon.-Thurs.), $47 to walk.

Carts: Walking permitted anytime, but cart fees are included

Amenities: Moderately stocked pro shop, bar and grill, banquet facilities; outings are welcome.

Rating: A shot-maker's hidden gem.

Maryland

70. Beechtree Golf Club
71. Bulle Rock
72. Chesapeake Bay Golf Club at Rising Sun
73. Greystone Golf Course

70. Beechtree Golf Club

Long and demanding, and certainly worth the trip

When he bought a parcel of old farmland here several years ago, developer Jim Knott's plan was to turn it into an industrial park. But Knott, an avid golfer, eventually thought better of it. Instead, he put in a call to golf course architect Tom Doak.

It was a wise decision.

The result is the year-old Beechtree Golf Club, another first-rate, upscale, daily-fee course in Aberdeen, along the I-95 corridor between Baltimore and Philadelphia.

If you don't mind the drive, and you don't have to dip into the kids' college fund for the $85 per round, Beechtree is definitely worth a try.

Think of Hartefeld National, of another "country club for a day" just over the Maryland border — you know, a bag drop where they scurry out to your car, a pro shop where they've got plenty of quality merchandise, a restaurant where you feel a little boorish if you don't take off your hat.

Best of all, if you prefer your golf courses long and demanding, think of a track that plays 7,023 yards from the tips, with a very intimidating course rating of 74.9 and a slope of 142.

A 142 slope is serious golf. Merion is 144 from the tips. Pebble Beach is 142. Even from the white tees, from which Beechtree measures just 6,086 yards, the slope goes 130, well above average. Playing a round at Beechtree this past week, I got the sense that Doak wouldn't have — couldn't have — settled for anything less.

The reason is simple. Doak, who also designed Stonewall, the very exclusive private club in Elverson, Pa., is an outspoken, somewhat controversial rising star among course architects. He wants very badly to be regarded among the handful of elites in the industry, and he can ill afford a misstep at this point in his career.

That made Beechtree quite the opportunity for him. Situated just six miles deeper into Maryland than the much-acclaimed Bulle Rock, Beechtree was a chance for Doak to go toe-to-toe with the legendary and even more controversial designer Pete Dye, under whom Doak apprenticed. Given the proximity to Bulle Rock, Beechtree was sort of the golf equivalent of the young football coach staring across the sideline at his mentor.

But, as Doak recently told Golf magazine, "I learned a long time ago that you don't try to outdo Pete Dye. You compete by building something different, but, hopefully, just as worthwhile."

While it doesn't offer quite the large-scale drama of Bulle

Scorecard

Hole	Black	Blue	White	Red	Par	HCP
1	432	414	355	313	4	7
2	186	162	126	103	3	15
3	347	337	294	260	4	17
4	234	204	185	170	3	13
5	426	394	363	274	4	9
6	466	397	378	303	4	3
7	529	487	460	433	5	11
8	588	575	555	493	5	1
9	432	424	400	333	4	5
Out	3,640	3,394	3,116	2,682	36	
10	423	401	371	315	4	10
11	346	324	298	276	4	16
12	446	427	406	366	4	4
13	186	176	154	137	3	12
14	441	430	386	344	4	6
15	475	465	432	409	4/5	2
16	155	147	122	114	3	18
17	354	347	314	266	4	14
18	557	523	487	454	5	8
In	3,383	3,240	2,970	2,681	35/36	
Total	**7,023**	**6,634**	**6,086**	**5,363**	**71/72**	

Rock, Beechtree is definitely large scale and unquestionably worthwhile.

Like so many new courses these days, it is built on what was once a farm. The front nine, the less interesting side, meanders across fairly open hill and dale, bringing water into play on a couple of holes and native-grass-waste areas into play on several others. The back nine, with a terrific stretch from the 12th on in, wends its way through more wooded terrain.

Beechtree has a modern feel to it, to be sure. But Doak, a student of the great architects of the last 100 years, here and abroad, has also made sure to integrate more classical design features throughout the course.

Fairways, often sloped or banked, are generally generous enough to higher handicappers, but they also offer better golfers a risk-reward scenario — i.e., carrying a distant and strategically placed fairway bunker. The bunkers, which are more plentiful in the fairways than around the greens, tend to be large and jagged, in the old style. But my favorite feature of Beechtree's is Doak's greens — they are large, gently undulating and subtly treacherous.

Much like Hartefeld and Bulle Rock, the entire course has an impressive, large-scale feel to it. Long and risky second shots are the norm, not the occasional test. Only one of the three par 5s is remotely reachable in two. There's not an easy — or, for that matter, short — par 3 on the course.

Because of the wide-open terrain, the front nine is the lesser half of the course, though it is hardly weak — a fact driven home as soon as you hit the fourth.

It's a par 3 — 185 yards from the white tees, 234 from the tips — and it has an almost dogleg look and feel. It has a huge, bunkerless green that defies you to 2-putt. The 466-yard sixth, with its yawning fairway bunker cut into the face of the fairway, begs big hitters to try and bomb one. But it's the back-to-back par 5s — the seventh, a sweeping downhill hole that's reachable, and the eighth, an uphill beast that is not — that contribute the most personality to the front.

As Beechtree heads back into the woods and into more rolling terrain, Doak demands you find your "A" game.

The 10th, a dicey little dogleg over a creek, is good. So is the 11th, a dogleg left that bears a slight resemblance to the 12th at Pine Valley. But the meat of the back nine begins at the 12th, a long, straight par 4 aptly named Up n' Over.

Indeed, it is on the back nine that the hole names suddenly take on more meaning. The 14th, a 441-yard dogleg, is dubbed Sahara for good reason — the series of bunkers guarding the green calls to mind the nasty cluster of sand at the par-5 fifth at Hartefeld.

The 15th, another downhill, sweeping, dogleg par 4, plays every inch of its 475 yards.

If you haven't yet had enough, there is the final test — the uphill, unreachable 18th that plays into a bunkered, two-tiered green that is higher in the front than in the back — as if you needed one more bogey on your card.

All in all, with Beechtree, Doak hasn't surpassed the grandmaster Dye's Bulle Rock. But in his effort to join the luminaries of golf architecture, he has added a significant course to his resume.

— October 17, 1999

If You Go

Address: 811 S. Stepney Rd., Aberdeen.

Phone: 410-297-9700 or, toll-free, 1-877-233-2487.

Greens fees: Weekends, $85 to ride, $85 to walk. Weekdays, $85 to ride, $85 to walk.

Web: www.beechtreegolf.com

Carts: Walking permitted anytime, but cart fees are included.

Amenities: Posh country-club-style clubhouse, with restaurant and banquet facilities; locker room; well-stocked pro shop; driving range; putting green; snack bar. Outings welcome.

Rating: Excellent new four-star daily-fee course with posh amenities; pricey but definitely worth a try.

71. Bulle Rock

Use only superlatives

What do you get when you find a wonderfully raw piece of rural real estate, hire one of the foremost golf-course architects, and turn him loose with an almost limitless budget?

Bulle Rock.

Remember that name. If Havre de Grace, about 50 minutes south of Philadelphia International Airport, just into Maryland, can be considered part of our area, then we have a new undisputed "best public course."

We're talking first class on a national scale. We're talking shoo-in to join Pebble Beach and Pinehurst No. 2 in Golf Digest's elite handful of daily-fee courses awarded its ultimate five-star rating.

You think I'm overreacting to designer Pete Dye's resort-like, top-dollar creation, pronounced, by the way, Bully Rock?

It opened on March 30, and already Golf Digest's Ron Whitten, perhaps the most respected and well-traveled architecture critic around, said Bulle Rock has "major championship written all over it." He's recommending the 2006 U.S. Open.

"Masterpiece," "off-the-scale," and "Augusta National for a day" have been tossed out by other reviewers. You get the idea.

No argument here. If you told me I could play only one golf course for the rest of my life, and I could choose between world-famous Pine Valley or this place, well, I'd need some time to think about it.

So what's the catch?

Other than the drive, which is Interstate 95 except for the last three or four miles, the only other caveat would have to be the $126 green fees. Eye-popping, yes. But if you don't wince at forking over $110 to play Hartefeld National, trust me, you won't mind springing for $145 to play Bulle Rock.

When I played a round there last week, with a golf writer

from Washington and a guy who's seen his share of courses as owner of a golf-outing company in Virginia, we no sooner hit the second hole than we were talking "signature hole."

The second hole at Bulle Rock, a 555-yard par 5, starts from an elevated tee, then sprawls downward for about 400 yards before rising another 150 yards to an elevated green. Woods line both sides of the fairway. A huge fairway bunker squeezes the left side. A creek runs across the fairway at just the spot to give big hitters pause as to whether to go for it.

"Got to be the signature hole," I said.

The other writer, who had played one previous round at Bulle Rock, shrugged. "Just wait," he said.

Sure enough, at the sixth, we had a new candidate for signature hole. Then again at the par-4 ninth that wraps around a pond, and again at the 11th, the 13th, the 14th, the 18th.

The 13th may be the best of all. At 476 yards from the

Scorecard

Hole	Black	Blue	White	Red	Par	HCP	Red HCP
1	358	343	322	287	4	11	13
2	572	555	524	459	5	5	1
3	177	164	156	121	3	17	17
4	417	380	368	298	4	9	11
5	483	453	405	355	4	1	3
6	413	387	363	299	4	15	9
7	202	157	143	113	3	13	15
8	546	519	481	413	5	7	7
9	478	418	366	315	4	3	5
Out	3,646	3,376	3,128	2,660	36		
10	393	373	358	282	4	16	10
11	665	624	596	519	5	6	2
12	190	174	155	135	3	12	12
13	476	438	415	380	4	4	8
14	372	330	319	283	4	14	14
15	529	511	493	426	5	8	4
16	425	387	330	274	4	10	16
17	194	171	144	122	3	18	18
18	485	459	422	345	4	2	6
In	3,729	3,467	3,232	2,766	36		
Total	**7,375**	**6,843**	**6,360**	**5,426**	**72**		

black tees, it is a long carry just to reach the fairway. Anything to the right is down an ominous ravine that leads to woods. The second shot, with a fairway wood or long iron, is another long carry down a hill into a green riddled with bunkers.

By the time we finished, we had seen no fewer than six breathtaking holes, any of which could have been a candidate for having its picture on a scorecard.

By the time we finished, we were also whipped. No doubt thinking major championship, the legendary Dye has given us a 7,375-yard layout from the tips, carved out of a onetime horse farm within sight of the Chesapeake Bay.

True to Dye's style, it's also plenty: a 76.4 rating and a 147 slope from the black tees. From the blues, it goes 74.0/139.

Bulle Rock was the dream of Ed Abel, a construction company baron from Lancaster County, Pa., who sold his company in 1993 and walked away with millions. Not long before he cashed out, he took up golf and found himself addicted.

"When I started playing six years ago, I was fortunate enough to get invited to play some great courses," said Abel, rattling off names such as Pine Valley, Sawgrass and Seminole.

Problem was, he said, they were all private, unattainable to all but a few members and their guests. With time, money, and energy on his hands — he's only 53 — Abel decided to develop an equally impressive course for any and all.

As a developer, he knew land. He searched for several years before coming across this horse farm. (Bulle Rock was the name of a horse.)

Once he settled on the land, Abel hired Dye, the famous, prolific and somewhat eccentric designer of such layouts as Harbour Town, PGA West, Crooked Stick and Sawgrass, where he invented the island green.

At this stage of his career, Dye, in his mid-70s, doesn't take a job unless the land and the budget are right. The budget is important because Dye doesn't draw plans, as most other architects do. He designs with his eye. If a hole doesn't look right, he orders the bulldozers and shapers back again and again. The process is expensive but ultimately worth it.

With the land, the two miles of 10-inch water pipe, the impressive clubhouse, Dye's fees and construction costs, Abel figured he has got $18 million in Bulle Rock.

"I spent $250,000 just on jet fuel flying him [Dye] back here from other projects he was working on," Abel said.

For golfers, anyway, the result is worth it. Is Bulle Rock going to unseat Pine Valley as No. 1? No chance. Pine Valley has the mystique, and it is, after all, an original, a masterpiece unlike any other. But Bulle Rock will immediately join the front ranks of the new breed of fabulous courses.

This fall, on land adjacent to Bulle Rock, Abel and Dye expect to break ground on a second 18 holes, with a hotel and conference center.

Abel acknowledged that at $145 per round, Bulle Rock might as well be private as far as many golfers are concerned. But he said he has to charge that much to recoup the investment in the land and in Dye, and to maintain it.

For his part, Dye, still spry and witty the other day, credited an even higher power. "I did not undo God's work," he said of the land.

— June 14, 1998

If You Go

Address: 320 Blenheim Lane, Havre de Grace.

Phone: 410-939-8887.

Web site: www.bullerock.com

Greens fees: Weekends, $145 to ride, $145 to walk. Weekdays, $145 to ride, $145 to walk.

Carts: Walking permitted anytime, but cart fees are included.

Amenities: Country-club-style clubhouse with restaurant and banquet facilities. Well-stocked pro shop. Grass driving range and putting green.

Rating: Five-star course. Premier daily-fee course within 100 miles of Philadelphia.

72. Chesapeake Bay Golf Club at Rising Sun

Semiprivate, semi-interesting

Chesapeake Bay Golf Club at Rising Sun, (formally Chantilly Manor), only a few miles south of Chester County into Maryland, will never be confused with Merion, Philadelphia Cricket or Aronomink.

On the other hand, at Chesapeake Bay, anyone can walk into the pro shop, plunk down $49 and get a hearty welcome and directions to the first tee.

Chesapeake Bay, about 45 minutes south of Philadelphia International Airport via Interstate 95, is another country club that has gone semiprivate and opened its arms and its golf course to daily-fee players. In the year since the course went semiprivate, daily-fee golfers have come to make up about 80 percent of the rounds played at Chesapeake Bay . There are still members, of course, among them Cal Ripken Sr., who was out enjoying a loop on a recent weekday afternoon.

Chesapeake Bay, which began in 1968 as a private club owned by the members, has the look of a small-town "country" country club, which is exactly what it is. No pretensions, no apologies.

The country club is a member of three different golf associations, including the Golf Association of Philadelphia, and draws golfers from Baltimore and much of Delaware and Chester Counties. The course is 12 miles south of Wynote Golf Club in Oxford, and gets 25 percent of its players from Chester County.

The course, at 6,593 yards and 130 slope from the blue tees, offers a mix of wide-open holes and tighter, tree-lined water holes. If Golf Digest were to rate it, Chesapeake Bay would probably go 2 1/2 stars out of 4.

The most interesting holes are evenly dispersed between the front and back sides, although the back is a little tighter and has more trees. Neither side will wow you; neither side will bore you.

Designer Russell Roberts, a Maryland native who also laid out Lebanon Country Club, Penn Oaks and Hidden Valley, starts you off with a lazy dogleg right, but at 403 yards (with the No. 5 handicap) it can be a little testy for an opening hole.

That's followed by the No. 3 handicap hole, a 395-yard par 4 with a sloping fairway and trees on both sides. But the toughest test on the front side doesn't come until the seventh, the No. 1 handicapper, a 465-yard straight-away par 4 with another sloping fairway that takes two serious pokes with everything in your bag.

For my money, the most interesting hole on the front nine is the ninth, a 532-yard par 5, 90-degree dogleg right with a

Scorecard

Hole	Blue	White	Red	Par	Ladies' Par	HCP	Ladies' HCP
1	403	381	335	4	4	5	3
2	395	368	357	4	4	3	1
3	307	291	274	4	4	13	5
4	219	185	158	3	3	7	15
5	530	500	376	5	5	11	7
6	193	170	92	3	3	17	17
7	465	425	425	4	5	1	9
8	358	344	310	4	4	15	13
9	532	508	404	5	5	9	11
Out	3,402	3,172	2,731	36	37		
10	399	381	3634	4	4	8	2
11	192	176	162	3	3	16	8
12	337	320	307	4	4	18	12
13	355	342	292	4	4	6	14
14	203	184	112	3	3	10	18
15	501	472	349	5	4	12	6
16	417	396	342	4	4	2	4
17	361	339	265	4	4	14	16
18	426	412	400	4	5	4	10
In	3,191	3,022	2,592	35	35		
Total	**6,593**	**6,194**	**5,323**	**71**	**72**		

lake on the right side and a line of tall evergreens that shrouds the elevated green and dares to you try to reach it in two.

The back nine is pretty easy sailing until you hit the 13th, a 355-yard par 4 with trees and a small lake on the right side and a mid- to long-iron approach shot to test you.

After a downhill 203-yard, par 3 at the 14th, the 15th is back up the hill, a dogleg left, with trees left and right. It's a hole that's more interesting than its ranking as the No. 12 handicap would suggest.

At the 16th, a 417-yard par 4, you have to try to fade your tee shot around a troublesome stand of trees on the right side, then play a mid-iron into a green guarded by a small pond and bunkers, which is why it's the No. 2 handicap hole.

In the end, for some golfers, what may be most appealing about Chesapeake Bay is the small-town feel of the place. It's a change of pace from most of the daily-fee courses in and around Philadelphia, and one you might like.

— April 27, 1997

If You Go

Address: Route 272, North East.

Phone: 410-287-0200.

Web si8te: www.chesapeakegolf.com

Greens Fees: Weekends, $49 to ride, $49 to walk. Weekdays, $40 to ride, $30 to walk.

Carts: Walking permitted anytime, but cart fees are included before noon on weekends.

Amenities: Reasonably stocked pro shop, driving range, snack bar and grill, banquet facilities. Outings welcome.

73. Greystone Golf Course

This Maryland course is worth a bit of travel

When Greystone Golf Course began taking shape a number of years ago, the idea was to create a new top-dollar country club — the most exclusive club in Baltimore County.

But along the way, the investors ran into financial problems and construction eventually ground to a halt. For the next six years, Greystone, hard by the Pennsylvania line in the northern tip of Baltimore County, lay fallow.

It's fallow no longer.

In the mid-'90s, the quasi-governmental Baltimore County Revenue Authority, which operates several public courses, saw potential and bought out the property. Respected designer Joe Lee, who designed Bay Hill in Florida and La Costa in California, was sent in to finish the job.

Now, open a little more than two years, Greystone has blossomed into a reasonably priced, first-class, upscale, daily-fee course midway between Philadelphia and Baltimore. To be sure, it's a drive for many area golfers. But if you live within 90 minutes or so, you may be glad you made the trek.

While it's not as upper crust a facility as, say, Hartefeld National, where you pay dearly for country-club amenities and a Tom Fazio design, the more understated Greystone can be counted among the region's growing list of quality upscale daily-fee courses.

From the tips — the gray tees — Greystone measures a hefty 6,925 yards, and plays even longer. Thanks to the rolling topography of the former farmland, a flat hole is rare.

Nor is Greystone easy. From the back tees, you'll suffer though every bit of the considerable 139 slope. Even from the mid-level white tees, from which the course measures only 6,161 yards, it has a 132 slope. Just for the record, the pro, Joe

Rahnis, generally plays Greystone from the white tees, sometimes the black (6,600), but rarely from the grey.

"I think its 5 or 6 shots harder from the greys," Rahnis said during a round last week.

Now you tell me.

From the balcony of the comfortable hilltop clubhouse that lords over the course, at least portions of almost every hole on Greystone are visible. It's enough to make you want to grab a cold beverage and sit down to watch others struggle as you just did.

Like so many modern farmland courses, the feel of Greystone changes several times as it wends its way through wide-open areas and woodlands. At times, as you look out over the open rolling hills, you might think you were playing a links-style course. Other holes, where the fairways are tight and tree-lined, you're sweating bullets trying to keep the ball

Scorecard

Hole	Grey	Black	White	Green	Red	Par	HCP
1	552	523	487	456	390	5	15
2	355	340	310	276	268	4	17
3	402	379	364	334	267	4	13
4	192	181	152	125	105	3	11
5	446	426	416	326	316	4	1
6	546	534	507	446	437	5	9
7	432	420	398	372	297	4	3
8	227	202	154	126	100	3	7
9	450	422	387	372	330	4	5
Out	3,602	3,427	3,175	2,833	2,510	36	
10	527	495	463	432	395	5	14
11	405	394	381	275	263	4	10
12	161	146	134	119	111	3	8
13	515	492	456	430	302	5	12
14	149	143	130	95	81	3	18
15	337	326	316	305	209	4	16
16	235	206	175	140	130	3	6
17	422	411	390	347	330	4	4
18	572	560	541	524	469	5	2
In	3,323	3,173	2,986	2,667	2,290	36	
Total	**6,925**	**6,600**	**6,161**	**5,500**	**4,800**	**72**	

in play. Perhaps the overall strength of the course is the good mix of holes. Lee has devised a fair sampling of short and long par 4s, doglegs, reachable and unreachable par 5s, and a couple of thoroughly intimidating par 3s.

If Greystone has weaknesses, they are relatively minor visual quirks, not serious design flaws. To add a little spice, several man-made ponds were built. While effective, certainly, as hazards, in places they seem a little forced and unnatural.

All in all, Greystone is a quality track that seems a safe bet to earn four stars in the next edition of *Golf Digest's 4,200 Best Places to Play.*

One final note: Greystone is off the beaten path. It's not deep into Maryland, but it is rather inconveniently situated between Interstate 95 and Interstate 83. You have to want to play this place, but you may be glad you did.

— July 11, 1999

If You Go

Address: 2115 White Hall Rd., White Hall.

Phone: 410-887-1945.

Web site: www.baltimoregolfing.com

Greens fees: Weekends, $64 to ride, $64 to walk. Weekdays, $45 to ride, $45 to walk.

Carts: Walking permitted anytime, but cart fees are included

Amenities: Well-stocked pro shop; comfortable, modern clubhouse with grill room and excellent view of the course from the balcony; banquet facilities; outings welcome; putting green and grass-tee driving range.

Rating: Potential four-star daily-fee course; difficult, varied layout.

About the Author

Joe Logan covers golf for The Philadelphia Inquirer. In addition to writing his popular "Playing a Round" column most Sundays for the Inquirer's Golf Report, Logan travels the country and the world to follow the PGA, LPGA and Senior Tours, as well as the top amateur circuit.

A native of North Carolina, the award-winning reporter played competitive junior and small-college golf, before conceding that his future was at the keyboard rather than on the tour. He promptly transferred to the University of South Carolina, where he earned a degree in journalism.

Prior to stumbling into his dream job in 1995, Logan spent almost two decades at the newspaper writing about topics as varied as presidential politics to movie stars. Logan is also a frequent contributor to several national golf publications.

Thanks largely to his job description, Logan manages to maintain a handicap of just under 5.